Praise for

"In *The Heart of Homestay*, Jennifer Robin Wilson captures the essence of the homestay experience: a unique opportunity for families and students to engage in the diplomacy of knowledge. Through precise research, balanced reporting, and beautiful storytelling, Wilson inspires readers to think more broadly about what it means to be a global citizen and how to engage in cross-cultural understanding. This book gave me hope for a better world—one built on curiosity, kindness, and respect for human diversity and dignity."
THE RIGHT HONOURABLE DAVID JOHNSTON, C.C., 28th Governor General of Canada (2010-2017)

"Jennifer Robin Wilson's *The Heart of Homestay* doesn't just open your eyes—it touches your heart. This is a beautiful, inspirational book about the power of human connection, as told through the experience of homestay families and international students. Wilson's understanding of cross-cultural competency is nuanced and deep, making this a great guide for how to live and work with anyone—whether or not they are visitors from another country."
DOLLY CHUGH, award-winning psychologist, NYU professor, and author of *The Person You Mean to Be* and *A More Just Future*

"Connections between communities and countries are built through people-to-people exchanges across kitchen tables, not by politicians. When we listen to different cultures, histories, and points of view, we create the ties that build coherence and tolerance in communities to tackle the most critical challenges. This book is a road map to a better future."
OSCAR TRIMBOLI, award-winning author of *How to Listen*, *Deep Listening*, and *Breakthroughs*

"*The Heart of Homestay* is relatable, insightful, and heartwarming, and it gave me goosebumps! It provides hosts with the tools to create and nurture healthy, optimal homestay relationships. Profound experiences and lifelong connections lie ahead for those willing to embrace the uncomfortable—to be open, trusting, and curious—and to grow!"

BONNIE MCKIE, executive director of the Canadian Association of Public Schools-International

"An insightful and heartfelt guide. Through a collection of real-life stories, Jennifer Robin Wilson highlights the joys and challenges that culture and personality bring to homestay relationships. Her examples provide valuable lessons on cultural understanding, setting boundaries, and, above all, treating students like family. This book is an essential resource for anyone looking to create meaningful and lasting connections."

GEOFF BEST, director of international student programs at the Ottawa-Carleton District School Board

"*The Heart of Homestay* is an excellent read that gets to the heart of the benefits and challenges of living in a culturally diverse home. Homestay organizations will benefit from making this essential resource available to all their host families."

DAVID BYCROFT, founder and director of the Australian Homestay Network

"*The Heart of Homestay* is an essential guide for both veteran hosts and fresh faces. It is a celebration of the deep, meaningful connections that come from embracing cultural diversity, and a heartwarming reminder that hosting is a thrilling journey of growth, discovery, and shared experiences."

ADAM LEE, CEO of StudentRoomStay and Melt Education

Spread the Word!

- Share *The Heart of Homestay* with a colleague, a friend, your family, or anyone else who might be interested.

- Purchase this book for your team or host family network. Please contact me or **orders@pagetwo.com** to learn more about bulk discounts and special offers.

- Join the conversation by sharing your stories and key takeaways from this book on social media, and tag **@jenniferrobinwilson** and **#HeartofHomestay**.

- Leave a review on your favourite online retailer's website. Positive reviews really help connect the book with new readers.

Work with Me!

- Invite me to deliver an inspiring keynote or an engaging fireside chat at your next event.

- Ask me to lead workshops or provide coaching on leadership, cross-cultural learning, writing, and/or homestay.

- Reach out to me to chat about how we could work together.

- Sign up for my newsletter and discover more resources, articles, and services at **jenniferrobinwilson.com**.

@jenniferrobinwilson

"As a four-time study abroad student to Switzerland, Mexico, Colombia, and Brazil in my teens and early twenties, I can attest to the critical role host families play in exchange success. *The Heart of Homestay* will ensure that both host families and visiting students get the most of what is a life- and family-changing adventure. I recommend it for every host family!"
PAMELA SLIM, author of *Body of Work* and *The Widest Net*

"*The Heart of Homestay* tracks beautifully how families and the international students they host forge relationships, often for life. It provides an intimate close-up of the journey of learning and perspective-taking on which parents and students embark. This book is not only a go-to guide for parents considering the adventure of hosting international students, but is also a must-read for anyone interested in an intimate portrayal of intercultural relationships. It is a realistic depiction of growing close relationships between different cultures, and a testimony to their rewards."
BATJA MESQUITA, award-winning author of *Between Us*

"Jennifer Robin Wilson has organized a wealth of experience to provide a comprehensive analysis of hosting international students. With unvarnished insights and practical advice drawn from compelling case studies and research, *The Heart of Homestay* is a must-read for all homestay stakeholders. This book is a timely reminder that a central value of international education is to bring people from different cultures together to combat prejudice."
JOHN TAPLIN, author of *Easier Said Than Done* and founding director of Global Village Calgary

Creating Meaningful Connections When Hosting International Students

the Heart of Homestay

JENNIFER
ROBIN
WILSON

PAGE TWO

Copyright © 2025 by Jennifer Robin Wilson

All rights reserved. No part of this book may be reproduced, stored in a retrieval system or transmitted, in any form or by any means, without the prior written consent of the publisher or a licence from The Canadian Copyright Licensing Agency (Access Copyright). For a copyright licence, visit accesscopyright.ca or call toll free to 1-800-893-5777.

Every reasonable effort has been made to contact the copyright holders for work reproduced in this book.

Some names and identifying details have been changed to protect the privacy of individuals.

Cataloguing in publication information is available from Library and Archives Canada.
ISBN 978-1-77458-498-9 (paperback)
ISBN 978-1-77458-499-6 (ebook)

Page Two
pagetwo.com

Edited by Emily Schultz
Copyedited by Indu Singh
Proofread by Alison Strobel
Cover, interior design, and illustrations by Taysia Louie
Printed and bound in Canada by Friesens
Distributed in Canada by Raincoast Books
Distributed in the US and internationally by Macmillan

25 26 27 28 29   5 4 3 2 1

jenniferrobinwilson.com

For Mum and Dad

———

IN LOVING MEMORY OF

Humberto Alonso Robles
Nadia Battani
Cathy Byrnell
Carol Goerke
Pam Harvey
Maria Hildebrandt Cereija
Robyn Inman
Hyo Kim

Contents

Author's Note *ix*

Introduction: It Can Be Beautiful *1*

PART ONE PART OF THE FAMILY

1 Lock Your Door, Open Your Heart: How to Begin *11*

2 Don't Be a Stranger: Getting Settled *33*

3 Love Is a Verb: Stories of the Heart *51*

PART TWO CULTURE IS EVERYWHERE

4 Creating Safe Spaces: Empathy and Belonging *71*

5 There's No Accounting for Taste: Stories about Food *93*

6 Let's Not Get Physical: Expressing Affection *115*

7 This Is Life: Bathrooms and Bodies *125*

8 That's Not What I Meant: Communication and Language *141*

PART THREE KNOW YOURSELF

9 Being Good-ish: Fighting Bias *167*

10 When It's Harder Than You Expected: Difficult Conversations *193*

11 We're Not Perfect: Second Chances *223*

12 When It Doesn't Work Out: Relocations *243*

Conclusion: Remember Your Purpose Upon Departure *259*

Acknowledgements *275*

Notes *279*

Author's Note

THIS IS A WORK OF NONFICTION. The people in this book—the hosts, the students, the employees, and the educators—are real people. I am grateful to everyone who agreed to be interviewed for sharing their stories and opening their hearts. I've changed some of the names to ensure privacy, but I have not knowingly changed any facts or details about their lives. The events and incidents chronicled in the book happened, and scenes are constructed based on my interviews or my own personal experience. Some of the conversations with dialogue in quotation marks may not be exact reproductions of the original conversations, but are based on documentation provided by people who were part of the conversation at the time it happened. All of my interviews with the hosts or students were recorded in writing or with an audio file. I recognize that each person's memories of the events described in this book may be different than mine, or than other people's whose stories are also included. I have done my best to present them with respect and care.

Introduction
It Can Be Beautiful

> *The best part about hosting is the sharing,*
> *the getting to know the different cultures,*
> *the life they bring into the home.*
> *Sometimes, you are lucky and get students*
> *who are like little blessings sent on loan.*
> **AMANDA**, host from Saskatoon, Saskatchewan

WHEN HALEY ARRIVED in Ottawa, Canada, in 2010, she was an outgoing teenager, which made her a good match for her host parents, Susan and Robert. Whereas Susan is more introverted, Robert loves to get people talking and poke fun. Haley would dish it right back at him.

In addition to her sense of humour, Haley had another talent: she played the *guqin*—a seven-string traditional Chinese instrument known for its rich, harmonious tones. Written accounts of the guqin go back three thousand years, and playing it was considered an essential art form, along with calligraphy, painting, and an ancient form of chess. Haley brought it with her to Ottawa so that she could keep taking lessons while she finished high school.

In the beginning, Haley was shy about practicing in the living room, within earshot of the rest of the family. She didn't have much choice, though, as the guqin is not a diminutive instrument; at about a hundred and twenty centimetres long and twenty centimetres wide (four feet by eight inches), it must be played while resting on a broad surface, like a table or desk. Every time Haley wanted to practice, she would ask Susan's permission.

"The first time she asked, I came out to look at the instrument to see what it was all about," Susan said. "It was absolutely beautiful—made of polished wood and inlaid with ivory. We're a musical family, with eclectic interests. Right away, I told her, 'Of course you can play!'"

Haley would practice, and Susan would be doing dishes in the kitchen, listening. The beauty of the sound would bring Susan to tears.

After Susan told me about Haley and the guqin, she went quiet for a moment, gathering her thoughts. Haley was their first student, but Susan knew she was experiencing something special. "What a blessing, having that in our home!" she said, a slight hitch in her voice. "That's the kind of story you want to tell about homestay. You get a student who comes with this delicious little surprise, a jack-in-the-box thing, and you think, 'Oh my goodness—really—aren't we lucky?'"

I've been hearing stories like this for decades.

My first introduction to the world of homestay was in high school, when I participated in an exchange program to Australia. I lived with four different families during a five-week trip, learning about the culture, falling in love with the landscapes and wildlife, and trying to pick up some Aussie slang along the way. In turn, my family hosted one of the girls from my school's "sister school" in Mittagong, just outside Sydney. It was a thrill for all of us—especially my older brother, who developed an adolescent crush on one of the students.

I was in university when my mother, Robin, started a little business managing the homestay program for a language school in downtown Toronto, in 1995. Her success grew, and her company—Canada Homestay Network (CHN)—expanded across the country. In 2000, my dad, Fraser, joined her in the business. By then, I had settled in Victoria and had started hosting students myself. A few years later, I became a homestay coordinator after a sudden divorce left me looking for work that allowed me to be at home with my then-toddler and preschooler. After five years and an MBA, I took over the reins as Robin's successor in the business and led CHN for another twelve years.

Our organization partners with dozens of educational institutions across Canada to manage their homestay programs. This entails recruiting and screening families, matching the students with hosts, and managing their relationships while they are here to study.

In addition to my roles as a host mother, international student, homestay coordinator, and business leader, I've been on the other side of this service as a "natural parent"—a term used in the business to distinguish a student's biological parents from their host parents. Both of my kids, now young adults, have lived in homestay—one in France, the other in Canada.

My impressions of the value of homestay are not only formed by my own experience, but also by research. The data shows that hosts tend to start hosting for a few reasons: they do it for the cultural exchange, for their own enjoyment, to support the students, and to benefit their families. Homestay is an opportunity for families to bring the world to their doorstep: to travel without ever leaving home. Building intercultural communication skills can enhance relationships in one's family, workplace, and community. In the same way that parenting offers a mirror to one's strengths and weaknesses, being a homestay parent can teach people about themselves. It's a way for families to open their children to the gift of diversity, especially in communities that are largely homogenous. It can bring purpose, companionship, and laughter to an empty-nester.

Students choose homestay because it's safe and affordable and for the intercultural exchange. Often, the students are leaving their family for the first time and homestay provides a soft landing in a foreign country full of new experiences. For both students and hosts, homestay fulfills a basic human need for connection and belonging.

Some programs depend on volunteer hosts. When hosts are paid, the extra income is appealing. The monthly allowance is intended to offset essential costs, such as food, gas, and utilities; indirect costs such as general wear and tear to the home; and some extra treats such as takeout, hobbies (some hosts buy art supplies, for example), and family outings. Most hosts find they have a little left over each month, and some of our hosts rely on this extra income to help pay their household bills. In a national survey of Canadian hosts conducted by CHN in 2022, we asked several questions about hosting motivators, benefits, challenges, and so on. Responses from over seventeen hundred hosts were coded and analyzed for statistical significance. Of all the families surveyed, 9 percent said they rely on their allowance "a lot," 25 percent rely on the allowance "a moderate amount," and 32 percent rely on the allowance "a little." However, our team actively screens out families who are solely motivated by the money. Students can tell, and the quality of the experience for both host and student invariably suffers in those situations. Homestay is not about the money.

While I celebrate these rewards, I've also seen the downside. Hosts often want to be paid more, whereas students' families want to pay less. When feelings are hurt and disappointment overshadows common sense, money is a proxy for respect. Homestay can be people at their worst: scared, ashamed, angry,

Intercultural competence is *not* built by learning cultural rules, but by learning about your own culture, and how to behave in ways that facilitate understanding.

hurt, and petty. In my work, I've dealt with clogged toilets, burned rugs, stolen cars, bed bugs, bed wetting, ruined dishes, and broken family heirlooms. Conversations get really heated, really fast. I've answered phone calls in the middle of the night reporting a missing student, late for curfew. School closures during COVID forced listless teenagers to wither on endless Zoom calls when they should have been out making new friends. My team and I have confronted sexual misconduct, immigration scams, underage drinking, teen pregnancy, mental health crises, eating disorders, and lots and lots of lying, sneaking, and all-around rule-breaking. Homestay is people being people, teenagers being teenagers, cultural misunderstandings layered upon language barriers, and the lost illusion of unmet expectations. This is not for everyone.

And yet, homestay is so much more. I've seen it bring unmeasurable love and joy and meaning to countless lives. Both the hosts and the students grow as people. My colleagues and I stick at it because of the blessings it brings.

Homestay is lifelong friendships: many of our hosts have been invited abroad years after their student's departure. Haley's hosts, Susan and Robert, who looked after twenty-five students before they retired from hosting in 2021, still keep in touch with their international "daughters" in China, Germany, Brazil, Turkey, Italy, France, and Spain.

Homestay is fun, funny, adventurous, exciting, educational, and meaningful. And most of the time, it works; our organization's relocation rate—the proportion of students who need to be moved to a new host family—has remained at around 11 to 15 percent for decades. Every day, we see the relationships between hosts and students grow into something meaningful, impactful, enduring.

That's why I wrote this book.

In *The Heart of Homestay*, I will help you understand what you can do to enhance your experience living with international students. I'll take you on the journey of hosting, from arrival through to departure, providing dozens of examples of people who embrace their work as hosts, even if that's not what they would call it. Some stories are included because they are unique, and others because they are common—but all offer important insights. I've combined my decades of experience in the homestay and international education industry with host survey data our organization has collected and dozens of interviews I conducted for this book. My work has revealed three ways you can improve your chances of success and enjoy the many rewards of homestay: treat your student like family, learn about culture, and learn about yourself.

In the first three chapters, I'll explore the importance of treating your students like members of your family—from the day they arrive all the way through to their departure. Susan and Robert naturally approached hosting with this attitude, and their ongoing connections with their students are a testament to the bonds they formed. When you start with the premise that your students are part of your family, it's easier to extend trust, establish clear boundaries, and make an effort to get them settled.

The next five chapters delve into culture, the second theme of the book. Building cultural awareness is critical to success in homestay, as well as in your communities and workplaces. Bringing people together to get to know each other will help you learn about others, but that's not enough. Intercultural competence is *not* built by learning cultural rules, or how behaviours are different across cultures, but by learning how to behave in ways that facilitate understanding. This requires self-reflection (to understand your own culture first), an open mind, and a plan for future behaviour. To that end, I'll talk about how to create safe spaces and empathize with others using a cross-cultural lens, and explore the ways in which culture influences food, physical touch, bodies, hygiene, and communication.

My dad loves a good sports metaphor for explaining concepts. In hockey, "the left wing doesn't apologize for the centre or a goaltender. And a goalie doesn't criticize a defender for not wearing pads," he says. "We can learn how to work together, and to say, 'You're different, and that's good. Tell me more.' At its essence, that's our work in homestay." My dad's metaphor is a good reminder that success in homestay also depends on self-awareness and a willingness to grow. The final four chapters of the book will help you learn about yourself as you navigate the harder parts of homestay: bias, racism, conflict, difficult conversations, and mental health.

This journey might be daunting if there weren't a clear reward at the end. In the final chapter, I'll explore what happens around and following departures—when your students are no longer strangers, and you'd like to keep it that way.

My parents taught me that homestay gives us the opportunity to do something important. They challenge me and our community of dedicated homestay professionals, hosts, students, educators, agents, and parents to dream big and imagine creating a positive future of intercultural understanding together. My parents and I believe in our hearts that when there's value in what we're doing—and we care about it and stick with it—we have the power to create our own future.

For us, homestay is not a job. It is a calling. For some it sounds like a whisper. For others it rings with the resonance of a guqin. Either way, my hope is that you hear that calling, too, and when you embark on this journey of intercultural exchange, you find a way to nurture the seed of discovery between you and your students, and watch it grow into something beautiful.

PART ONE

Part of the Family

I.

Lock Your Door, Open Your Heart
How to Begin

---

*This concept is so bizarre. I mean,
you lock your door, but you open your home to
a complete stranger... You have to believe in
the best of people to even think of doing this.*
JEN, host from Victoria, British Columbia

"MAMA LEE," as her students call her, started her hosting journey with May, a German high school student. May was a beautiful, charismatic young woman with sweet eyes and blonde hair, a talented artist who liked to hang out with her friends. She chose to study in Fredericton, New Brunswick, a charming city of about a hundred thousand residents, near the east coast of Canada.

A few months after May's arrival, the local alpine ski resort opened for the winter season. Located about forty-five minutes from downtown Fredericton, it was an easy day trip for May and Lee's daughters, who would make the journey by car most Saturdays. On the weekends when Lee's daughters weren't available to drive May, Lee would take her to the Crabbe Mountain shuttle bus in the morning and then return to pick her up around 5:30 p.m.

One Saturday afternoon in December, May wasn't on the shuttle bus at the end of the day.

They had enough of a pattern by then that right away, Lee started making calls: to her daughters, to May's friends, to the homestay coordinator. Her daughters didn't know what had happened to May. None of her other friends had any news, either. When more time passed, Lee called the mountain to ask if anyone had seen a blonde girl. They couldn't be much help.

Lee's concern and frustration grew with each passing hour. After a while, she packed May's bags—she was done. When May got home, she wasn't going to stay long. But her agitation turned to panic, and by 11:00 p.m., Lee was debating whether or not to call the police. She was consumed by the worst-case scenario, imagining the awful things that could have happened to May, all the places she could have been abandoned between Fredericton and the mountain. "Here's this kid, she's new to Canada, and it was my first student," Lee says. "What in the hell am I going to tell her parents if something happens to her?"

The darkest fears thrive in the absence of information.

Lee replayed conversations, questioned her judgment, begged the universe for grace, tried to breathe. She ached with a mixture of guilt and dread, bargaining with herself just to get through this.

Anger is a secondary emotion, and is often an expression of pain, or fear, or both. In this situation, there was also a betrayal; the best-case scenario here was that May had gone off without telling anyone. But then, that fuelled a story Lee invented about May's total lack of care and consideration. When May breezed through the door near midnight, Lee was angry.

Fuming.

And she wanted May to know it.

Ask a dozen families why they started hosting and you'll get a dozen different answers, but it's fair to say that nobody is looking for the anguish and frustration that Lee felt that night. Nevertheless, there are no guarantees about what will happen when you open your door to a stranger. You can't assume it will be easy, because sometimes—as Lee discovered—you won't be so lucky.

"Hi, Mama Lee," May said, oblivious to how much trouble she was in.

"Where in the name of God were you at?"

"I was out... I met some friends."

"Look at the time! Who did you meet? From where?"

May had met a few college guys at the ski hill, caught a ride back into town with them, and then hung out for the rest of the evening.

But Lee didn't really care about the details. She kept thinking about her own girls, and her protective mothering instincts were in full flight. This was all new to Lee, and she felt lost in her frustration and fear. She ordered May to sit down on the sofa.

At this point, Lee had a choice: She could tell herself she didn't sign up for this and couldn't cope with a teenager who didn't follow her rules. She could have stopped hosting, or considered trying again with a different, better-behaved student. But that wouldn't be Lee.

When I ask Lee what she values most about herself, she says, "just being there for people who need me... when times are tough." This was a tough time, and Lee had already embraced her role as a host mother to May. As long as May lived under her roof, Lee would treat her like a member of her family.

"I was a 'beat my own drum' kind of person," Lee says. "I was very firm with my own girls. I raised my daughters to be kind of rugged and tough." That tough side comes out in her language; she's a welder by trade and has worked with young offenders. Swearing comes easily. Lee and her husband, Danny, give all their new students a friendly warning on their first day:

they curse a lot, and if that's not okay, you'll need to find a new homestay. The second thing they tell their new students is how to find the cookies, chips, and other food.

So instead of kicking May out, Lee taught her something, the way she taught her own girls: "Either you communicate with me, or you're out of my home!"

"What do you mean?"

"I mean, your bags are packed and you'll be out of here unless you can do as I ask," Lee said, raising her voice. "I told you when you first arrived: Call me! Keep me in the loop about what you're doing!" Her kids knew how important this was. She's sure she had explained this to May, too. "If you can't keep in touch, to give me respect in our home like I asked, I don't want you here. You can leave."

May broke down and cried. Lee kept going.

"I'm getting old! I didn't sign up for this! You realize there's probably forty-five places between here and Crabbe Mountain where you could have been—those fellas you were hanging with—you could have been raped and thrown in a ditch. Do you understand that?"

"Never. That was never in my mind," May said to Lee, still crying. "Nobody has ever talked to me like that. Nobody has ever explained anything like that to me."

When Lee shared her fears—that May could have been in serious danger—it opened up an opportunity for them to talk. Sharing your perceptions like this slows down the pace of dialogue, exposing assumptions and allowing you to talk about what really matters. Often, your perceptions are based on your past experiences—especially old wounds, tender spots, or traumas. Parenting someone else's child was a big tender spot for Lee.

Lee learned that May's parents were divorced, and her father remarried a woman who was a few years older than May's elder sister. May and her sister had a lot of freedom, and could come and go as they pleased. It didn't matter where May or her sister went, who they were with, or when they came home. Living with an adult who cared about her well-being and worried about her like this was a new experience for May.

The next morning, May came to Lee and said she was very sorry. She had listened, appeared remorseful, didn't argue or contradict. There was no blaming, half-hearted apologies, or deflected accountability. She understood her mistake and was motivated to do better. In the end, Lee's approach with May was effective, and May's response garnered her a second chance.

"You're not here to be free," Lee told May. "You have to let us know what you're doing. This is part of what homestay's about. You gotta learn from it."

New Challenges

It wasn't just May who had learning to do. Like every new host, Lee was encountering new challenges, testing what she thought she knew about parenting. It may help to remember that when anyone tries something new, chances are good that something will go wrong. It's like a scientist conducting an experiment. The learning happens in the doing, and every lesson brings the scientist closer to the answers they seek. The experiment may hit a snag, but it's more accurate to call it an "intelligent failure" than a mistake. Mistakes happen when you already know better. Intelligent failures happen when you are growing. As you gain experience as a host, learning from failures and mistakes alike, it gets easier and more rewarding.

Hosts learn that they can't default to blaming the student when things go sideways. It's tempting to fix a problem by requesting the student to be transferred, and it's true that some students aren't suited for homestay. But those cases are the exception, not the rule. Yes, the student has to approach this experience with a willingness to learn, good intentions, and an open heart. The majority of the time, they do. Even when you recognize the role you play in building (and repairing) a relationship *and* you expect that to take time and effort, applying your usual strategies may not be enough. A lot of misunderstandings arise from cultural and language barriers that require new approaches and skills.

There's work to do.

I'm not suggesting that hosts shoulder all the responsibility for positive outcomes (and I lament the cases where hosts are unfairly blamed by agents and parents). Yet it's not a fifty-fifty partnership, either. As the host, you create the conditions for an optimal relationship with your student. You are the host, after all. You're providing the space for this relationship, the way a gardener turns a plot of land into fertile ground. When the student comes along, they join you as a fellow gardener of this soil, working side by side with you to nurture the growth of your relationship. If you approach hosting with this mindset, adding the right nutrients to the soil, ensuring there is light and air and water available, you have a better chance of success when it's time to plant your first seed—or your hundredth.

Begin with Trust

Lee makes a fundamental choice about how to approach her relationships with her students: she begins with trust. This is one of the many ways that hosts like Lee create the conditions for an optimal relationship with their students. A few years later, when Lee went to Germany to visit May, May introduced Lee as her Canadian Mom and "the woman who saved my life." She meant that Lee saved her from all the bad things that *could have* happened. "She grew from it," Lee says. "She made good choices after that. She became responsible. By February, she was a new person."

Trust is "choosing to risk making something you value vulnerable to another person's actions." That sounds a lot like what hosts and students do in homestay *every day*. It's the premise upon which homestay rests: to open your home to a stranger for a cultural exchange, granting them easy access to your home, your reputation, your heart. Students make their whole selves vulnerable to their host's actions, relying on them for their most basic needs of food and lodging but also care and support and guidance.

If you don't begin with trust, can you begin at all?

If you wait to see if your student can be trusted, you're keeping score in a way that creates winners and losers. Since your student doesn't know there's a scorecard, they are at a disadvantage from the beginning. When they make a mistake—because everyone makes mistakes, especially teenagers—what does that prove? While you're waiting for signs that your student is trustworthy, your student will feel your distance.

I'm a giver of trust, and encourage you to be, too.

The alternative—to wait and see if someone has earned my trust—is to hold myself back, to protect myself. And by holding back, I make *myself* less trustworthy, and threaten the depth and vulnerability I'm seeking from my relationships.

Nevertheless, giving trust doesn't mean letting people take advantage of you or ignoring your needs. That's where boundaries come in.

Set Boundaries and Expectations

May was Lee's first student with "free bird" habits, but she wasn't the last; Lee says she has seen this happen again and again with her students. "Some of these kids have no idea about how to communicate," she says. "And this was before we had the phones like today. Now there's no excuse not to stay in touch."

Most host orientations and handbooks recommend setting clear house rules with students from their day of arrival, the way Lee told May about her communication expectations. I've seen a lot of variations of these rules, from a verbal reminder about curfews and locking the doors to laminated multi-page documents posted to the laundry room walls. Rules ordinarily encompass daily routines (especially when bathrooms are shared by multiple family members), use of household appliances, chores, curfews, and other practical aspects of life. Most host families develop and expand their rules over time, as they gain experience and experiment their way to harmony.

Lee learned how to reinforce boundaries and structure while loving her students like they're her own kids. "I give them all different scenarios—what could happen. If you're in this situation, you're best to walk away. If there's drinking, drugs, etc., I'll come and get you." Lee doesn't try to restrict their every move. It's about being responsible. "You don't have to be their boss; you want to be their friend, but you also want to be a parent, in the sense that we're here to keep them safe. And then to do all the fun stuff."

For a student like Robby, a sixteen-year-old from China who didn't want to leave home in the first place, it was hard to see past the rules to enjoy the fun stuff. When Robby was in grade ten, his parents told him he would finish his last two years of high school in Canada. He didn't want to leave his home and

By holding back trust, you make *yourself* less trustworthy, and threaten the depth and vulnerability you're seeking from your relationships.

---

all his friends in China. He didn't have a choice. When he first arrived at the home of Denise and Mike, he had already made up his mind that he would be going home in two or three months.

Robby was nervous all the time and felt a general sense of panic at his situation. He could barely talk; he was embarrassed about saying the wrong thing or making a mistake when speaking. He spent a lot of time in bed, or up late at night, chatting online with his friends back in China. He was disengaged at school and wasn't interested in his homestay.

Denise and Mike were experienced hosts by the time Robby arrived, and had a list of expectations and rules. He had to be home by 6:00 p.m. on school nights. He had to walk the dog (and pick up after him), do dishes, and tidy his room. They would ground him if he was late for school, tell him not to stay up too late at night, and remind him not to play on his computer all the time. They even threatened to cut off the internet a few times.

To Robby and his friends, it felt like there were too many rules; his friends used to call his host parents "insane" and "so mean." But Denise and Mike knew how to be kind and firm at the same time.

The examples of their kindness started on his second day in Ottawa after he gave himself a sloppy haircut. It had looked terrible, but he was too embarrassed to ask for help. He didn't have to: Denise just fixed it for him. "She just understood," Robby says.

A few weeks later, one of his best friends in China was badly injured in a car accident. When he got home from school that day, he retreated to his room, wanting to be alone. Despite himself, he began to cry. Soon there was a knock on his door from Mike.

"Are you okay?"

Robby's response was reflexive and stoic. "I'm good."

"Can I come in?"

Something in the gentle tone of Mike's voice gave Robby a moment's pause. "It's open," he said.

Mike sat on the edge of Robby's bed and started to talk. He asked a few easy questions about Robby's day, followed by silence, then more easy questions. Gradually, Robby began to talk about his friend, and the tears started all over again.

"It's going to be okay," Mike said. "I promise."

That evening, Denise made Robby chicken wings—one of his favourite meals—because she hoped it would make him feel better.

When Robby failed his first English course, Denise and Mike asked him if he needed the help of a tutor and offered to find one for him. They suggested he spend more time with them practicing his English and offered to look over his essays and other homework. They gently persisted while he learned what responsibility meant. He began to connect their concern for his overnight computer habits with his fatigue in the morning, and realized that when he slept better, he did better on his schoolwork.

Over time, he grew to appreciate how much Denise and Mike cared for him. By enforcing their rules, they were showing Robby that he was part of their family. Robby talks about this realization with a self-effacing charm that could be clichéd if it wasn't so sincere. "They helped me through. They taught me. I started to feel part of a family. I was growing up. Their rules are there because they really care about me. They are being parents. So, I follow the rules that they made. It's good for me; it's good for both of us. I started to like this family. I figured out that if you want them to treat you as a family, you have to treat them as a family, too."

As Denise and Mike know, whenever you need to set or enforce a boundary around a behaviour, it's critical to be detailed about your expectations, explain the consequences for failing to meet those expectations, *and* explain why you have the rule in the first place.

Consider curfews. As much as every family in your country handles curfews and discipline differently, the same is true for families around the world. When you set a curfew, is there any leeway around the curfew time? If so, how much leeway would you give? Is there a different punishment for being fifteen minutes late versus an hour late? What if the student calls and explains why they are running late and updates you on their expected arrival? Would you change the punishment if they were late for curfew three times in a row? At the same time, do you explain that curfews are in place to keep your student safe, not to punish them or prevent them from having fun? Like Lee did with May, it's okay to talk about your fears and worries; it makes you human and helps them see curfew less as an arbitrary rule and more as a healthy boundary based on respect and care.

Nobody wants to be surprised by an unexpected reaction to a blurry rule. Being clear with your student—and yourself—in advance is hard, and it can feel awkward at first, but it does not have to be heavy-handed or rude.

Robby stayed with Denise and Mike for two full school years. When I ask if he would have considered living on his own, or in a residence, he says some of his friends have done that, but it would have been so different. "They care about you; they're someone you can depend on," Robby says. "When you're living in a new country and need help, they are like your new parents."

As he makes plans for his upcoming first year of university in Ottawa, it's clear that he intends to keep in touch. He feels ready, thanks to them. They've softened this upcoming transition with a gift of second-hand dishes, and a standing invitation for him to come for dinner any time. "Maybe I'll stay and make them suffer," he says with a grin. "Just joking. We had a lot of good times."

Boundaries and Culture

Many hosts struggle to find a balance between enforcing a rule and being culturally sensitive. As one of CHN's longest-term employees, the former registrar at a busy language school in downtown Toronto, a host and a mother, Deirdre brings a wealth of experience to homestay. She has several examples of scenarios where this balance was particularly tricky. She is a light sleeper and tends to go to bed earlier than a lot of her adult students. She was concerned about noise disrupting her sleep and disturbing her neighbours. She hadn't had a problem, but she wanted to be clear and diligent—just in case—so she asked her students to be quiet when they came home late at night. Somehow this topic came up in conversation with friends of hers, who happened to be from Brazil. When they found out what Deirdre had been telling her students, they said a comment like that would be considered pretty rude in their culture.

"How would you express that to a student, about being quiet?" Deirdre asked, now puzzled about the best way to broach this subject.

"You don't," her friend said. In Brazil, noise is not an issue.

After this conversation, Deirdre adjusted her approach. "I usually don't say anything, but I would if they end up being noisy. Interestingly enough, I've never had to address it."

Deirdre has also learned that encouraging students to "help themselves" to the refrigerator doesn't always work. One of her students, a thirty-year-old man from Brazil, said thank you whenever she invited him to help himself to some extra cheese or a glass of milk, but steered clear of the fridge.

About a year after he moved out of her homestay, he was accepted into a community college program near Toronto. He returned to stay with Deirdre for a few weeks while he looked for his own apartment. His English had improved a lot by then, which may have contributed to his response when she invited him to help himself to the fridge again.

"He said to me, 'I have to tell you, in my culture we would never open a fridge in somebody's house,'" Deirdre says. She touches her hand to her chest in surprise as she remembers that moment. She assumed he was being polite, so she insisted: "As a host mother, I'm giving you permission!"

"Although you gave me permission, I am very uncomfortable about opening your fridge," he replied.

I ask Deirdre how she approaches this with her students now. "Do you offer them extra food, or serve them yourself?"

"Yes, both," she says. "Especially with students who are in homestay for a short stay." She agrees that this dynamic could shift over longer periods, or with younger students.

A lot of the time, your guest won't tell you that you've crossed a cultural line. It takes a certain amount of familiarity, comfort, and trust to say something potentially hurtful.

Being firm about house rules and preferences in the face of a possible cultural gaffe is risky, and hosts need to decide for themselves when that risk is worth the potential downside. For Deirdre, living in an environmentally conscious way is a value that she isn't willing to compromise on with her students. When it comes to recycling and composting, Deirdre's students don't resist her efforts to teach them. "If they aren't sure how to sort it, I tell them to ask me," Deirdre says. "Sometimes I have to fish something out and put it where it belongs. But that's a good place to start."

Energy and water conservation are top of mind for many hosts. Students who run the thermostat too high in their bedrooms, or complain about the time limits on showering, are often not aware of the financial implications of their choices. Nor should they be: our team advises our hosts to avoid discussing financial matters with their students; it often doesn't end well and can damage goodwill in the relationship. Even if the student is aware of the cost of electricity, oil, gas, and water, they may not care; after all, their monthly fee helps to pay for that heat and water. But approaching these topics from an environmental perspective can shift the conversation, turning an arbitrary rule into a low-impact, eco-conscious way of living. For instance, in Australia, you may need to explain that water scarcity requires everyone to turn off the tap while brushing their teeth or washing dishes.

Deirdre's last student loved the cold, and he was from the hottest part of Brazil. She says he never complained about the temperature, but that was unusual compared to other students she's had. Energy conservation is one of Deirdre's boundary-setting conversations that takes place when her students first arrive. She talks about the thermostat temperature and explains that it's programmed by time of day. She asks her students to tell her if they're cold, and she shows them where the extra blankets are kept. She places a space heater in their bedrooms, but she is clear about when and how to use it. "I remember students saying they hated when the hosts started talking about saving money. So, I usually say, 'Use this when you are cold. But I prefer that you don't leave it on at night, because I'm concerned about the danger, and it uses a lot of electricity.' I try not to say that I'm saving money."

"Those small steps do matter," Deirdre says. "I'd love to think that I'm helping them form new habits. You don't want to throw it down their throats... Like, my students often ask for paper towels, and I give them cloth. You hope they might go home and say, 'My host uses cloth napkins.'"

As the host, you create
the conditions for
an optimal relationship
with your student.

Normalize the Discomfort

Setting boundaries is not just about rules and lifestyle preferences. It also means carving out time and space for you as an individual, a couple, or even a family.

This is especially true with long-term students, as hosts Jen and Stew found out. When one of their students stayed over the Christmas holidays, his mother and sister came to visit. "The entire Christmas dinner was about them... at the sacrifice of connecting with family," Jen says. "It got to the point where sometimes my parents would ask us to come over without our students. It happened with some friends, too. Sometimes people just wanted to see us, without folding our new teenage children into it."

Jen also realized she needed to protect her alone time. She told me about another student, Bai, who was pursuing a master's in music. Bai bonded with the kids right away; he brought joy and beauty to their home. At the same time, Jen and Stew weren't expecting someone with such a big presence.

"He was an opera singer, like *that*," Jen says, spreading her arms wide and gesturing to indicate the sheer physical space that his energy occupied. "It wasn't a good fit for me. It was too much. I'm an introvert, so I had to physically remove myself in order to get that alone time to recharge."

Jen said she learned from this experience that she had to be very clear about her need for personal time and space. "It can take a lot of energy to pull that back if you don't do it at the beginning. It can get out of control," she says.

It's also okay to take a break from time to time. This can happen between students, but hosts with long-term students can also get a few days off by requesting a "respite." Whether this is planned (a vacation or out-of-town business trip) or unexpected (being called to care for a family member or to attend a last-minute event), the homestay team will arrange for the student to stay with another host temporarily. Even just knowing this is an option can make all the difference.

Jen's experience is also a good reminder that not every placement is going to be magical. Many families would describe their relationships as just okay—and that's okay. It's nobody's fault.

After hosting seventy students, Deirdre knows what this is like. "It's the same in your own personal life. Sometimes you connect with someone, and those people become part of your circle of friends, and sometimes you meet people and you get along with them fine, but there's not a big connection. You don't have that chemistry. And that's fine."

All the same, as Lee demonstrated, it's important to not give up just because you don't have that great connection, or you're worried about hurting your student's feelings, or you don't know what to say. Don't be afraid that your rules are too harsh, or won't help, or will lead to repercussions. Boundaries can be uncomfortable to establish and hold, which is why it's important to *normalize discomfort*.

It's *uncomfortable* to offer feedback, and to parent other people's children. It's *uncomfortable* to welcome a stranger in your home in the first place. It's *uncomfortable* to live with someone whose interests don't align with yours, who keeps a different schedule than you, who has different hygiene habits. It's *uncomfortable* to communicate with someone who may completely misunderstand your meaning. It's *uncomfortable* to challenge the status quo of your life.

Yet isn't this precisely a reason to do it? In discomfort, don't we see a unique opportunity for ourselves, our families, and our communities? As author and educator Seth Godin says, "When you identify the discomfort, you've found the place where a leader is needed. If you're not uncomfortable in your work as a leader, it's almost certain you're not reaching your potential as a leader." Embracing your role as a host means embracing your role as a leader, and growing into that role with every uncomfortable moment. Hosts create the conditions for an optimal relationship with their student, partly by normalizing discomfort.

Can you imagine saying to your kids, spouse, and students, "We believe growth and learning are uncomfortable. It's a normal part of the learning process, and it's an expectation of being in homestay and being part of this family. You're not alone!" Normalizing the awkward parts of homestay is a powerful way to shift your experience as a host.

Set Yourself Up for Success

For homestay to work, it's critical to adopt the default approach to hosting demonstrated by Lee, Denise and Mike, Deirdre, Jen and Stew, and the many other hosts you'll meet in this book: treating your students like they're part of your family... from the first day, and every day thereafter. There are two other steps you can take to set yourself up for success: learn about culture and learn about yourself. Being open to the ways you may need to grow and change through this experience will also serve you well.

All of this learning requires a belief in yourself and your ability to improve by activating a "growth mindset." According to Stanford University psychologist Carol Dweck, there are two belief systems about one's basic qualities: a fixed mindset and a growth mindset. The fixed mindset says, "My qualities are predetermined and cannot change," whereas the growth mindset says, "I can improve my qualities through my efforts, strategies, and help from others."

Everyone has a mixture of both. People tend to embrace both fixed and growth mindsets at different times, and for different areas of their lives. One day you may feel motivated and excited to learn how to solve a problem, and another day you may throw up your hands, believing that there's no way you'll accomplish your task. The evidence suggests that the patience and resilience required to persevere through the ups and downs of being a host—and an international student—requires a growth mindset.

It's been fifteen years since May lived with Lee and Danny. Now a grown woman with her own children, May still chats with Lee at least once a month. May has been back twice to visit Fredericton, and Lee and Danny have been to Emden, Germany, in return.

"Me and Danny are now grandparents to four wonderful kids in Germany," Lee says. "The last time we spoke, May said, 'I want my children to know their Nanny,' so she introduced her children to me as Oma Nanny in Canada."

From a late-night crisis to a lifelong friendship: this is the potential of homestay. If you're up for this adventure, the work is worth the effort.

CHAPTER SUMMARY

- Begin with trust. By holding back trust, you make *yourself* less trustworthy.

- Set clear boundaries with students from their day of arrival, like Mama Lee did.

- Treat your students like they're part of your family... from the first day, and every day thereafter.

- As the host, you create the conditions for an optimal relationship with your student.

- Activate a growth mindset, remembering that you will also be learning and experimenting as a host. Discomfort and awkwardness are normal in homestay.

2

Don't Be a Stranger
Getting Settled

When people say to me,
"How can you live with a stranger in your house?"
I say, "They're only a stranger for the
first two minutes"... I have a lot of love to give.
LAURIE, host from Cornwall, Ontario

MORGAN, THEN fifteen years old, was off to Paris for a five-week exchange trip. In the wee hours before dawn, it was hard to tell if our eyes were puffy from the lack of sleep or the tears. I expected my daughter to be nervous. I willed her to know she was brave. She clung to me in our goodbye hug as if she didn't want to go—not the kind of lingering that was expected, but the kind that was regretful—and as much as I fought with myself to be stoic, I was crying, too.

Morgan had started asking about studying abroad a couple of years earlier. In Canada, children have the option to study in French immersion programs, which both our kids did, so France was a natural choice of destination. We had also visited Paris as a family in the spring of Morgan's grade ten year, and she had fallen in love with the city.

We started planning her trip about six months in advance. International students often select their destination city first, followed by their preferred school district and/or school. Many students contract with a travel agency in their home country to advise them on these choices; the agents are specialists in international education (rather than tourism) and earn most of their revenue by charging the student's family and collecting a commission from the educational institution in the destination country. In contrast, all the European agencies we contacted explained that Morgan would be allocated to whichever city and school they selected for her after she applied. The chances of her getting a spot in Paris were slim.

Instead, we found a Parisian family through a personal connection. They had four kids, three of whom had studied abroad already. The youngest, a daughter named Philippine, is a year younger than Morgan.

After dozens of emails, less paperwork than you might expect, and some logistical planning, Morgan was finally leaving. I once read that having children is like taking your heart and letting it walk around outside your body for the rest of your life. As I stared at the tiny dot on the flight tracker app on my phone that afternoon, the tether binding me to my child stretched with every passing moment, following her into the sky.

When she landed all those hours later, she was fine. Tired and nervous, but fine. She breezed through passport control and made it to the location in the airport where we agreed she would meet her host mother, Sophie, and Philippine.

Only... they weren't there.

Morgan's dad, my mother, and my closest friends were all texting me at the same time I was texting Morgan to find a Wi-Fi network; Sophie had been using WhatsApp to communicate with us and she couldn't reach Morgan directly.

Where is Sophie? Why is she late? my ex demanded.

I've been on the receiving end of these kinds of messages from parents on countless occasions, so his reaction was predictable. I've seen dozens of legitimate reasons why students aren't picked up on time, or can't find their driver in the arrivals area. Sometimes shit happens. People make mistakes. It's nobody's fault. Relax.

All the same, it gave me a newfound appreciation for the parent's perspective. As much as I could see this from the homestay parent's point of view—after all, that was my default mode—I was also upset and disappointed. Maybe even angry. My baby, my brave girl, was eight thousand kilometres away from home and utterly alone. How hard was it to arrive at the airport on time? Was this a harbinger of neglect to come? Had we made a terrible mistake?

We had not made a terrible mistake.

Sophie arrived about an hour after Morgan's plane landed, thwarted by transit delays. She was lovely and kind and apologetic. The event was swiftly subsumed by other, more pressing challenges (Morgan's homesickness) and delights (Morgan's view of the Eiffel Tower from the apartment).

For me, it was a good reminder that first impressions are lasting, and they affect our opinions about people even when we are faced with contrary evidence. Hosts create the conditions for an optimal relationship with their students, starting with their first greeting. When efforts to create a soft landing and help a student feel welcome overlap with strategies to address homesickness, the impact is even greater.

Morgan's journey to Paris also gave me an intimate understanding of the degree of trust parents place in these strangers— that's you, the host—when they send their children halfway around the world. All I wanted, all I could hope for, was that I could trust Sophie to be there for my daughter when I couldn't.

Be Present—Right from the Start

As Morgan and I discovered, and as I've seen countless times in our business, being present for your student is critical. This includes physical presence: If you do airport pickups, arrive on time. If your student is dropped off at your home, be there to greet them. It's what you would do if family were visiting. And, as many hosts know, physical presence is only the beginning when it comes to establishing a solid relationship.

Deirdre, whom I introduced in the last chapter, has unique insights about the qualities and behaviours of successful host families. Deirdre believes a big predictor of success in homestay is the amount of effort the host makes to build a connection, especially in the first few days. "I had a student about three years ago whose English was this high," Deirdre says, lowering her hand a few inches off the floor. "But we had an immediate connection because he tried so hard."

This emotional presence is the kind of attention and care that tells someone you are interested in them, you want them around, and you understand that this transition can be challenging at first. The homestay family is a student's first social support system, and your approach will have a lasting impact on the student's adjustment. Students who feel welcomed, connected, and well supported will find it easier to deal with culture shock and homesickness.

This takes a lot of effort.

In CHN's 2022 survey, 14 percent of hosts said the initial adjustment period of building trust, bonding, adapting to new routines, and working through cultural differences is the hardest part of hosting. Students are trying, too, but hosts often feel like they're the ones doing all the work. This can also be true in a family: sometimes relationships feel a little lopsided. Deirdre would agree. "I always made a huge effort," she says. "You do have to put out a lot. It is an expectation and responsibility. I think if you're taking a homestay student, you should have some obligation to work at it. In real life, it may not be worth your time to explore that relationship, but I think it's part of your obligation as a host." Trust me: your effort matters, and will pay off in the long run.

Johanna, a German high school student who visited Ottawa in the summer of 2018, loved her time in Canada. She still keeps in touch with her hosts, and says she is sure they will meet again one day. They made sure her first day was memorable. "We drove to a pool, which I thought was a good idea to relax and to get to know everybody better," Johanna said. "[My hosts] introduced 'Canadian pool traditions' like eating chips and cookies. We had fun... I was allowed to help myself to lunch and eat what I want. It was a fantastic experience to feel so welcomed in this family."

It didn't stop there. "The first evening my host mum asked me to go shopping with her for dinner, to show me a Canadian supermarket. Unfortunately, I was too exhausted to join her but I believe this gesture was very friendly," Johanna explained. "The next morning, I was asked if I needed anything to start school or get around... I got the chance to buy everything I needed after twenty hours in Ottawa."

On the first day of school, Johanna's host father dropped her off and picked her up, driving the bus route and explaining everything as they went. It was more than just shopping and logistics, though. Johanna praised her host family for their open-mindedness and interest in her as a person. They wanted to talk, and were curious about her views on politics, family, travelling, and more. "Every day they did so much to integrate me in their family, and I felt accepted and respected," she said.

Suzanne, another Toronto host, understands this obligation to be emotionally present. She shared an anecdote about one of her students from Argentina who wasn't comfortable at first.

"She was particularly self-contained and reticent to go out much beyond the trips to and from school," Suzanne said. "I formed the opinion that she was depressed and unsociable." Nevertheless, Suzanne continued to make an effort, offering warmth and kindness. After a couple of weeks, the student felt safe enough to share more personal details about her life. "She began to reveal her experiences of abuse and harassment in her hometown," Suzanne said. "She assumed that every city was full of the same dangers. Her opening up allowed me to help her feel safe in Toronto and with others in the house—and eventually she went for walks in the parks and out with friends to restaurants."

Show Them the Things You Love

In addition to being present from the start, another way to build a connection—and satisfy your student's expectations—is to be a tourist in your own town. To be fair, for many busy families, spending time and money on overpriced, crowded, and often underwhelming tourist attractions does not sound fun. However, showing your student around your city doesn't necessarily mean lining up for the CN Tower, Empire State Building, or Sydney Opera House.

Sharing things you already love to do is a great way to break the ice with students. For example, Deirdre loves to watch documentaries, plays clarinet, sings in a choir, and goes hiking or walking around Toronto most days. She would often take her students on a walking tour of downtown Toronto—Ontario's capital and Canada's most populous city—through a busy shopping district, along a scenic pathway through the University of Toronto campus, and past the parliament buildings and other landmarks. She also enjoys taking her students to the St. Lawrence Market, a famous public market in downtown Toronto, parts of which have been in operation since 1803.

One student stood out in her memory. "It was a horrible day; he was cold and I was cold," Deirdre says. "But he loved it. He loved the new museum and walking through the University of Toronto and seeing these old buildings from the 1900s. I tried to think of all the famous Canadians like Dr. Banting and Dr. Best, and I asked if he's heard of them... At the end, he said, 'I learned more on that walk than I did in the whole four weeks I was here.'"

In addition to walking, Deirdre invites her students to go to movies with her—knowing that most of the time, they will say no. It delights her when they do reciprocate: "It was cute when they would say, 'I'm going to a movie tonight, would you like to come?' And they'd be going to some awful movie, so then I'd say, 'You know that's not my taste, but thank you so much for asking me!' It's so much give-and-take. It's so important to be invited."

Be Open to Moments of Beauty

Charlene and her husband started hosting "to pay the universe back for this beautiful gift" of their adopted son, Mason. Going into it, they expected to provide housing for somebody and share a bit of their home life.

Their first experience hosting was somewhat unique in that Paolo arrived in March 2020, as COVID was shutting things down. "We realized he wasn't going to get the opportunity to see New Brunswick and Canada through the lens of a student [because schools were online during this time]... We decided to make this a three-month vacation for him! As soon as we were able to leave home and start to explore, we took him

Students who feel welcomed, connected, and well supported will find it easier to deal with culture shock and homesickness.

everywhere—to Hartland, to Shediac, to Hopewell Rocks—and he became part of our family."

They were delighted by the unexpected gifts hosting brought them. "We got to see our world through a different lens," Charlene says. "Our meals are so different. The way we speak is so different. Then to see the beauty of a little thing like a snowflake... we take it for granted and we complain about it when we get thirty centimetres of snow. Then we go out and make a snowman and take pictures of all the different snowflakes, because Paolo was never exposed to snow before."

Charlene expressed a tremendous amount of gratitude for this realization, this opportunity to pause and appreciate their world, and see it through the eyes of her students.

One spring day, Charlene and Paolo were driving from Saint John to Fredericton along a quiet highway surrounded by forest. All of a sudden, Charlene spotted a moose down the road. She pulled over as soon as it was safe to do so. Paolo was sound asleep at that moment, his seat fully reclined. Charlene tapped him on the leg to wake him, exclaiming with her trademark passion, "There's a moose! There's a moose!" He grabbed the handle on the seat, jerking himself upright, and rubbed his sleepy eyes, trying to focus. They ended up sitting there for thirty minutes, taking pictures and enjoying the moose. They named him Geary, after the nearest town.

Charlene estimates she's seen thirty or forty moose in her life, but this moose was particularly special because of Paolo's reaction. As a parting gift, she gave him a moose stuffy named Geary, so "he'll always have Geary the Moose in his life."

Charlene and Paolo still keep in touch regularly. When I spoke to her, he had been back in Brazil for a few months already. She told me she had just gotten an email from him a few days earlier.

He wrote, "It's one o'clock in the morning. I'm [lying] here in bed at home thinking of all the things you did for me while we were in that pandemic. And I can't thank you enough for going above and beyond."

As soon as Charlene shares this with me, she's stepping in to editorialize; she believes that her work as a host was to help her student make the most of his time overseas, in spite of the pandemic. "For me, it wasn't going above and beyond," she says. "I knew I needed to do it, because if my son was in Brazil, I would want his host family to do this."

Be Prepared for Homesickness

Like Johanna, Morgan was excited about her adventure: she thought it would be fun and she looked forward to exploring the city with a local family. She wasn't expecting to be homesick, because she was a seasoned international traveller and she had been moving back and forth between my home and her father's since she was four years old. But everything was a little harder than she had anticipated, from the moment she arrived. Looking back, she remembers a series of small, seemingly insignificant events, starting with the late pickup. She was exhausted from her journey, but there was no time to relax; they had to rush to catch the next train back to the city. Morgan didn't have a transit ticket, and she vividly recalls pushing through the barricade to the train platform while passing her suitcase overhead.

On the train into Paris, she was explaining something about her stepbrothers to Sophie and Philippine in French, when Sophie corrected her for a grammatical mistake. I asked her how that made her feel. She said it was fine; it was an example of the French being direct—and yet, this is one of the conversations that stands out in her memory, five years later. "I guess I was self-conscious about it," she said. "It wasn't rude; it was just different. I thought my French must be terrible, and then they said my French was better than they thought it would be, so that made me feel slightly better."

When I asked what else happened in the first twenty-four hours, Morgan said they left her in the apartment alone at one point—she doesn't recall why, or for how long—and someone knocked on the door, but she was too frightened to answer.

Her lasting impressions are all about the contrasts.

"Everything was so different. The light switches, and the kinds of food, and what times we ate, and how strict it was at school, and speaking French—that was really hard. And we didn't do any touristy things. We saw other parts of Paris, which weren't as... picturesque." She says this with a self-effacing chuckle, realizing how it sounds—but the point is a valid one. In hindsight, she says it would have made a difference if her hosts had wanted to show off their city. It might have helped if Philippine hadn't hated living in Paris. Morgan finally made it to the Eiffel Tower on her second-last day. By herself. "Sometimes I felt bad being there," she says. "Like it was bothersome for the family. Like I was a burden." Nothing in particular made her feel that way, but it did contribute to the homesickness.

For students like Robby from chapter 1, who don't want to be in homestay in the first place, homesickness can seem unbearable. Try not to take this personally. As host Laurie explains, "For a lot of the students, their parents make them come. It wasn't their choice. They would never tell their parents they didn't want to. They're crying at the kitchen table the first night, and I know this is going to be hard. So we all cry together."

That's presence. After raising five children, Laurie wasn't sure she wanted to be a host mother. The homestay coordinator convinced her to try it out, and reassured her by telling her to do what she did with her own kids. She did, and it worked. Laurie has stayed in contact with all of her students over the years. "It's like a mini adoption," she says. "I keep accumulating children."

It's normal for students to feel sad and lonely from time to time. In fact, struggling is good for young people. These tough experiences help them learn to believe in themselves, cultivating the potent cognitive process we call hope, which is linked to well-being. Being a witness and holding space for these feelings, like Laurie does, is a powerful way to connect.

However, if low mood persists beyond a few weeks or starts to interfere with school, the student may benefit from professional help to identify more serious mental health concerns, such as depression.

In North America, the UK, and Australia, talking about mental health still carries a stigma for many people, but a shift is taking place—especially among young people. You can add momentum to this shift by reinforcing the message that depression and other mental health conditions are no different than physical conditions, like breaking a leg. There is no shame in going to a doctor to get better. Getting treatment is normalized in schools and health care settings. However, many international students live in countries and families where the stigma against raising mental health concerns is deep and powerful. Students may not be comfortable talking about these issues; they may be afraid of the way it may be seen by their family and friends back home. I will discuss mental health further in chapter 12.

Diana, a host in Victoria, BC, remembers a moment of holding space for sadness with her first student—an experience that was one of the most impactful for her, despite lasting no more than a week. Her guest was a young kindergarten teacher from

Japan who was travelling abroad for the first time. Not long after her guest arrived, Diana took her up to the top of PKOLS (formerly known as Mount Douglas Park) to enjoy the viewpoint. When the teacher spotted Mount Baker across the Strait of Georgia, she covered her mouth in surprise and started to weep. The mountain was as clear as could be, rising up from the horizon in a nearly perfect triangular shape.

"Oh, Mount Fuji," she said. "It reminds me of home."

Understand Acculturation Stress

While not every student will experience homesickness, everyone who moves from one culture to another will experience some form of stress as they learn to adapt. This "culture shock" can start immediately and last for months—much longer than homesickness. Several factors are known to exacerbate or mitigate acculturation stress: individual personality, age, gender, language proficiency, support networks (including hosts and peers), distance from home, and previous travel. Naturally, the more similar one's culture is to the new environment, the less stressful the change will be. But what do we mean when we talk about culture, anyway?

Culture is "the way of life of a people, including their attitudes, values, beliefs, arts, sciences, modes of perception, and habits of thought and activity." It's taught to us as children and reinforced through socialization in religious groups, age groups, social classes, genders, families, communities, and organizations. Kids learn how the world is supposed to work and how they are supposed to behave by watching and listening to parents, teachers, coaches, religious leaders, and other authority figures. We all learn these things without knowing we're learning them.

Diversity expert Steve Robbins says people absorb these messages the way they absorb the lyrics of a song, "not because you studied them, but because you heard them repeatedly. Moreover, you didn't have to pay attention to the songs as they wafted through the air and into your ears. Your brain grabs the words for you, outside of your awareness." This is why the rules that govern your behaviour are often invisible to you until you encounter difference.

For example, when I visited the Forbidden City in Beijing, I was confused and offended when a man walked up to the ticket booth and stood shoulder to shoulder by me as I paid for my ticket. Like other children who grew up in North America, the UK, and Australia, I learned to wait in line in kindergarten. Still, as an adult, I line up and wait my turn.

I assumed my Canadian cultural rule was universal: everyone knows that it's polite to wait in line. To me in that moment, this man was being disrespectful. However, in places like France, India, or China, people have learned to push through the crowd to get what they want. When I reframed the man's actions to be cultural—not universal—it changed the meaning of the behaviour. Not only did I gain a new appreciation of my own cultural norms—a critical first step in learning about culture—but I also avoided unfairly judging the personality traits of a stranger. That man in line wasn't being rude after all.

As students spend more time in a new culture (or hosts live with someone from another culture), they are better able to suspend their automatic cultural responses and choose behaviours that are most appropriate for the situation. In my case, I accepted the man's presence at my side, bought my ticket, and moved on. I'll explore culture and its impact on hosting further in part two.

Encourage Peer Relationships

As much as hosts can make a big impression on their students through their own care and attention, homesickness and acculturation stress are deeply impacted by peer connections, too. When students make new friends, their problems seem more manageable, and the stress of adapting to their new life is reduced.

Morgan had a hard time making friends, despite hanging out with Philippine and her friends at school every day. She could speak French, but she still struggled to understand them. They spoke too quickly, or they used slang that Morgan hadn't learned in French class in Canada.

Besides encouraging students to sign up for extracurricular activities and supporting an active social life, hosts can help their students make new friends by helping them practice their English (or French) skills. As your student's comfort in their new language expands, their ability to connect with their peers will also improve.

If you are new to parenting teenagers and young adults, the homestay program can offer guidelines for curfews and help you set reasonable expectations to ensure a healthy balance between school and socializing.

What started as an awkward relationship between Morgan and Philippine ended up being at the centre of Morgan's favourite memory from her time in France. Her host family took her and Philippine to a historical theme park called Puy du Fou, about a four-and-a-half-hour drive from Paris. It's one of the most popular theme parks in France. "That was finally when things had changed," Morgan says. "We were driving back in the car, and I don't know what we were laughing about—we weren't talking; we were just laughing. Yeah. That was..." she trails off, smiling as she recalls the unexpected joy of that moment.

Paradoxically, the very things that made Morgan feel homesick at the beginning were also the things she liked best by the end. "The differences were also fun," Morgan says. "Once I got used to it... I started enjoying the different foods, and got used to eating later... It was fun becoming friends with Philippine, and seeing different parts of the country."

Homestay can be beautiful, even when the beginning is bumpy.

Remember Your Purpose

Be present from the start, share what you love, be open to moments of beauty, hold space for homesickness, and encourage peer relationships: these techniques will go a long way to establishing a solid footing with your student and enjoying the experience. Regardless of how you choose to connect, the important thing is to remember why you're doing it. The photos and Instagram posts will be lasting reminders of the excursion, but the most impactful moments may end up being seemingly small things—like Robby's bad haircut, or Paolo's moose—that demonstrate to the student that you're paying attention and including them in your family.

This is especially true when the memorable parts are more significant, difficult, or deeply saddening. In these moments, your purpose will be your guide. When you set out to grow your family by creating a home-away-from-home for a stranger, you're building connections that are a form of love. This is the heart of homestay.

CHAPTER SUMMARY

- First impressions are lasting. Being present for your student is critical—physically and emotionally.

- Fourteen percent of hosts find the initial adjustment period of building trust, bonding, adapting to new routines, and working through cultural differences to be the hardest part of hosting, but the extra effort is worth it.

- Feeling welcomed and shown around can help a student adjust to homesickness. German high school student Johanna found her first day memorable.

- Share the things you love. Through your student's eyes, ordinary things may seem new and beautiful. Paolo had never seen snow, or a moose.

- Overcoming acculturation stress (culture shock) can take several months.

3

Love Is a Verb
Stories of the Heart

We love our students. Seeing their faces when we show them something new, or having a heart-to-heart conversation about their dreams and goals, is so touching.

KATHY AND KAREN, hosts from Ottawa, Ontario

THE FIRST SNOWFALL of the season didn't stick. It seldom does, but the air still has that crisp bite to it, a harbinger of winter, darkness, silence. The November sky is overcast now, a uniform grey spitting cold droplets of rain. Leon finishes his morning cigarette quickly. As he turns to leave, he flicks it with a practiced twist of his wrist. He doesn't notice that it deviates ever so slightly to one side, landing not at the side of the house where he intended, but in a tidy paper yard waste bag full of yellowed leaves.

A few hours later, Leon's host mother, Liz, is in the kitchen at her friend Melissa's house. They have been getting some things together for a snack when her cell phone rings. It's a Sunday afternoon, around two, and Liz's husband, André, is not at home, either. All three students—Fernanda, Shun, and Leon—are at home.

It's Leon, speaking urgently. "Mama Liz, come home now! There's fire!"

"What?"

"There's fire! Come home now!"

"Get out of the house!" Liz says, registering what she just heard. "Go to a neighbour!"

Hanging up, she knows at some level that she needs to call 911, but her whole body has tensed up; her brain and hands are not cooperating.

Fire is so fast.

Melissa takes the phone and makes the call for her.

"Nine-one-one, what is your emergency?"

"My house is on fire," Liz manages to say.

"What is your address?"

Liz answers. This had been their home for the last seventeen years. Seventeen years of her husband's thoughtful renovations, seventeen years of pouring his heart into every update and improvement.

"Thank you. I can see here, we've had several calls about that address. We have trucks on the scene."

Trucks on the scene. The scene. Our home.

The next call is to André, who says he's at the checkout of Home Depot, ringing through his purchases—supplies for a deck he has been planning. She knows her husband; he will shut down. He will go on autopilot. Liz tells him he is going to have to leave immediately. Drop everything and get home.

Fire is so fast.

Liz knows something about fire. When she was seven, her eight-year-old brother was playing with matches in a closet when a plastic dry-cleaning bag caught fire. The blaze destroyed part of their home before it was brought under control.

Fire is so fast.

The refrain keeps looping through her mind as Melissa drives Liz from her home in Kanata back into Ottawa. The twenty-minute trip seems to take an eternity as she rocks to and fro in the front seat.

Fire is so fast.

Liz and André's house is on a quiet, tree-lined street of modest bungalows. The lots are generous; every home has a driveway. The houses across the street back onto the Crestview green space, a field-turned-scrubland furrowed with trails. The neighbours know each other by name.

When Liz and Melissa arrive, there are five firetrucks on the street and the sound of chainsaws in the distance.

This is not good.

They park the car as close as they can—which is not close at all, as the fire department has blocked the street and is not allowing any traffic through. Liz can see the smoke. She gets out and starts walking toward the house, dreading what she's about to see. The pounding in her chest won't stop, the cloudy fog in her brain won't clear, her hands won't stay still.

When she reaches her home, the first person she sees is Fernanda: their little ray of sunshine. The girl who hadn't stopped smiling since the day she'd arrived from Mexico nearly three months ago is standing on the street now, sobbing as she stares at their burning home, tears streaming down her beautiful face.

For Liz, things suddenly snap into focus. She grabs Fernanda, taking her into a big hug.

"It's going to be okay, baby," Liz says, trying to soothe herself as much as Fernanda. "It's going to be fine. Don't worry about it."

She asks after Leon, Shun, the two dogs and three cats—all are safe. The firefighters are on the roof, cutting it open with chainsaws. When they have to ventilate a house in this way, it usually means the fire is growing.

Liz notices André approaching, his eyes fixed on their home. She knows they're thinking the same thing: *We're done. It's gone. All is lost.* His steps slow to a halt, and Liz watches as he falls to his knees on the street. Glancing around at her neighbours, she realizes none of them are going to help. *Thanks a lot, guys. What's wrong with you?* Liz helps him to his feet so they can stand together.

Hours pass.

Liz and her family—André, Fernanda, Leon, Shun, and the animals—take refuge in a neighbour's house. They have a glass of wine; they wait for news.

Eventually, the fire chief appears.

"Which one of you smokes?"

What? None of them are smokers. *What is he talking about?* Liz looks around at the others, searching for an explanation.

After a pause, Leon slowly raises his hand.

"Come with me," the fire chief says, beckoning to Leon. Glancing at each other, Liz and André follow without a word.

The chief leads the group back to the remains of their home, down the driveway to the side of the house.

"You see this V pattern?" he says, pointing at a blackened patch that's wide at the top and narrow at the bottom.

"Yeah," they say, nodding.

"That means the fire started here. Do you see what's at the bottom of that V pattern?"

Liz follows his gaze down to the ground, where she sees a pile of dozens of cigarette butts. They look at Leon, and Leon doesn't speak. He raises his hand to his head, the only acknowledgement he can muster.

"It's okay, Leon," Liz says. "We forgive you."

After the Fire

The next day, one of Liz's first calls was to the insurance adjuster. He tells her he thinks they're not covered for the fire because they have boarders in their house.

"We do not have boarders," she says. "We have international students. The government likens it to having foster children." *This is not a money-making endeavour.*

"Well, I'm pretty sure you're not covered."

"What the fuck do you mean, I'm not covered?"

Looking at her, André says quietly, "This is bad. This is really bad."

Liz refused to give up. She called my colleague Jennifer, who filled me in on the crisis. Of course, I was shocked; in all our years in homestay, and from all the stories I've heard from other homestay companies and international student programs, this kind of catastrophe had never happened before.

I composed a letter confirming that Liz and André were hosts in good standing. I explained what hosts are expected to do for their students, caring for them as they would care for their own children. "Given these expectations," I wrote, "The entire amount of the monthly allowance paid to host families is intended to offset expenses related to the proper care of the student, and should not be considered income… Furthermore, students are not considered 'boarders,' 'lodgers,' or 'tenants,' and there is no lease agreement in place to characterize this type of arrangement."

Two days later, Liz met with the insurance adjuster. She walked in the door and handed him her phone, saying her lawyer would like to speak to him. "I didn't have any problems with him after that," Liz said.

We're in This Together

Leon was sixteen at the time, attending the local college for ESL (English as a Second Language) before heading to university. He's six foot three, and from a northern part of China that borders with Russia. When he first arrived, he told Liz that he was a "bad Chinese person" because he hated school. Liz responded, "You're not a bad person; you're just normal." In our interview, she said he was funny, and they were charmed by that side of him.

He was not funny after the fire. For the first four days, he shut down, unable to speak.

Five days after the fire, she found a home for rent with enough bedrooms for all of them. It was her sole criterion. The place was so big, they closed off the lower level so they wouldn't have to clean it.

Liz sat the students down after the first day in the rental and said, "Okay guys, here's the thing. This place is too big for André and me to do everything. You're going to have to help." They wrote down all the chores on slips of paper and placed them into a jar.

Fernanda was thrilled to draw vacuuming. Liz laughed, surprised and delighted at her reaction. Shun had to clean the bathrooms. Leon had to wash the dishes after dinner. All he had to do was a few pots and pans, whatever didn't go in the dishwasher.

On the third night in the rental house, Liz went into the kitchen while Leon was at the sink. "And he's got this face on," she says. "I said, 'what's your problem?'"

"I don't like this," Leon said. His voice was low, grumpy. Like a petulant child.

Liz was livid. *How dare he say he doesn't like washing a couple of pots?* Liz believes that confrontation is not a bad thing; if you're having a confrontation, it means you're confronting the issue. She took a breath before speaking.

"Okay, Leon. I'm going to say this once to you, and you're going to hear me. And I promise I will never bring it up again." She paused, took another breath. She spoke slowly, deliberately, calmly. "I don't like living here. But I have to. And you're the reason I do. So suck it up and wash the fucking pot."

The Heart in Loss

Liz and André started hosting in 2005, after their eldest daughter moved out, and ended up having forty-five students over the next fourteen years. When people would ask Liz what hosting was like, she'd say, "It's been one of the greatest experiences I've ever had in my life. I never realized how wonderful it was going to be and how much I was going to learn about other people."

Her two teenagers took on their own "jobs" with the students. Her daughter was in charge of helping them get settled: how to take the bus, how to find their way home, where to go shopping. Their son taught them how to play hockey. Liz's job included all the things you might imagine, plus another perk she hadn't expected. "When I was younger, I wanted to be a teacher," she told me. "It didn't happen—I ended up being an IT manager. But about five years into hosting, I'm doing homework with the kids, and I'm like, 'Oh my God, I'm an English teacher!' It was a lot of fun for me."

Besides having fun, she says their family became more polite to each other—not only the way they talk to each other, but at a deeper level. Knowing that they were setting an example for others raised the stakes. "You become better people," Liz says. When we talk about bias and prejudice, she says she's much less tolerant of other people making inappropriate comments or jokes around her. "Maybe it's because we had this multicultural experience."

Liz and André's positive feelings about hosting didn't diminish after the fire. After suffering such a devastating loss, I wanted to understand what was behind their decision to keep the students with them—especially Leon—and how they resolved things with him afterward. It begins, as many things do, at the beginning: their initial motivation for hosting.

Liz thought joining the homestay program would be like having more children, and in hindsight, she says she wasn't wrong. In fact, that ended up being the most meaningful part of it for her: the students became "part and parcel" of their family. She says their whole family felt the same way. She describes her affection as akin to parental love. She was engaged in their lives and wanted to make an impact on them by teaching them some of the values that have served her and her family, while learning about their culture in return.

This fundamental belief that her students were part of her family showed up in her philosophy about rules. "If you're in my house, you're one of my kids, and you have to live by the same rules as everyone else," Liz says. Growing up in a military family, her childhood was nothing but rules. Hosting forced her to examine whether or not she was setting a rule that was necessary—like having ten-minute showers, so everyone gets enough hot water—or if it was something she was "inflicting" on her kids and students. For example, she relaxed her "you must be home for dinner" rule to allow the kids to enjoy time with their friends, adapting it to "you must tell me where you're going to be" instead. If her students made mistakes, she confronted them head-on with the same consequences that her kids would get. The same was true of their Christmas traditions—all the students were given gifts and stockings. "If you're part of the family, you're part of the family," she says.

Feeling "at home" is another way of talking about love and belonging.

———————

When they talked to Leon after the fire, they told him he had screwed up, but everybody screws up. "Some screw-ups are bigger than others," Liz says.

Well, yes, I thought, many people would say this was a colossal screw-up.

"Tell me about that decision to keep him with you," I say, nudging toward my question. "Why weren't you angry at him?"

"Why wasn't I angry with him," Liz says, but it's not a question. Her answer begins with her story about the fire her brother accidentally set as an eight-year-old. "My dad was horrible to him," Liz explains. "Horrible. My brother burned part of the house down, and my dad made him sleep in it. He was a terrible man. Terrible. He should never have had children...

"My brother was permanently scarred and filled with self-loathing. I think that was in the back of my mind... I remember saying to André on the night of the fire, 'Leon can't define himself by this. It will affect the rest of his life if he does.' We had to go on as normally as we could. And that meant he washed the damn pots."

The family bond that Liz described came up again and again in my interviews, the host survey comments, and student testimonials. While some hosts are quick to identify this as love, others use related words like "bond," "connection," or "friendship," but they share the characteristics of familial love. Psychology professor and researcher Barbara Fredrickson, who is known for her work in positive psychology, defines love as "the preoccupying and strong *desire* for further connection, the powerful *bonds* people hold with a select few and the *intimacy* that grows between them, the *commitments* to loyalty and faithfulness."

In a nutshell, love is large. It is an emotion, but it's also a verb. All loving actions, gestures, words, and commitments produce meaningful connections between hosts and students, but some of the most profound examples come at moments when we are most vulnerable. In the anguish of a devastating loss, or the depths of grief, or the intense pain of heartbreak, love persists.

The Heart in Grief

You might think that Mama Lee, who managed the curfew incident with May, would recall that case when I ask if she had ever felt stretched as a host. Instead, she shares another story.

"I'm going to tell you something, Jennifer... and I'll probably break down," Lee says, gathering her strength as her voice begins to wobble. "My dad got sick. Within three weeks he had passed away. And I had offered to [the students] to go to another home. And there was no way they would leave." The two girls, one from Germany and the other from Brazil, had been with Lee and Danny for two months at that point. "Still to this day—that was eleven, twelve years ago—they keep in touch," Lee says. "That, to me, was a real bond. They saw the whole process of losing and going through the grieving. They told me they were part of my family. That was overwhelming for me."

Grief expert David Kessler says, "What everyone has in common, no matter how they grieve, is a need for their grief to be witnessed. The need is for someone to be fully present to the magnitude of their loss." This is what the girls offered to Lee in those moments: a profound connection.

Sometimes these bonds form swiftly, as with Lee and these two girls. In other cases, they are nurtured over the course of several years. Paul and Tina have been hosting in rural Ontario since 2014. As parents of an only child, they made a conscious decision to introduce other "kids" to their lives. They are an active couple who like to have fun and didn't want to spoil their son. They also wanted him to "get a feel for what it's like to have another person in the house with whom you should negotiate and compromise." They explored the Big Brothers Big Sisters program (wherein adult volunteers are trained as mentors for youth facing adversity), but chose homestay after seeing a Facebook ad that emphasized the cultural exchange aspect. Paul had a specific story to share with me about the most profound experience he had as a host father.

Tales and Yuri are brothers from Brazil. Tales was sixteen when he arrived in Canada for grade eleven. He lived with two other families before moving in with Paul and Tina toward the end of that school year. He returned for grade twelve the following September, staying with them until he graduated.

Tales continued his education at the University of Toronto, about a hundred kilometres (sixty miles) away from Paul and Tina's place. That year, it was his younger brother Yuri's turn to study abroad—so he chose to live with Paul and Tina. Yuri was fourteen when he arrived in August for his grade nine year. Every once in a while, Tales would come to visit Paul and Tina's for the weekend to hang out with their family and his brother.

Not long after Yuri arrived, his parents came for a visit and stayed with Paul and Tina. They became acquainted over family game nights, enjoyed a local hockey game, and travelled around to various attractions. During that visit, Yuri's father extended an invitation to Paul and Tina to visit them in Brazil.

About a month later, in early November, Yuri's mother called Paul and Tina to share the devastating news that Tales and Yuri's father had died of a sudden heart attack. "It was a horrible evening here," Paul says. At first, their mother wasn't sure if the boys should be told before or after they returned home. In the end, they decided Paul should be the bearer of the news. He was also asked to accompany the boys back to Brazil the next day.

When he arrived in Brazil with the two boys, they drove straight to the funeral. "The number of family members who knew us from the stories that [the boys' mother] and the family had shared... and how *everybody* was so thankful, from grandparents, to brothers and sisters, to uncles and aunts... there were so many different people who knew of us and what we'd been doing and how we were involved, it was just so touching," Paul says.

Yuri chose to come back to Canada after the funeral to continue his studies. In the months following, Paul and Tina continued to support his grieving process. "He'd say, 'I'm fine, I'm fine,' and then his emotions would bubble up out of nowhere," Tina says. "He would be sitting watching TV... and then burst out crying. I'd go over and hug him for about five minutes and let him cry it out. And the dogs would come and lick his face and he'd start laughing and say, 'Okay, okay, I'm okay.' So yeah, it was a rough time. But thankfully, we had the prior relationship with the family and with Tales. I think if he'd been in a different home it would have been really difficult for him."

What is this, if not love?

The Heart at Home

Melanie, a host from Brisbane, Australia, says of her expectations of hosting: "I didn't realize I would love them as much as I do." Melanie is known at the Australian Homestay Network (AHN) as having set a record for the longest placement: her first student arrived more than seven years ago and hasn't left yet. "I mean, they're part of the family. Now they're young adults, they've both got boyfriends. The thought of them moving out is *horrible*. It's like having my children move out again."

When I ask Melanie to share an example of a special experience, she doesn't hesitate. It was in April of the year she started hosting—a few months after Laura and another student had arrived from China. Laura loved lizards, and wanted to see a water dragon. These long-legged lizards are greenish-grey with black bands and can grow up to one metre (three feet) long.

One morning, Melanie and Laura took Poppy, Melanie's black miniature poodle, for a walk along Enoggera Creek to look for the lizards. This area is considered an endangered rainforest ecosystem, lush with soaring canopies of native elm, white booyong, and red bean trees. The paths are lined with yellow boxwood, figs, black plum, and weeping lilly pillies. In addition to the lizards, this beautiful area is home to the endangered yellowish-green Coxen's fig parrot and the Richmond birdwing butterfly with its striking iridescent blue-green wings.

On the way back to the house, they encountered a woman coming toward them with a pair of forty-five-kilogram (hundred-pound) chocolate Labrador retrievers. "Her dogs were less than friendly," Melanie says. "So I stepped off the path to give her plenty of room." That's when Melanie lost her footing and fell about three metres (ten feet) down an embankment, landing in a green ants' nest.

Melanie broke her ankle in the fall—so badly that she couldn't walk. "So I'm sitting there, green ants crawling all over me... and so many bites," Melanie says. "I don't know what hurt more: the broken ankle or the green ants."

Melanie ended up needing surgery and was incapacitated for a few weeks. She told Laura and her other student, who were both seventeen at the time, that she would ask AHN to find them a respite homestay until she was back on her feet. "They refused," Melanie says. "They said, 'We want to stay here with you. We can't leave you on your own!'" She understood they didn't want to be uprooted again, but this wasn't just a matter of convenience for the girls. They carried her knee scooter from her bedroom on the lower level up to the main floor every morning and took it down every night. They did all the cooking for the first couple of weeks. "I discovered that I really could eat tofu, and it wouldn't kill me," Melanie says with a laugh. "They were so considerate. They made everything mild enough for me. I still won't eat durian or chicken feet, though.

"I'm not going to be vain and say they liked me so much they wanted to stay," Melanie says. "But to go through the bonding process again, to get used to another homestay, when they were so far from their own homes... they'd been here long enough to feel that *they were at home*."

Feeling "at home" is another way of talking about love and belonging. Research has confirmed that a sense of home "offers a psychological refuge that provides security, safety, protection, and assurance... a haven from the stresses of the external world. Such a home can reduce anxiety and help us cope with change." It's understandable that students, who are undergoing tremendous change, would protect and nurture the bonds that create such a haven.

The Heart in Love

Stew and Jen, the couple from Victoria who hosted the opera singer with the big personality, developed a bond with each of their students. Yoma was a good student and a dutiful son who came to Canada from Japan and pursued his studies based on his father's wishes. He started dating when he was in Victoria and fell hard for another international student. Sadly, their relationship would be ending when they finished the semester, soon going their separate ways, back to their lives overseas.

Jen knew Yoma had been dating, but she hadn't heard many details due to the language barrier. Research has shown that second-language learners prefer their first language to talk about emotional topics; linguistically, the second language has less emotion in it. For instance, people tend to curse in their original language. They also prefer to love in their original language. But he didn't need language for Jen to notice that he was suffering as the semester neared its end.

"His body changed, the way he was walking, the way he would sit at breakfast," Jen told me. "He was in physical pain. I mean, heartbreak at the age of twenty? I can identify with that."

In their last few days and weeks together, Yoma and his girlfriend would spend hours at Tim Hortons until it closed, then hang around parking lots in the dark just to be together. Around that time, Yoma also began to open up to Jen.

"I encouraged him to spend the night with her," she says, giggling conspiratorially. "I said, 'Yoma, you're twenty, you're in love, she's leaving, and you may never see her again. If you want to stay somewhere with her, you can book a room at the Howard Johnson.'"

In the end, the young couple did just that. After Yoma's girlfriend left the country, Jen was still there for him, reminding him that every day he would feel a bit better. She had been through it, and she chose to share her experiences. She told him, "Your heart is broken, and that takes time. It feels awful, and it will keep feeling shitty for a long time, but it will heal."

Eventually, it was time for Yoma to leave as well. The day Jen took him to the airport, it was quiet with just the two of them in the car. As she drove, she pondered the strength of their relationship, feeling glad Yoma felt comfortable enough to not have to speak. Jen described it as a "shared silent space," one that honoured the weeks they had bonded over his lost love. As she describes this scene, I'm right there with her, imagining that special moment, contemplating the sweetness of their connection.

Then Jen pauses, looks at me, and says with a tone of knowing self-deprecation, "And then I glanced over at him, and he was asleep."

CHAPTER SUMMARY

- Love is large. It is an emotion, but it's also a verb.
- When Liz and André lost their house in a fire, they forgave Leon. They saw this as caring for their students as they would care for their own children.
- Hosts often identify the nature of their relationship with their students as familial love—and use words like "a bond," "connection," "part of the family," or "friendship."
- Some of the most profound experiences in homestay happen in difficult moments, but these are powerful reminders of the value of connection.
- Feeling "at home" offers a psychological refuge for students that will help them deal with stress and anxiety.

PART TWO

Culture Is Everywhere

4

Creating Safe Spaces
Empathy and Belonging

*Empathy and tolerance go hand in hand
when you're dealing with people from different cultures.
Superstitions, food, clothing, how they behave in a family...
hosts can't be like, "Oh my god, what are you doing?"*
CHRIS, host from Ottawa, Ontario

THE EMERGENCY CALL from Evelyn came late on a Friday night in September. Evelyn is one of CHN's longest and most loyal hosts; she has looked after more than one hundred students in Toronto since 2003.

"Artem has disappeared," she said, rushing and breathless. "He just took off, and I don't know where he is. It's past curfew. I'm worried about him, and I don't know how much more of this I can take. He's more interested in being with his friends than going to school." Her voice had a high-pitched tremor, warbling with intensity.

Fern, the homestay coordinator who answered the phone, told Evelyn she would try to track him down and make it clear that he had to return to Evelyn's home immediately. As a seventeen-year-old Russian student, Artem was still a minor and had certain rules to follow.

It took a few stern text messages and voice mails, but eventually Artem returned her call. It was well past 1:00 a.m. by this point.

"I'm in a shelter," he said, his voice nearly a whisper.

"Why did you go to a shelter? Where is it?"

"It's too embarrassing. I cannot say. I cannot face my host for shame. I don't want to talk about it," he said. Muffled sniffles and a hitch in his voice betrayed his emotion.

"What's the name of the shelter, Artem?" Fern needed to make sure he was safe, and needed to get him back to Evelyn's home as soon as possible. *How did he check himself in to a shelter? Don't they have rules about minors?*

"I have a clean room and food," he said, avoiding Fern's questions. "It's in a secure location. I want to spend the night here."

"You cannot stay there! It's completely against our rules. We are responsible for making sure you are safe, with one of our hosts. I will talk to Evelyn. She'll be okay, I promise. I'll make sure she is calm, so you can go back tonight."

"No! I cannot! Please don't make me—you don't understand..." His voice cracked, and he sniffled again. "I'm begging you. I'll call you in the morning. Please don't tell my parents!"

"I can't promise that, Artem. You are a minor and we have to tell your parents where you are."

"Please don't. I will call you tomorrow, I promise."

Fern relented on the understanding that Artem would call by 8:00 a.m. the following day, or sooner if he had any trouble in the meantime. She contacted Evelyn to relay her conversation. Evelyn sputtered with frustration, saying she couldn't believe he had taken it this far.

"It was nothing!" she said, raising her voice. "He phoned me at the last minute to say he wouldn't be home for dinner. I reminded him about the rules that he has not been following. I told him we would have to have a conversation when he gets home. His dirty laundry is all over his bedroom, and the lunch I made him on Tuesday—which he said he loved, by the way—was on the floor. I told him I had found the food. On top of that, there's mould in his toilet. I saw that once before—with another student who threw up all the time. I don't think he's eating enough. He's skinnier than my eleven-year-old grandson, for heaven's sake!"

"Have you talked about this with Artem's homestay coordinator, Danny?"

"Yes, he's aware. I've been struggling since Artem arrived. I'm worried that he's harming himself in ways that we don't know. Why would he take off over such a minor incident? The lying, the broken promises. It's too much."

In some ways, Artem resembles many seventeen-year-old boys. He keeps his hair cut in a manner reminiscent of Harry Styles: long on top and short on the sides and back, with a few wild wisps and a fashionable amount of volume. A sparse scruff of facial hair dusts his upper lip and chin, and his sharp Adam's apple nudges out of his long neck. A prominent upward sweep of his right eyebrow gives his otherwise neutral expression an air of mischief. But Artem is not a mischievous young man. On the contrary, he is exceptionally focused, resourceful, articulate, and intelligent.

He also suffers from depression.

In a lengthy email to Danny and Fern that Saturday afternoon, Artem opened up about his mental health. He was already so overwhelmed that he couldn't handle his host mother Evelyn's response. He wrote, "It's getting colder, darker. I need to go to school, where I'm an outcast. I'm in a new country (which I don't like, by the way). I can barely handle it, and a minor inconvenience can completely destroy me." He understood that it might have been better to disclose his condition up front, in his homestay application. Artem admitted to breaking Evelyn's reasonable rules, said he was irresponsible, and that he had made a few mistakes already. "Even if she is a kind and caring person, I'm too embarrassed to face her and admit my fault, because I'm weak. Besides, she doesn't trust my sincerity anyway."

He escaped to the shelter because the alternative was too bleak. "I don't want to harm myself. I can't throw all of my mental progress into trash. I'll do anything for my well-being, even if it's radical. I don't want to feel depressed." Artem would work on his relationship with Evelyn, as long as she understood that he was truly sorry.

Whether Evelyn would have him back, however, was moot. The lack of trust in their relationship combined with his undisclosed depression and rule-breaking were grounds enough to dismiss Artem from the program.

But that email! It was filled with heartfelt remorse, logic, and vulnerability. Artem's homestay coordinator, Danny, wanted to give him another chance.

When Danny tells me this story months later, he says Artem's reaction to Evelyn reminded Danny of his own experience growing up in Vietnam. He moved to Canada as an international student when he was in high school. "I understand [Artem] because when I was younger, in my household, people would yell at me all the time," Danny says. "It's how my culture works. Back then, I could not talk back, so I understand that completely. That anxiety, I used to have that in high school and college, too."

Danny had a long conversation with Artem later that Saturday. "I told Artem, 'Okay, I understand where you are coming from. But you have to promise me that you're never going to do this again. If you have any problem, you text me. You call me.' I gave him my personal number. 'Promise me you won't go to the homeless shelter again. It's not safe for you, and it's against our rules. You could be asked to leave the program if you do this again.'"

Artem agreed, leaving Danny to find a different host who would take him.

Mike and Lee-Anne had hosted Artem during his two-week pandemic quarantine period when he first arrived from Russia in August, before he moved to Evelyn's. A retired couple in their sixties, they have over twenty years' experience hosting international students. Mike's salt-and-pepper beard frames a gentle smile. Lee-Anne is warm and inviting; she is a self-proclaimed talker and loves people. The only problem was their location, more than an hour from Artem's school on public transit. Nevertheless, Artem was comfortable with them and they had no problem taking him back, with full disclosure of the issues he had faced with Evelyn. This would suffice as a short-term placement until Danny could find a host in a better location.

For the first week, Danny called Artem every night. Artem preferred deep topics—politics, religion, geography, and social matters—but he also had a soft spot for trains. He enjoyed taking a ninety-minute train trip to the Hamilton Museum of Steam & Technology. Over time, Artem began to open up about his history of depression, his struggles at school, and his friends.

During those conversations he told Danny he'd like to stay with Mike and Lee-Anne, despite the daily commute: they didn't question him about his eating habits and he liked their energetic environment. If Artem made a mistake, Mike would explain, in great detail, what he had done wrong. It made him feel guilty, but it didn't trigger his anxiety.

The conversations with Danny reduced in frequency to a few times a week. In October, he told Danny that he was considering applying for refugee status.

Danny was shocked. "I asked him why. He told me that he is bisexual, and in Russia that's not okay. He is from an Eastern Orthodox family and his parents would reject him if he returned, as would his neighbours and church—it's a small community. He was bullied and traumatized at a young age by his peers due to his sexuality. He said, 'This is my way out.' He said his parents didn't know, and asked me not to tell them. I took a moment to understand it, and we left it there that night."

Being a Wisdom Keeper

When Artem told Danny that he was applying for refugee status and asked Danny to keep it a secret, Danny felt torn. This promise was critical to reinforcing trust in their relationship, and yet, our organization is generally obligated to disclose all information about minors to their parents.

Danny's first step was to call his supervisor to discuss the case. With the help of legal advisers, our team determined that we didn't have to inform Artem's parents, which was a huge relief to both Danny and Artem. Artem's journey was far from over, and Danny wanted to continue to support him as best he could.

This is one of the great rewards of homestay: the chance to connect deeply with others. In CHN's 2022 host survey, 24 percent of respondents said they started hosting to provide care and support to the students. They see hosting as an opportunity to be a good role model and influence young people, providing love and care in the process. Some of our hosts are immigrants or were international students like Danny, and understand what it's like to adapt to life in a new country. One host said, "English is my second language and I know how difficult it was to learn, and how scared I was." Another host said, "As an immigrant I know how it feels to miss your home country and the warmth of family life, so I decided to provide that kind of experience for foreign students." Regardless of background, good hosts want to help students adapt to their new life so they can have a positive experience.

In my experience, this motivation is an essential element for all successful host-student relationships. Susan, a host in Ottawa, explains, "I think you have a responsibility to guide the student. If that is taken away, then you might as well be renting your room out... It's the guidance that brings you together—they're young, scared, in a new country, and may not be used to going to someone for help. All of a sudden, all they have is you. If you become that safe place, if they know they're going to get good advice, and comfort, and someone to sympathize with what they're going through, that's what matters. I guess it's the mentor thing... what's the word? Someone who is a 'wisdom keeper' for the new culture they're in. The host needs to be the person they can go to who's not going to judge them, but will give them truths. Deep truths. It builds a tremendous amount of trust."

Hosts and coordinators alike can create these safe spaces, as Susan explains, by providing judgment-free guidance and "deep truths" based on wisdom drawn from their life experiences. It's what Lee did with May, when she taught her to be cautious with strangers. It's what Danny did with Artem.

Being a wisdom keeper requires a good deal of empathy, as Danny demonstrated. Recognizing and talking about someone's struggles by saying, "I've been there, too" can be a powerful source of connection. But it can fall flat when you find out—due to cultural differences—that you haven't, in fact, "been there." The good news is you can improve your chances of creating safe and supportive environments by learning about the ways emotions differ across cultures, allowing you to express empathy more effectively.

There's no such thing as universal basic emotions or predictable facial configurations.

Empathy Is More Than a Feeling

Empathizing with your students' experiences can seem easy: many people have travelled abroad, learned a new language, faced awkward social situations, lamented embarrassing changes in their bodies, been left out, or suffered from mood disorders like anxiety or depression. However, when you try to be empathetic by imagining how someone must be feeling based on your own experiences, you run the risk of misinterpreting their emotions. Likewise, your efforts to improve someone's well-being—another facet of empathy—can fall flat if you don't know what would make them feel better. We just can't know everything about someone else's reality.

Even if you are aware of the gap between your reality and another person's, you may be tempted to gauge someone's emotion by reading facial expressions or interpreting physical gestures. This, too, is risky. Despite early research suggesting otherwise, there's no such thing as universal basic emotions or predictable facial expressions.

A smile in Japan does not always convey happiness—it could be a way to mask an underlying emotion of sadness or disgust.

Holding eye contact in many cultures is considered rude or disrespectful.

Nodding means "yes" in some cultures, and "no" in others.

Winking in Latin America is considered a romantic invitation; in Nigeria it's a way to tell your kids to leave the room; in China it's considered rude.

If I pucker my lips it mimics a kiss, but in Latin America, the Philippines, and Puerto Rico, I could be mistaken for trying to point at something.

A student who appears withdrawn, distant, or quiet may *not* be unhappy or maladjusted.

These kinds of variations in how we express emotions are also true within a given culture. When I'm nervous, I laugh. It's awkward, but it's a chuckle nonetheless, and it doesn't mean I'm amused. When my kids say that something is "good," it can mean mediocre, acceptable, or outstanding, depending on the context. Anger looks and feels different when someone cuts you off in traffic versus when your student stays out late after a day of skiing and doesn't call to update you on her plans.

In other words, your understanding of emotions—what's healthy or unhealthy, rude or not rude, bad or good, right or wrong—is based on your own experiences. Those experiences are informed by your family of origin, gender, socio-economic status, race, religion, and of course, culture. And they aren't universal.

Batja Mesquita is a social psychologist who specializes in the study of emotions across cultures. In her compelling book *Between Us: How Cultures Create Emotions*, Mesquita makes the case that emotions are "social practices," and understanding how different cultures experience emotions requires insight into that culture's social norms and expectations. These norms are taught to people by their parents when they're very young.

For example, I'm from a culture that values individual achievement. When my children perform well in school, succeed in a sport, or learn a new skill, I praise their effort to help them feel good about themselves. In other words, in my culture, I'm teaching my kids that pride is good—what Mesquita calls a "right" emotion. In a culture like Taiwan's, praising a child like this would be unacceptable, or "wrong," whereas shame would be "right." There is no good translation for *self-esteem* in Chinese. This is because the norms and expectations in the Taiwanese cultural context depend on propriety. Children and adults alike need to know their place in the social network.

Anger also shows up differently across cultures. In the US, when someone is wronged, the cultural context condones defending one's rights, extending blame where it's due, and insisting on fairness. In these ways, anger can be a justifiable means to an end, and is a "right" emotion. In Japan, on the other hand, anger (*ikari*) is considered destructive to relational harmony and is therefore "wrong." Instead of displaying anger the way an American would, Japanese people are encouraged by their cultural context to try to apologize for their contribution to the conflict and understand the other person's perspective.

Bridging cultural differences in emotions can be tricky, but it doesn't mean you shouldn't try. Decades of research support the idea that people can grow their empathy and become kinder as a result of practice. Empathy is not a fixed trait—we can turn it up and down like the volume knob on a stereo. Hosts can also get better at understanding the role culture plays in their experience of emotion, and in turn, avoiding the assumption that they know what someone is feeling. Learning about others requires a certain humility: a willingness to question nearly everything we do, and feel, and think, in an effort to open ourselves to another person's perspective.

In practice, Mesquita recommends three steps to unpack the meaning behind someone's emotional experience.

1 **Ask how or why what happened matters to them.** Consider questions like, "When X happened, did it affect your self-esteem? Your honour? Your status in your community? Did it say something about you or your family? What is important to you in this situation? What would your parents or friends say about what happened?"

   In his email, Artem gave Danny insight as to what was at stake for him: his fragile mental health and his reputation with Evelyn. If his parents found out what happened, he knew he would be in trouble and couldn't bear the thought of facing them.

2. **Inquire into the emotions being felt, and ask what the words mean to them.** Labelling emotions is difficult for many people; this is a skill that must be cultivated. Furthermore, your student may not know the right word to translate their feeling into English—indeed, the word may not even exist in English. Even if they know the translation, it may not mean what you think. There are many ways to understand anger, love, grief, shame, and so on. You could say something like, "What expression would you use to describe the feeling? What does the emotion want to do, or what does it accomplish? Does it help you be the person you want to be? How would your family react to this emotion?" You can also ask what their bodily reactions, like smiling or crying or being quiet, mean to them.

Artem wrote words like *embarrassment, shame, weakness, depression*. His emotions meant he needed to escape the situation, because the alternative would have been too harmful to his well-being. His family probably would have approved of his shame, but his choice to break the homestay program rules would have lowered his standing in their eyes, jeopardizing their relationship.

3. **Ask how this situation should end, or what the next step should be. Don't assume there's a right answer.** Think about how emotional episodes engage people with each other, or the way they impact relationships. You could say, "How would you like this situation to resolve? What should happen next? What are your goals in this relationship?"

Artem's final message was that he wanted to work on his relationship with Evelyn, but that he needed her to believe he was remorseful. His goal was to repair the relationship, and he was willing to be more vulnerable and open with his feelings going forward. On this basis of deeper understanding, Danny could help Artem begin anew with Mike and Lee-Anne. It also laid a foundation of safety for further disclosures—about his plans to apply for refugee status, and why—which might have been impossible otherwise.

These steps for unpacking emotions may feel clunky at first, especially if you are pretty sure you understand your student already. However, Mesquita reminds us that there's no shortcut to this process. Like any new skill, it will take time and practice to get better. And if you stick with it, I am confident that the tools will help you in your journey to the kind of rewarding relationships you hope for in homestay.

With the help of an immigration lawyer, Artem submitted his application to seek protection as a refugee in late November 2021, three months after he turned seventeen. As a refugee claimant, he had access to the Interim Federal Health Program and other services, such as subsidized temporary housing, loans, life skills training, and referrals to community resources. By January, Artem's application for housing was approved. He could move out of homestay into his own apartment by February 1. "It brought me huge joy at the end by being able to help Artem," Danny says.

An Emotional Burden

Bonding with a student over a shared experience, as empowering and meaningful as it can be, can come at a cost. In CHN's 2022 host survey, 18 percent of respondents said the most challenging part of hosting was the emotional burden: stress and worry over the student's well-being, having to be available

24/7, having to address behavioural issues, and the overall added responsibility of caring for another person's child. It also includes logistical pressures, such as being "on" all the time, or dealing with the lack of privacy.

The weight of concern for students certainly rings true for Danny, who continued to check in with Artem long after he left our program. In April 2022, Artem told Danny that he was getting along with his new roommate. He was living in Hamilton, Ontario, a university city a couple of hours west of Toronto, while finishing high school online and trying to navigate his new life. He had mustered up the courage to tell his parents about his decision to immigrate to Canada. Artem told Danny they were furious at first, but they were coming around.

In October 2022, a couple of months after Artem's eighteenth birthday, Danny called Artem again. He had recently moved to Montreal, "to start a new journey." To Danny's delight, Artem said his application for refugee status was accepted, which gave him "protected person" status. It meant he could stay in Canada and apply to become a permanent resident.

"I congratulated him and received the usual awkward laugh in return," Danny told me. "We talked about politics, ideology, and then the war [between Russia and Ukraine] and I learned something new about him. His dad is Ukrainian and his mom is Russian. They moved to Moscow so their kids could have a better future... Sadly Artem told me he is no longer in contact with his parents. Maintaining a relationship with them is hurtful. He has been seeing a therapist to help him overcome the pain of facing his parents with the hope of one day finding common ground."

At that time, Artem was still working on finishing his Ontario diploma, with the hopes of attending university in the future. He may need to enroll in a trade school in the meantime to gain the skills necessary to support himself.

By supporting students through difficult experiences, helping them find their way, you are sending a message that you accept them as they are.

When Danny hung up, he wasn't sure if he should feel happy or sad for Artem. He was excited that Artem's status was approved, yet taken aback to learn Artem's relationship with his parents was so strained. He was relieved that Artem was happily settled in Montreal yet concerned about how lonely he must be. A few minutes later, Danny's phone vibrated with a new text message from Artem.

Thank you for reaching out to me. I really don't have anyone to talk to.

Artem searched for refuge in Canada because he feared for his life in Russia as a bisexual man. What of the students like him who have to return home? Deirdre, one of our homestay coordinators, recalls a young woman from Taiwan who studied at a language school in downtown Toronto back in the '90s. On her last day at school, she had come out to her teacher as a lesbian, and she was terrified of going home because it was illegal there. Same-sex marriage has been legal in Taiwan since 2019, but this was 1998. Deirdre and the teachers were concerned for her. "She came here and figured out who she was, and felt comfortable, and then she had to go back home," Deirdre says. "What do you do? Do you go back to your old life? Some of them have found a community and feel safe, but some of them…" Deirdre trails off in mid-sentence, considering the consequences for this young woman.

Some emotional burdens come from supporting students who aren't mature enough or independent enough to leave home, and struggle to adapt. Others don't want to be here in the first place. In one such instance, a host said, "Every outing was a painful event and we had no support from the parents. He never adhered to the homestay agreement and missed the school bus minimum three times a week."

Kenda, a host from Ontario, said she has noticed students being sent abroad "because the parents don't know what to do with them at home." Kenda has the impression those parents are hoping their kids will be "fixed" by this experience. With these students, "it's hard to turn them around. The ones who really wanted to come, it works; those are the ones who are sitting at supper with you and talking and asking questions, and showing you photos of their home, and calling you mum and dad. The others... it's kind of sad. But we never give up on them." If these students act out by not going to school, breaking curfews, or being belligerent, it helps to recognize that they may be dealing with some deeper issues.

Supporting a student through emotional upheaval—such as homesickness, going through a tough breakup, having doubts about the future, and so on—can be exhausting. As I explored in chapter 3, one of the most painful experiences to witness is grief, which turns one's empathy all the way up.

On the morning of April 16, 2014, the Korean ferry MV *Sewol* sank off the coast of South Korea. It was a standard overnight crossing from Incheon to Jeju Island, one of three regular sailings a week. This trip was unique in many respects, perhaps most significantly because it was carrying twice the legal limit of cargo. A sudden turn caused the boat to list to the right. Within minutes, it was leaning thirty degrees—and then it started sinking. Three hundred and four people died in the disaster, including 250 youth from Danwon High School.

It was a devastating tragedy, sparking national mourning and intense public criticism of the government, which was partly blamed for lack of adequate oversight. The captain and fourteen other members of the crew were convicted on charges related to the sinking.

At the time of the *Sewol* disaster, Susan and her husband were hosting a Korean student, Lucy. Supporting Lucy as the news unfolded, and beyond, was a profound learning experience for Susan. "When things happen in different parts of the world, you get a first-hand view into it," Susan says. "It becomes personal." This wasn't just another sound bite, a tragic event on the other side of the world that would fade into the background of Susan's busy life.

Each of these opportunities to empathize, as emotionally difficult as they can be, contribute to a sense of safety and comfort in your home. By supporting students through difficult experiences, helping them find their way, you are sending a message that you accept them as they are. In other words, they belong.

Belonging

Chris and her husband, Simon, have hosted more than a hundred students in thirty years, and she loves it just as much now as she did at the beginning. "When I started in 1991, my oldest son had left for university and we had a spare room. We replaced him with a better model," she says, with a wry grin. "We hosted a friend of our son's from a local university. When he left, I put up a sign, 'room available,' and we started getting a lot of students. After that, it was mostly word of mouth."

Chris is a retired federal government worker, and Simon is a software engineer. They live in Ottawa, the capital of Canada and a beautiful city of about one million residents. Chris didn't have any expectations going into hosting—it was all "kind of brand new." Her husband was in the military and they were used to having a lot of structure and rules in their home. "We wanted someone to fit in to the house and follow what we wanted," she says. But after they started hosting she realized this wasn't how it worked. "That was a long time ago," Chris says. "Expectations change. I have a lot more information about different cultures in my toolbox. Things like their values, food preferences, likes and dislikes. We've become an international family. My children have benefitted as well, helping these students, being ambassadors."

One of Chris's favourite experiences as a host mother involved a German high school student who lived with them for a full school year. A few months after Rika arrived, they were sitting at the kitchen counter together, chatting. Out of the blue, Rika said, "You know, it's been four months and there's been no screaming."

Chris knew she had to respond carefully. She started by listening without judgment. Rika's father had high standards. If she scored 90 percent on a test, he would demand to know why she didn't get 95 percent.

Not living up to your parents' expectations can be part of the heartache of not feeling a sense of belonging at home. Peer pressure can have the same effect, leading people to change who they are to be accepted in their social group, putting the need to fit in as an artificial version of themselves above the need to belong as they are.

Chris created the opportunity for belonging with Rika—not only by listening, but also by being open about her own experiences as a teenager. "I always tell my students, 'Stop beating yourself up; nobody's perfect,'" she says. "You can't pick your parents. My mother had her issues, too."

Susan has also seen the academic pressure put on her students. "I had one student who was struggling with perfectionism," she says. "My heart went out to her because she's an artist, but wasn't allowed to be herself... You have to follow your bliss; that's where your genius will come from. It will blossom if you pursue it." Susan's perspective is born from a culture that values the individual over the group. This is not the case for many homestay students who grew up in a collectivist culture, like those in South America, China, or South Korea. These cultures place more emphasis on relationships, loyalty, and the well-being of the group. The pursuit of individual goals and "following your bliss" will be a foreign and, possibly, unappealing concept to them. Nevertheless, allowing a young person to feel seen, heard, and valued for who they are, rather than who they're supposed to be, builds connection and contributes to their sense of self-worth.

Sometimes, feeling seen and heard means *not* becoming part of the family. Asuka had been staying with Mary, her husband, John, and their two-year-old daughter, Kiera, for a couple of weeks, but was clearly not enjoying herself. She had been reclusive, spending a lot of time in her room. When the family would play "dance party" after dinner, for the first few days she would sit on the floor and watch, but not participate. Mary offered to play games or cards, asking what she wanted to do but, again, Asuka showed no interest.

One night, she didn't even want to sit and watch, so Mary invited her to the kitchen to help clean up after dinner instead. In the quiet of the kitchen, Asuka finally spoke up.

"I hate to say this, but I do not like kids," she said.

Mary was surprised; the application from the school had indicated that Asuka's only homestay preference was "a clean house." Mary's response was to empathize. "That is okay," Mary said. "When I was your age, I didn't like kids, either! It took me a long time to want one of my own! Clearly, this is not the right house for you. Let's get you to a house that has all the things you want and need." Asuka did move to a new home, but in the meantime, she could finally be herself.

Besides displaying empathy and making genuine efforts to connect, each of these adults—Danny, Mike and Lee-Anne, Chris, Susan, and Mary—are grounded in themselves and who they are. They approach their relationships with their students with humility and a willingness to grow, aware that when dealing with other cultures, they will never stop learning. And they take on the emotional burden of hosting, trusting that the rewards will make the challenges worthwhile.

CHAPTER SUMMARY

- Be a wisdom keeper for your student, offering them support and deep truths as they adapt to this new place and culture.
- Ask for help if you are struggling with the emotional burden of hosting, and know that your efforts are meaningful.
- Remember, you can't tell what someone is feeling by their facial expression, physical gestures, or even their words. Check your assumptions by asking questions.
- Don't forget Batja Mesquita's three steps for unpacking emotional episodes, from *Between Us: How Cultures Create Emotions*.
  1. Ask how or why what happened matters to your student.
  2. Inquire into the emotions being felt, and ask what the words mean to them.
  3. Ask how this situation should end, or what the next step should be. Don't assume there's a right answer.

5

There's No Accounting for Taste
Stories about Food

I've loved preparing meals for my kids: having their breakfasts ready in the morning, making their lunch bags with goodies to share... and dinners with family, other hosts, and their students.
JUDY, host from Cornwall, Ontario

THEY SAY that if you drink the water in Dangriga, you are bound to return. The superstition struck me as endearing when I heard it on my first trip to Belize, in 1997. I was there as a tourist, on holiday with my university roommate for a sea kayaking adventure. I returned in 1999 with a new purpose: to work as a student midwife. My midwifery school required all students to attend a minimum of a hundred births in order to graduate. To satisfy this requirement, most students had to travel to a high-volume birth centre or hospital, and most of these were in the developing world.

Dangriga is a small coastal town in Belize with a population of fewer than eight thousand people, mostly Garifuna, Belizean

Creoles, and Mestizos. For adventurous tourists, it's also a popular access point to the Belize Barrier Reef, but they don't linger in this gritty town.

For five weeks, I lived in the "nurses' quarters" of the Dangriga Hospital, a building elevated on stilts to protect it from flooding, like most of the houses. Short staircases descended from the doorways and breezeways to reach the sandy ground. Its wind-battered wooden siding had been white at one time, but the paint was faded and peeling. The staff room had one of the only refrigerators on the property. The long, narrow ward along the side facing the ocean was for in-patients; children recovered from fevers alongside aging grandparents with broken bones.

Nobody else lived at the hospital, so I had two bedrooms, a bathroom, a shower with no hot water, and a kitchen with a broken stove and no refrigerator. I didn't have a phone or computer, either. Belize was a developing country in 1999; there was no such thing as a smartphone yet.

My first night there tested what I thought I knew about heat and bugs. Summers in Ontario, where I grew up, were nothing compared to January in Dangriga. With no screens on the windows and no air conditioning, I was at the mercy of the mosquitoes. I couldn't cover my face with the sleeping bag lest I suffocate. I hardly slept that night. I arose the next morning with my face covered in mosquito bites. I was hot, itchy, and buzzing with anger and exhaustion. My first purchase at the market that afternoon was a mosquito net, which I hung with care over my bed.

It wasn't just the climate that I found hard. The culture shock of attending births as a student midwife was draining, frustrating, and often frightening. I worried about my skills and lamented my inability to speak to most of the patients (who only spoke Spanish or Creole). I tried to stay up for the night shifts, and slept during the oppressive heat of the day—but if a woman arrived in labour, I would need to be awake, no matter when it happened.

On top of all this, I struggled with the food: what to eat, when to eat it, where to get it, and how to store it. The weekly farmers' market had a dazzling array of tropical fruit and vegetables, but I had no means to cook or refrigerate anything. The two or three restaurants in town only served local cuisine.

The national dish of Belize is rice and beans—not to be confused with beans and rice—and most locals eat one or the other every day for lunch and/or dinner. The primary difference between the two dishes, of course, is the preparation. Rice and beans is a one-pot dish of white rice and kidney beans cooked with onions and garlic and a blend of spices known as *recado*: annatto, oregano, cumin, clove, cinnamon, black pepper, allspice, garlic, and salt. It's often served with stewed or barbecued chicken, beef, or pork, and a side of coleslaw or potato salad and plantain. For beans and rice, on the other hand, the beans are cooked separately and served over a bed of rice, also with a protein and fried plantain.

Other Belizean dishes—fried fish, coconut fish stew, vegetable and pigtail stew, pupusas, tamilitos, and soups—were hard to find, unlike the rice and beans and beans and rice, which I ended up eating almost every day. Just like a local, but with far less enthusiasm.

One afternoon, I stopped at the tiny general store for some sunscreen. The shop was about three square metres (about thirty-two square feet), with a counter running along the length of one wall. The shelves were stocked with dry goods, meat, pharmaceuticals, and a few souvenirs. Much to my surprise, they also carried a product that gave me a singular glimpse of home: Kellogg's Corn Flakes. I was overcome by nostalgia, relief, and hunger, and had to stop myself from weeping right in that dusty little shop. Thankfully, they also carried powdered milk. I suddenly felt like I could cope again.

From that day on, my favourite meal was breakfast. Every morning, I would take a cereal bowl to the staff room and fetch a single ice cube from the freezer, making sure to top up the tray if it was running low. Upon returning to my quarters, I would mix up the powdered milk with some tepid water and the ice cube and wait for it to melt, which never took long. Finally, I'd pour in the corn flakes. The chalky texture of the milk didn't bother me. With a bowl of corn flakes for breakfast, the cold showers were more tolerable, the lack of sleep more bearable, and the lonely stretches of time with nobody to talk to a little less lonely.

Living in Belize gave me a new definition of comfort food. It used to mean a handful of dishes my mother made when I was a child, or fed me when I was sick—Chicken à la King, apple crumble, scrambled eggs and toast. I now understand it to mean something much broader, much deeper. Comfort food is not about the food. It's about the memories, rituals, and people; it's about familiarity, love, and home. When I talk about food in the context of homestay, I'm not just talking about ingredients or nutrition, I am talking about culture: family culture, regional culture, national culture. I'm talking about the very things that make us who we are, and define us in relation to others.

Food Culture

Food culture refers to the traditions, rituals, beliefs, values, and habits connected to growing, preparing, eating, serving, and celebrating food. Food culture is influenced by ethnicity, climate, social and political history, family history, and geography. Food is intimately connected to time and place, making it an important way to connect and relate to others. Given the link between food and home, people will always choose what to eat and how to prepare it based on what it means to them. When hosts and students come together over a meal, in addition to sharing food, they are also creating an emotional connection and sharing a cultural experience.

Therefore, it isn't such a stretch to learn that complaints over food are among the most common issues faced by homestay organizations. In CHN's 2022 survey, 14 percent of hosts said the most difficult or challenging part of hosting related to food: the logistics and time involved in meal planning, grocery shopping, and food preparation; the headache and stress of satisfying picky eaters, dietary restrictions, and diverse palates; and the overall burden and financial cost of this daily responsibility.

While these issues are vast and varied, questions over what to eat can be grouped into three broad themes: quantity, quality, and preferences. In other words, our team at CHN manages conflicts over hosts who don't serve enough food and students who eat too much. Students expect a certain quality of food to be served as a family, and will complain when they're tired of eating takeout and frozen dinners while watching television with their hosts—or worse, without anyone at all. And naturally, stories about food preferences abound.

Thankfully, there are also a lot of wonderful stories about food. My colleagues and I love seeing photos and videos of students enjoying their first taste of pumpkin pie, roast lamb, pavlova, or poutine; hosts being treated to a delicious spread of foreign delicacies carefully prepared by their student; and students meeting extended family and neighbours at barbecues and birthday parties. Mealtimes provide hosts a chance to encourage students to practice their English, while sharing details from their day at school or working through a challenging social situation. In the end, when you remember that food is not just about the food—it's how you connect, how you express yourself and your culture—you give yourself a chance to deepen your relationships while celebrating difference.

In her TED talk "The Hunt for General Tso," Jennifer 8. Lee says, "what you want to cook and eat is an accumulation, a function of your experiences—the people you've dated, what you've learned, where you've gone. There may be inbound elements from other cultures, but you'll always eat things that mean something to you."

Quantity

Mama Lee, whom I introduced in the first chapter with her student May, embodies the love and caring that gives Maritimers their legendary reputation for hospitality. She's the mom whose kitchen is always full. "The kids never go without," she says. For example, she likes to keep five or six loaves of bread in the refrigerator or freezer—whole wheat, multigrain, white, sourdough—whatever they want.

Lee was already hosting three boys from China and Vietnam when Fred arrived at her home. Originally from Bangladesh, he had been living with another host family nearby and needed to be moved, but the homestay coordinator hadn't told her why. When Fred arrived, he said he was on a special diet and was trying to lose weight. She didn't question him further.

The next morning, the bread was gone. All six loaves had disappeared overnight. It had to have been Fred, Lee concluded. He didn't deny it.

"Are you hungry?" She asked him, with a smile and a strong hint of sarcasm.

"No," he said, somewhat sheepishly. "I just love bread!"

Lee bought more bread, but not before explaining to him that he had to leave some for the rest of the family. Her instructions didn't get through to him, but she wasn't sharing this story with me to criticize or complain. "That's what he would eat," she says, with a shrug. "I would make pasta, salmon pieces, white rice, quinoa... all for him. He'd cook a five-pound bag of quinoa and eat all of it within a day. I'd make a pot of spaghetti, and he'd mound his plate, like he wasn't going to get any more. And then he'd finish and want some bread. That's the way it was."

Lee continues, her voice rising with delight as she recalls how ridiculous it was. "I'd say, 'Okay, boys, hide that loaf of bread for the lunches tomorrow, or it will be gone!'" The other students in the home would chuckle about it. "Anyway, that was one of my funnier ones."

The question of what constitutes a "normal" serving size, or how much students should be expected to snack between meals, or what food should be available for students to eat, is a matter of individual taste, as Lee and Fred's story illustrates. As a homestay organization, we provide general guidelines to help manage expectations on both sides, but most of it comes down to common sense.

For instance, eating six loaves of bread—or even one loaf a day—is too much (though some students, such as athletes, pay extra for more daily calories). Limiting a student to two pieces of bread at breakfast—and counting how many pieces have been consumed—is too little. (Hosts who ration their student's food in this way won't last long in our program.) Eating all the family's leftovers for lunch is too much, and sending a student to school with a package of instant noodles is too little. Eating the organic, gluten-free bar that was being saved as a special snack for the toddler is too much; having no snacks between meals is too little.

Comfort food is not about the food. It's about the memories, rituals, and people; it's about familiarity, love, and home.

Your homestay coordinator can help with conflicts over the amount of food being served or consumed. In some cases, our coordinators have advocated on the host's behalf with students' families for additional compensation for large appetites or specialized diets. When hosts aren't serving enough food, our team can reset expectations and address any underlying concerns and assumptions.

When I ask Lee how she coped with Fred's eating habits, she agrees that it was a lot, but she never asked him to move to a new family. "I made sure that the agency knew," Lee says. "Fred would get angry if he didn't get a loaf of bread to eat. It was astonishing," she adds. In fact, she suspects he may have been asked to move to her home because the previous host couldn't cope with his appetite. She says it helped that she had three other students, and she was used to keeping a lot of food in the house. I press the matter, wondering if there was some wisdom she could offer to other hosts. She agrees that he *was* eating too much bread, and would remind him to share with the other students. But Lee also points out his qualities. "You know, he'd learn some things," she says. "He was so helpful. He was right there to be an assistant to anything you wanted to do. Like, he knew I was treatin' him good, but then he'd try to treat back." Lee could overlook the inconvenient aspects of hosting when she saw him as a "good kid" who deserved care and support and empathy, and he demonstrated a willingness to learn and adapt. "I've had so many experiences over the years," says Lee. "But the students are all looking for some type of know-how. They want to grow up. To learn how to do stuff differently."

Some disputes over quantity of food are related to a cultural norm or expectation. On a business trip to China in 2015, I was amazed by what I learned about Chinese food. Not only was it delicious, nutritious, and bore no resemblance to any Chinese food I've eaten in North America, but also the quantity of food served at every meal was remarkable.

I had the good fortune of staying with a host family one night—a teacher from one of our partner schools in Suzhou—and she held a small dinner party for me with six other guests. Since the host didn't cook much, the international school director asked her husband to come over to prepare the meal. When the first four dishes landed on the table (marinated chicken in sauce; shrimp; lotus root; and a mixture of celery and corn), I ate enough to be satisfied. Then came a huge plate of roasted pork belly drenched in a sweet sauce that melted in my mouth; eight fillets of grilled fish with a simple seasoning; and fried rice. It was like another whole meal, and I wished I had paced myself for this feast. Next to arrive was a plate of green beans; a big bowl of soft tofu swimming in a brown sauce; and soup. I was stunned. I've never been served so much homemade food at one sitting.

I would have attributed that meal to an overly generous host, but every meal at every restaurant followed a similar pattern. I would order one dish for myself, and my companions would order double. I left every meal stuffed—the table still laden with half the food.

Every hotel I stayed at in China served a complimentary buffet for breakfast. In contrast to the pastries, cereal, and eggs for the Western visitors, the rest of the spread resembled an evening meal: white rice, fried rice and rice porridge; egg pancakes with scallions, sausage, and greens; steamed buns, dim sum, and dough sticks; steamed vegetables like bok choy and spinach; spring rolls; pickled plums; a salad bar; fresh fruit such as dragon fruit and rambutan; cold deli meats; a wide assortment of cheeses; roasted salmon, tofu, and fish balls; noodle soups; and simmered meats. Indeed, while a "typical" Chinese breakfast varies across the country's vast and complex cultural landscape, it often includes rice or porridge, along with savoury cooked dishes such as soup, noodles, and steamed buns. Breakfast is considered the most important meal of the day in China, for both nutritional and cultural reasons. It's often eaten as a family. This gave me new insight to the adjustment required by students who are shown a box of cereal and cold milk for breakfast and left to fend for themselves.

When Chinese students complain that there isn't "enough" food, they may be referencing these customs from home. They may also be saying there aren't enough cooked fresh vegetables or leafy greens. Chinese students tend to consider instant noodles to be akin to junk food, and given the emphasis on fresh ingredients in traditional Chinese cooking, frozen food is considered unhealthy. When an important staple is missing from the diet, it can feel like there's no food at all. I recall a Japanese teenager who complained to her parents that she wasn't being fed any dinner. When I called the host to ask for her side of the story, I was puzzled to discover that the student was eating regular meals along with the family. What the student meant was that she wasn't getting any rice.

Rice is not just a carbohydrate served for dinner in Japan. It is a key dietary staple eaten three times a day. Japanese people have been cultivating rice for thousands of years; it has shaped their landscapes and economy due to its use as a currency. It signifies evolution and perseverance. There's an old Shinto saying that "There are seven gods on each grain of rice," representing the soil, water, wind, sun, clouds, insects, and people who worked to bring the rice to the table. This saying is taught to children to encourage them to eat every last grain.

Some complaints from students about the quantity of food are really about the timing of the main meal. For example, in many Latin American food cultures, lunch is the largest meal of the day and is eaten as a family, and dinner is a small meal that's served late in the evening. You may notice students wanting more food in their packed lunches and eating a lot more snacks between meals to make up for the adjustment to your mealtimes. Snacks don't have to be expensive or heavy; raw fruits and vegetables, fresh juice or smoothies tend to be popular choices.

Quality

Jen, who hosted the opera singer with the big personality, grew up with international students. When she and her husband, Stew, started hosting, Jen took it upon herself to prepare three gourmet meals a day for the students and her two children. With hindsight, they think Jen's mother had a strong influence on them—it's what she would have done. Jen shopped at Costco weekly, going to great lengths to ensure they had enough amazing food in the house at all times, and spent hours in the kitchen on top of her full-time job.

Some of their students would appreciate her efforts, and some wouldn't.

A few months into their first hosting experience, Jen took her two kids to visit her parents in Florida over spring break. Stew was left alone with the three teenage students. As Stew says, "It was bachelor week, and I wasn't hung up on what to have for dinner." He served smokies (seasoned sausages) cooked over a barbecue. Every single night.

When Jen returned, the students raved about their week with Stew, saying, "Oh, Jen, Stew is such a good cook!"

Far from being offended, Jen found it hilarious. "These kids are just as happy eating smokies and Kraft Dinner as they would be eating all these fancy three-course meals. I could have made it easier on myself, for sure." She wanted to give the students the best experience, and for her, that meant beautiful food.

After their students moved out, it was time to clean the empty bedrooms. That's when Jen discovered dozens of granola bar wrappers under their beds. "We could have just served granola bars," Stew says, laughing. "They were kids!" At the end of our interview, Jen offered this piece of advice to other hosts: "Pace yourself, so you don't burn out. It's okay to give them Costco pizzas on Friday night so you can go out on a date. Give yourself a break."

While it's true that some students would be perfectly happy on a diet of smokies and granola bars, the reality is that most of them would complain after a couple days of nothing but hot dogs and snacks. But the other extreme—three gourmet meals a day—isn't the solution, either. As with providing "enough" food, matters of quality are all about the happy middle.

My advice is simple: as long as you prepare the evening meal, instead of buying pre-made frozen dinners or ordering take-out every night, your students won't complain. As one student said, "My host hardly cooked me the main meal of the day many times because he worked (I made myself breakfast and ate out). I chose homestay so I wouldn't have to worry about cooking but it was not like that."

A lot of hosts lead very busy lives. I know what it's like to get into a cooking rut, and I know I'm not the only one with favourite recipes and meals that become go-to solutions on busy nights. But again, it doesn't take much to keep a student satisfied. Some hosts have a set meal for each weeknight: burgers on Mondays, pizza and a movie on Fridays, and so on. And when you get too exhausted to cook, it's okay to order in. This just can't become the norm.

Variety is critical not only for the nightly menu, but also for the way food is prepared and what is served. As much as culture influences perceptions of what constitutes enough food, it also influences how someone defines "good" food. This is why food manufacturers and restaurant chains customize flavours to satisfy international palates—a marketing strategy known as product localization.

Consider, for instance, the mighty Snickers bar. Although you can buy a Snickers in more than seventy countries and it's the bestselling candy bar in the world, it doesn't taste the same everywhere due to geographic variations in recipes and ingredients. As Harry Kersh said on *Business Insider*'s *Food Wars* video series, "People in the UK really turn their noses up at US chocolate. Our chocolate tends to be way richer and smoother... One potential reason... is that UK chocolate tends to have a higher fat and cocoa content." Some of this can be attributed to local regulations, but consumer preference for particular tastes also plays a role. The same is true for Pizza Hut, where you can order coconut shrimp pizza in South Korea, mac 'n' cheese toppings in Germany, and poutine pizza in Canada. McDonald's McNuggets are half as salty in the UK as in the US. Dunkin' Donuts, available in thirty countries, offers a dry pork and seaweed flavoured donut in China, and a grapefruit Coolatta donut in South Korea. If you like spicy food, you can order a Chicken Tikka Masala Burrito at Taco Bell in India.

So what's a host to do, in the face of all these culturally informed preferences and judgments about the quality of the food they serve? Our team reminds hosts and students that being in a new country means learning about, and hopefully growing to enjoy, the food in that country. It means students should be open to trying Balmain bugs or lasagna at least once, even if it doesn't become their new favourite food.

Understanding cultural food preferences can go a long way to making a student feel welcome.

As much as hosts aren't expected to alter menu planning to cater to a foreign palate, understanding cultural food preferences can go a long way to making a student feel welcome. Hosts can do some research on their student's traditional cuisine and ask them about the customs surrounding meals and food preparation in their home. You can offer to take the student shopping to pick up some of their favourite items, like my corn flakes in Belize. For example, offer kimchi as a side dish or condiment when hosting Korean students, or buy a rice cooker for Japanese students and invite them to make rice whenever they want.

Many students have some experience cooking, and would love to share a family recipe with their new hosts. Inviting students to prepare a favourite dish from their home country is a highlight of the hosting experience for many families, as it offers a unique cultural exchange opportunity. It's also a wonderful way for a student to eat some comfort food and, in some cases, to learn how to cook for the first time—perhaps with a parent back home coaching them over FaceTime.

My colleague Brenda recalls a wonderful host in Ottawa, Faye, who looked after a Korean boy. They had a good relationship, but he missed his food so much that he asked to be moved to a Korean Canadian family home. When Faye found out why, she offered him ten dollars every Saturday so he could get lunch at a local Korean restaurant. He went only two or three times and that was enough. He ended up staying with her for about a year and a half. "She gave him a way out that he controlled, and it stopped being an issue," Brenda says. "Brilliant problem solving."

Then again, some students are thrilled to leave their traditional cuisine behind. As Lee's student Alex told me, "I'd kill in China to get pizza, burgers, sandwiches. In Chinese culture, people drink a lot of tea, a lot of warm water. I never liked it. I always liked cold water right out of the fridge. Back home, there's nothing like the milk here in Canada. So, food-wise, drinking-wise, I blended right in."

As long as a host provides home-cooked meals with some regularity, ensures some variety in the meal planning, and offers some comfort food to alleviate homesickness, they've done a lot to address the most common complaints about food. The rest comes down to personal preference.

Respecting Food Preferences

Host Judy from Cornwall, Ontario, is a self-proclaimed "great cook and baker" who attended cooking school in England, and has worked as a pastry chef and bakery manager for a grocery chain, and cook/baker for an art gallery tearoom. She also ran her own catering business, serving individuals, a hospital foundation, and her local school district for many years.

Judy's culinary skills don't stop at cooking and baking. She loves to make preserves: zucchini and orange marmalade with maraschino cherries, peach and orange jam, rosehip and apple jelly with thyme, strawberry freezer jam, beet pickles, bread and butter pickles, and chilli sauce. Her beautiful corn relish, which she makes every year, is a favourite. She uses fresh corn on the cob—about twelve ears in all—as well as red and green peppers, tomatoes, English cucumbers, and onions.

One early afternoon in October, Judy set to work on the relish, scraping the corn off the cob with a paring knife while the jars sat in the oven to sterilize. She puréed the fresh vegetables, mixed in the sugar, salt, and vinegar, and let it simmer on the stove until tender. After adding the seasonings—mustard seeds, celery seeds, turmeric, and some flour for thickening—the mixture was ready to pour into the hot jars. She processed the jars in the boiling water bath, then set them on a rack on her counter to cool.

By the time she finished, it was close to five o'clock. She had been planning to make a meat-free shepherd's pie for dinner that night, as her Spanish student Biete was vegetarian. She had already taken a package of Yves Ground Round (a ground beef substitute) from the freezer to thaw. As she emptied the pot of boiling water and put the dishes in the sink, she remembered she still had to prepare for a catering function the next day, and her other student—Ahad from Switzerland—was at the mosque and would be eating dinner with the religious leaders there.

Why not grab some takeout? Burger King (known as Hungry Jack's in Australia) had just introduced their new Beyond Meat vegetarian burger, and she'd been wanting to try it. It would be a little treat for her and Biete. She jotted a note for Biete that she would be back in fifteen minutes and left it on the counter.

When Judy returned home, she carried the takeout bags into the kitchen. As she started to unpack, she called out to Biete: "Supper's ready!"

Biete joined her in the kitchen. "I'm not hungry. I ate that," he said, gesturing to the counter. Judy was puzzled. The package of Ground Round was still thawing, unopened.

"What did you eat?"

Biete pointed at an empty jar of relish.

"It was too hot," he said. "It burned my mouth. I didn't really like it. I prefer my soup to be not so thick."

Judy smiled, unperturbed by his criticism in her delight that he had tried something new.

"Biete, that was not soup! That was a relish to eat with meat. Usually you would only eat a tablespoon or two!"

"Is it going to kill me? Do I need to go to the hospital?"

"No, you'll be fine, but you might be spending the night in the bathroom!"

The following evening, Judy served a spoonful of her homemade corn relish with the shepherd's pie, as planned. Biete laughed but refused the condiment as politely as he could, saying, "I've had enough of that."

Judy is still in touch with Biete through his parents, now that he's back in Spain and attending university. A few days before speaking to me, she had prepared another batch of her famous relish, which she now refers to as "Biete's Corn Relish." Just for fun, she sent him a photo of the jars, as a reminder of his soup-that-wasn't-soup.

You have to give Biete some credit for trying something new. If you're like me, you tend to walk right past the exotic fruits and vegetables in the local grocery store in favour of the same staples you always buy, and you tend to frequent the same familiar restaurants to order your favourite dishes. Curious cooks and adventurous eaters aside, most people aren't just getting stuck in a rut with their cooking and consumption habits. It's partly psychological.

Researchers have found that taste is rooted in both biology and experience. Biologically, people are hardwired to prefer fatty foods that deliver an immediate calorie load, and most people like sweet and salty food as soon as they're old enough to develop preferences. The rest of the food you eat, such as vegetables or spices, you learn to like at a young age—partly based on what your parents exposed you to, and partly because your culture promotes those flavours. Those early experiences stick with you.

Take spicy food, for example. Spice tolerance has a genetic component related to the number of taste buds in the mouth, which are surrounded by pain fibres that detect the burn of a hot pepper. This explains why some families have a higher tolerance for spice than others. But tolerance can also be built up after ten or fifteen minutes of exposure. The compound that makes hot peppers burn is called capsaicin. Capsaicin desensitizes the pain receptors on the tongue, so the more someone eats hot peppers, the less intense the burning sensation becomes. But why would someone want to put themselves through that pain? Dares and pranks aside, people who enjoy spicy food have learned to like it.

We can also learn to dislike food. As anyone who has had food poisoning will know, it only takes one nauseous incident to turn you off a particular food. This can happen even if the person has no recollection of the illness. Some dislikes can lessen gradually, but this takes time and usually doesn't change much.

Likewise, a particular smell can evoke such strong memories that it's stressful to overcome a food aversion that is tied to a bad experience. When you eat, you aren't just tasting with your tongue, you are also smelling the food as it passes the nasal cavity at the back of your throat. Humans are not born loving any particular smells, but we learn to associate certain scents with past experiences. I'm taken to another time and place with the smell of my grandmother's perfume, or the smoky residue of a campfire in my fleece jacket, or the sweet, fuzzy warmth of a baby's head. Considering the emotional associations with smell, the complexity of our food behaviour becomes easier to understand.

The next time one of your students expresses a food dislike, have some compassion. It's not something to tease about, make fun of, or exert undue pressure over. Pay attention to subtle cues, as students are often reticent about their food preferences, for fear of offending their host. In some cases, it takes several attempts with plenty of cajoling and reassurance for a student to admit they don't like something.

The same can be true for hosts. Patricia's student Mako, a teenager from China, wanted to share a special dish with some of her friends. With Patricia's support, Mako invited three or four other girls to the house and made a Japanese dish called takoyaki. Takoyaki is a ball of batter filled with diced octopus, tempura scraps, pickled ginger, and green onion, and is cooked in a special moulded tin. The balls are brushed with takoyaki sauce—like Worcestershire sauce—and mayonnaise, and then sprinkled with green laver (a type of seaweed) and dried bonito flakes. Mako made all of it from scratch.

"I watched her, and took pictures. That was something interesting to let her go ahead and do," Patricia says, "But, oh my god, it was awful," she adds, expressing her own food preferences. "I've never eaten octopus. I like seafood, but not octopus."

Never mind. Sometimes it's best to keep such preferences to ourselves.

CHAPTER SUMMARY

- Food can mean more than ingredients or nutrition. It's how people connect, how they express themselves and their culture.

- Your homestay coordinator can help with conflicts over the amount of food being served or consumed.

- As long as you serve a home-cooked meal most nights, it's okay to give yourself a break and order takeout or prepare a freezer meal once in a while.

- If your student expresses a food dislike, have some compassion. It's not something to tease about, make fun of, or exert undue pressure over.

6

Let's Not Get Physical
Expressing Affection

Consent conversations can be uncomfortable, but it's a practice. And the earlier we start practicing it, the less stigma there is around it, the less weirdness. It becomes the norm.
ARYANNA CHARTRAND, educator and advocate

Content Warning: This section includes a discussion of unwanted physical touch.

I LEARNED THE ACRONYM "PDA" when I was in high school. When you're a teenager, life is fraught with opportunities to shatter your status and expose you as a loser; figuring out the range of normal "public displays of affection" was no exception. Should my boyfriend kiss me on the lips when saying goodbye to me, or keep it to the cheek? Should we hold hands when we're at a party, or would it be okay for me to sit on his lap on a crowded couch?

My culture and family taught me what I should and shouldn't do. In Canada, as in many parts of the Western world, some PDA is acceptable—such as holding hands, or hugging and kissing in greeting—unless I am part of a same-sex or interracial couple in a conservative place. I also know I shouldn't make out in public unless I want to hear the derisive yet affectionate exclamation, "Get a room!" Hugging my friends and family is expected when greeting or saying farewell, but the length and firmness of the embrace varies by context. I was taught these rules as a child, the same way I was taught how to wait in line.

These Western norms stand in stark contrast with South Asia and the Middle East, where holding hands with someone of the opposite gender in public can get you arrested. In places where PDA is not illegal, there may be strong cultural taboos against it that result in public disapproval and aggression. This can be true in regions like Eastern Asia, Africa, and Eastern Europe.

The gaffes I've witnessed in homestay related to physical touch are numerous and often embarrassing for both parties. Understanding that other people have different levels of comfort with physical affection is not difficult. It takes a little cultural sensitivity, intuition, and empathy.

Too Close for Comfort

Megumi, a young adult Japanese student, took some time to adjust to many aspects of life in Toronto. When her host parents hugged her in the first few days after her arrival, she was embarrassed by this breach of Japanese etiquette.

In Japan, there are strict codes of politeness, etiquette, and personal space. Being affectionate with a romantic partner in public is known as *icha icha*, or *rabu rabu*, and it's considered rude. Families rarely touch, hug, or kiss in public. In private, "hugging is generally deemed inappropriate... Physical contact is kept to a minimum, so as to show respect for personal boundaries. Instead of embraces, it is more common to bow or give a slight nod of the head to greet one another."

At the orientation on her first day at her language school, Megumi assumed Deirdre, the homestay coordinator, would share her shock at the hug and promise an immediate relocation.

Deirdre asked a few questions to ascertain the nature of the hug (when did it happen, where, how did he hug her, for how long). She then smiled and gently tried to reassure Megumi. "It's normal for a host mother and father to hug their family like this. You are part of their family."

Megumi blushed deeply. "Not in my family."

Deirdre tried again, approaching it from another angle. "I know it's not normal in Japan, and this must be confusing. Your host father was not trying to embarrass you," she said. At that moment, another student appeared in the doorway of the classroom. He was in his early twenties, with dark wavy hair and olive skin.

"Are you the homestay lady?" he asked. His Portuguese accent gave him away as Brazilian.

"Yes, that's me," Deirdre said, and stood to greet him. Without waiting for any further introductions, the young man crossed the room in two strides and reached out to Deirdre with both arms. They hugged, laughing.

"I'm Francisco."

"Nice to meet you, Francisco! I'll be with you in a moment."

When Deirdre turned around, Megumi's whole face had changed. Gone were the lowered eyes and red cheeks.

"Ahhhhhh," she breathed, looking back and forth between Deirdre and Francisco. "You... just... meet?"

"Yes," Deirdre said, nodding slowly. "Francisco, this is Megumi. Megumi, this is Francisco."

"But, you..." she started again, and stopped.

Deirdre could see the cultural understanding dawning on her face. She rushed to explain. "It's okay! We like to hug in Canada, even strangers, when we first meet!"

"It's the same in Brazil," Francisco said. "Everyone does this."

Megumi did not ask for a relocation that day, and never complained about her host father hugging her again. In this case, it turns out that a spontaneous demonstration was the secret to conveying a cultural norm, and was all the explanation this student needed to understand that the intent was not to harm.

However, as with any cultural norm, there will be variation between individuals. Where Megumi was reassured by Deirdre, other students in her position may not be.

Power Imbalance

One such occasion took place in the fall of 2005, during a program involving four hundred Japanese high school students who came to Victoria, BC, for a few days. The organizers had agreed to "double placements," wherein two students were placed in each home. Colin and his wife took two female students, Akemi and Hana. On Sunday evening after dinner, Colin was sitting in the living room on the couch with the two girls, looking through a family photo album. His wife was upstairs with their newborn baby. According to Akemi and Hana, at one point Colin touched the leg of one of the girls seated next to him. This gesture set the girls on edge. Not long afterward, the students retired to their shared bedroom for the night.

That could have been the end of it, but Colin went down to Akemi and Hana's room and sat on one of their beds briefly. I recall him telling us that he had picked up on a sense of discomfort from the girls, and left.

Touch is critical for connection *and* it requires consent.

Akemi and Hana were indeed uncomfortable. So uncomfortable, in fact, that his entering their room intensified things. They ran from the house in the darkness despite the pouring rain and flagged down a passing motorist. The stranger kindly drove them to the hotel where the group chaperones were staying, which set in motion a chain of events that culminated in a written apology from the host and a trip to Japan by my father and the head of the organization that booked the group. They were expected to apologize in person to the school principal.

Colin's apology letter was sincere and heartfelt. He understood he had frightened the students, and he was "very, very sorry." He felt terrible. He acknowledged that the girls' parents and teachers must have been worried about them, too.

In all such cases, our homestay team must act swiftly and with the student's best interests at heart, which often means removing a student from the home. Our team knows how unfair it may seem to a host in the moment. It's never our intention to label someone as predatory. Our intention is to protect everyone involved: the students from potential danger, the hosts from potential damage to their reputation due to further accusations, and our client educators and our organization from litigation.

This story persists in my memory as a remarkable example of a cultural misunderstanding and a man's lack of awareness of a power imbalance, compounded by the heightened stress of a short-term homestay placement. The situation was resolved by the swift response of our team and the other group organizers, and a culturally appropriate reparation that acknowledged how serious this situation had become. While it makes an interesting case study in international business relations, I share it here as an example of how quickly situations can escalate, and to help hosts learn from Colin's experience. I believed him when he said he meant no harm, but that's not the point. It may not be enough to have good intentions. Colin admitted, and I agree, that he needed to be more aware of the power imbalance and cultural norms in the situation: between adult and minor, male and female, Canadian and Japanese, authority and subordinate, host and guest.

The rise of the #MeToo movement in 2017 against sexual violence and sexual assault has brought a long overdue focus to the meaning of consent and its importance in both personal and professional relationships. However, consent is equally important for all forms of physical touch, from any gender toward another. As the National Sexual Violence Resource Center based in Pennsylvania states, "Consent is about always choosing to respect personal and emotional boundaries. By practicing consent in everyday situations, you show that you value the choices of others."

I've made mistakes with consent. When my daughter, Morgan, travelled to France in the fall of grade eleven, it was planned as an exchange. Her host sister, Philippine, came to stay with us for five weeks at the end of the school year. Day after day, she watched me hug my children when they left for school, when they came home, and when we said goodnight. Still, she made it clear to me that she didn't expect that kind of relationship with me. The couple of times I tried (when she arrived at the airport, and the first day of school), it was awkward and clumsy. I turned the aborted hug into a polite kiss on the cheek, wondering if it was supposed to be two or three pecks according to French custom. I respected her boundaries, but wish in hindsight that I had asked her how she felt before assuming she would appreciate a hug.

I could have said, "Is it okay if I give you a hug when we say goodbye?" Or "Can I hug you?" Or "I'm a hugger, but I know not everyone likes to hug. How do you feel about it?" It may feel awkward at first, because you aren't used to it. If you don't want to ask, then it's best to avoid any form of touch—no matter how innocuous it seems to you—especially with new students.

Part of practicing consent is to accept the other person's response. It's okay to feel disappointed or awkward if the answer is "no." Keep in mind that your reaction to a "no" may influence the person you're asking, to the point where they may end up saying what you want to hear. Again, there is a power imbalance between hosts and their students, regardless of age. International students are a vulnerable population, as there is a higher likelihood that they will experience harm while having insufficient ability or means to protect themselves. Addressing this power imbalance requires hosts to be open and honest, to make compromises in favour of the student, and to respect their boundaries. As the host, it's your responsibility to create the conditions for an optimal relationship with your student.

Social Touch

By this point, you may be wondering if any physical contact is worth the effort and the possible risk to one's reputation due to misunderstandings or false accusations.

The answer is a resounding yes. It is well documented in the scientific literature that social touch is a powerful bonding mechanism among humans and other primates. In infants, skin-to-skin contact has been shown in dozens of studies to significantly reduce the risk of mortality, infection, and hypothermia and to increase weight gain and growth. Tiffany Field, a leading authority on touch and touch therapy, explains: "Touch is ten times stronger than verbal or emotional contact, and it affects damned near everything we do. No other sense can arouse you like touch... We forget that touch is not only basic to our species, but the key to it." Another researcher found that touch can promote trust and generosity, even in the workplace and in sports: "In general, NBA basketball teams whose players touch each other more win more games."

This effect may persist across cultures. A 2020 study on the effect of physical touch among people from cultures that tend to engage less in physical contact (especially with acquaintances and strangers) found a small amount of contact can reduce the perception of loneliness. Their findings also suggested a positive physiological effect (measured by heart rate). The researchers speculated that "even casual touch may play a more important role in mediating human interactions than we typically assume," and "this could imply that physical contact can alter people's perception of the quality of a relationship."

For many host parents, their instincts are to show their students that they are part of the family and, therefore, to extend affection. It's why Megumi's hosts gave her a hug during her first weekend, and why I tried to do the same with Philippine.

Despite how important touch is to our well-being, Field asserts that many people don't get enough physical contact with others, a phenomenon which she evocatively refers to as "touch hunger." Your student may need that extra bit of reassurance, a sign that you care and you'll be there no matter what. Student Kiho, who liked to be called "Joy," told me about a time when she had to move to a temporary host family while her regular hosts were unavailable—a "respite" placement. Students meet their homestay coordinators at their school every month, which gave Joy the feeling that she had someone to talk to. When she had to move to respite, Joy said, "[The homestay coordinator] gave me a big hug. I was so nervous about the new host, but she helped me a lot."

Touch is critical for connection *and* it requires consent. The challenge is to stay curious about how you can express your delight, joy, and caring in a way that's true to your culture *and* respects other people's boundaries. When you can do that, you are well on your way to creating something meaningful.

CHAPTER SUMMARY

- Everyone has different levels of comfort with physical affection.

- Practice consent in everyday situations, including asking if a touch or hug is wanted. It shows that you value the choices of others.

- Part of practicing consent is to accept the other person's response.

- At the same time, social touch is a powerful bonding mechanism.

7

This Is Life
Bathrooms and Bodies

I knew they called us host parents, but I didn't realize I was actually going to be a mother. We had to deal with masturbation, personal hygiene... You're putting human beings together. This is life.
JEN, host from Victoria, British Columbia

PHYSICAL TOUCH and personal space are examples of boundaries that hosts and students must explore in order to build and maintain a healthy relationship. Just as some students will prefer to keep a respectful distance, most will keep their bodily functions to themselves, abhorring the thought of their hosts having to witness or clean up any messes.

Then again, some students couldn't care less about their mess. Jen and Stew, the couple from Victoria who hosted the Chinese opera singer, were young parents when they started hosting: their children were one and three years old. Hosting teenagers thrust them into a stage of parenting that, from time to time, caught them by surprise.

Among their first placements were two sixteen-year-old high school students from Brazil and Germany and the Chinese opera singer attending university. The two younger boys shared a bathroom, which Jen cleaned every week. One afternoon, after cleaning the floor around the toilet, she opened the cupboard where the wastebasket was stored. "It was *full* of crunchy tissues," Jen says. "And there was a *smell*."

After futile speculation about who might be responsible, Jen and Stew came up with a plan to trap the culprit. At dinner that night, Jen announced, "You have to start cleaning your own bathroom now. Who would like to take the bathroom garbage out?" Jen and Stew assumed that whoever had filled the basket would volunteer.

They were mistaken. None of the boys spoke up.

"That's when I should have said, 'Okay, who's been jerking off in the bathroom?'" Stew says, laughing.

Teaching Moments

Plenty of hosts like Jen and Stew know what it's like to share a home with a student—male or female—who hasn't been taught how to clean up after themselves, respect common spaces like family bathrooms, or do their laundry. Delegating cleaning duties to students is a valid way to manage a busy household and teach them important life skills at the same time.

In CHN's 2022 host survey, 11 percent of hosts said that the practical day-to-day chores of hosting are their biggest challenges. In addition to housework, hosts talk about the hassle of driving students (a perennial burden in rural communities); managing conflicting routines; trying to balance hosting and family obligations on a busy schedule; and budgeting for, planning, and engaging in activities to keep students happy. When I analyzed the survey data, I included financial stress and complaints about the amount of the hosting allowance, as these issues often overlap with each other. The cost of gas impacts the driving; the cost of food impacts meal planning.

When students participate in these family obligations, it can make all the difference. Chris, Rika's host from Ottawa, embraces her role as an educator of life skills, like cleaning up around the house. "Generally speaking, most of the Asian students do nothing at home. Nothing. Zero," Chris says. She counts off on her fingers as she continues, "They don't make their bed, they don't do their laundry, they don't clean up... they do nothing but study, study, study." She strikes the palm of one hand with the edge of her other hand as she says these last three words, the swift tap-tap-tap emphasizing the academic discipline.

Millions of teenagers in many parts of the world are raised from a young age to focus on their studies to the exclusion of anything else. As Robby shared in chapter 1, this is often a function of parental and cultural expectations, not personality. While Chris may be expressing a stereotype, there's also a conflict in belief systems at work. The students are not intentionally making the host's job hard; they are studying—doing the thing they travelled abroad to do.

I had to learn this the hard way when I first started hosting. I was also a new mother at the time, pregnant and parenting a sixteen-month-old toddler. Looking after two teenage boys from Japan added a lot of work. I realized pretty quickly that something had to give.

First, I asked the students to clear the table when we finished dinner. They were pleasant and cooperative. I wondered why I waited so long to suggest this.

Next, I asked them to wash the dishes. It's not an onerous task; thankfully we had a dishwasher and I was happy to keep loading it myself. I patiently pointed out the scrub brush, dish soap, and drying rack. I showed Hiroto how to operate the faucet and adjust the temperature, hoping he understood. I stepped away, seizing the moment to tackle the whack-a-mole game that was my life in those days.

A few minutes later, I returned to the kitchen to check on Hiroto's progress—just in time to prevent a minor disaster. He had dutifully followed my instructions to rinse the soap off each dish, but instead of turning the water on and off periodically, he let it run. The sink was so full to the brim with dirty water that some of it sloshed over the edge when I reached down to unplug the drain. He had never washed dishes before.

As I learned, expecting students to instantly adapt to a new culture and lifestyle that requires them to perform tasks around the home that they've never done before is unreasonable, but with a little guidance—and a sense of humour—behaviours can change.

Chris gets her students doing their chores around the house within a few days of arrival, but she makes it fun. "I give them a couple days to get settled, then I talk about what we do around the house." If she finds out they don't do any chores at home, she tells them, "Well, you know, that doesn't work for me." She chuckles, and gives me a brief, matter-of-fact grimace.

"So, you teach them all those skills?" I ask.

"Oh yeah, well, of course! And there's nobody who's ever said, 'Well I'm not doing that.' I involve myself in what they're doing, and we'll laugh, and we're joking, and we'll talk about things," she says. Her eyes widen and she wags a finger at me as she says, "I always tell them, 'Now this is a teaching moment!'" Her face relaxes. "So, yeah, we have a good time."

Melanie, the host from Brisbane whose students didn't want to leave when she broke her ankle, also expects her girls to clean their own bathrooms. At first, she didn't inspect their work; she wanted to give them privacy.

Melanie's third student, Carla, was eighteen when she arrived in Australia from China. She was starting her "foundation year," the precursor to attending university in Australia and a common pathway used by international students. And like many students, "I don't think she'd ever cleaned a thing in her life," Melanie says.

Carla had her own ensuite bathroom. The other student, Iris, cleaned her own bathroom every other Saturday morning. On those mornings, "Carla would walk out of her room wearing bright pink rubber gloves like this," Melanie says, holding her forearms vertically, palms facing inward, like a surgeon who had just disinfected her hands. "She'd stand in the hallway and go, 'I think you need to buy me some more cleaning product,' or 'I've gotta go out soon, but I'll just finish my bedroom.'" Melanie pauses, a grin spreading across her face, her hands still in the air. "I don't think she ever did anything more than put the rubber gloves on, the whole time she was here."

After Carla moved out, Melanie entered the ensuite bathroom to clean it, where she found six months' worth of accumulated grunge around the sink and mirror. "That bathroom was vile," Melanie says, her voice dropping to a growl. "Disgusting. The worst part was the toilet. It had not been cleaned at all. I don't know how anybody could cope with that. It was *black*."

It took two days and several rounds of thick liquid bleach to soften the scum enough to attack it with a scrubbing brush.

Thankfully, this was a one-time incident. She looks back on it now with a healthy sense of humour. "It was the fact that she put the rubber gloves on and made sure that I *saw* she had rubber gloves on," she says, grinning. "And she talked about cleaning products... But she never used them."

In addition to teaching students how to *clean* their own bathrooms—and checking that they're actually doing it—hosts may also be surprised to discover the need to explain how to *use* the bathroom and toilet. What is considered "standard" to you may not be a universal norm.

Toilets

People who grew up in North America, the UK, and Australia tend to take two things for granted: we flush our toilet paper and we sit on the toilet seat.

In many places like Southeast Asia, India, Japan, and parts of Southern Europe, people use water to clean themselves instead of toilet paper. They may use bidets, or they may rinse with a bowl or cup of water or their hand. Even in countries where toilet paper is used, chances are they don't flush it down the drain. Residents all over the world throw their used toilet paper in the rubbish bin due to the diameter of their sewage pipes, which is too small to handle anything other than human waste. In fact, the *only* countries with universally adequate sewage systems for flushing toilet paper are Canada, the US, Australia, the UK, parts of Northern Europe, New Zealand, Japan, and Tanzania. Teaching your students to flush the toilet paper may take some explaining and a lot of reminding. In the meantime, make sure there's a covered wastebasket near the toilet in case they revert to an old habit.

One of the biggest adjustments I had to make when travelling in China was to using a squat toilet in public facilities. Some of my guides would point me to the single stall that held the "Western-style" sitting toilet. (They would also invariably hand me a few squares of toilet paper—which are not stocked in public facilities and must be carried around with you in your bag or purse—because I would often forget.) All the other stalls held a basin surrounded by a non-slip surface. Some squat toilets are raised on a platform about thirty centimetres (twelve inches) high, but most are recessed so they are level with the floor. Some squat toilets can be flushed, and others are dry. Squat toilets are common in many Asian countries including South Korea, Taiwan, and Thailand. However, sitting toilets are gradually becoming the norm in major urban areas in several of these countries, as well as places like Russia and Japan, where the sitting toilet is starting to be seen as more modern.

Some students will squat on their host's toilet seat, which can loosen the seat and, over time, cause irreparable damage—and if they are wearing shoes at the time, it's unhygienic. Nevertheless, most students who are used to squat toilets will adapt to a sitting toilet. It can help to reassure students that the seat is cleaned regularly. Keeping a small step stool near the toilet for their feet to rest on while sitting can also ease the transition, as it facilitates a more familiar squatting position.

Bathing

While bathing habits reflect myriad personal preferences and factors that may change from day to day, there is a cultural aspect to the way we clean ourselves.

First, what is considered "normal" for the frequency and length of showers to you is not "normal" to many students. In Canada, the UK, the US, and Australia, men and women tend to shower five to eight times a week, with showers lasting around seven to ten minutes. For a few contrasts, consider Japan, where people take an average of five showers and six baths per week, and often bathe in public facilities. Brazil takes first place worldwide for the greatest number of showers per week, with the national average at twelve. It's not uncommon for Brazilians to shower two times a day, and some people will shower up to five times a day. Not all of these showers serve the same purpose; for example, the *chuveirda* is more of an "express" shower—a quick refreshing rinse in the middle of the day or before heading out for the evening.

It's clear that climate plays a role in shower frequency, but this is not the only explanation; consider Turkey or Spain, where showering is much less frequent. Likewise, asking a Brazilian student to shower less often because of your climate may not be effective. It would be like telling someone they couldn't shower after exercising; these are deeply ingrained personal habits. As with many other cultural issues, hosts will be more successful at encouraging behavioural change if they show some empathy and allow for an adjustment period.

It can help to explain the environmental impact of showering and the importance of water conservation. In regions like Australia that are facing drought conditions, there is some urgency to this lesson. If your home has a hot water tank, show it to the student and explain how it works and which appliances are drawing down the water. Many students' homes are equipped with on-demand (tankless) water heaters, so they may not appreciate the way their lengthy shower impacts other members of the family.

Just don't talk about the cost of water—as Deirdre explained in chapter 1, it's best to avoid conversations about money and the financial impact of hosting. It's natural for the economics of hosting to be top of mind for you, especially given the cost of utilities, gas, and food. But when you draw attention to that aspect of your relationship, it detracts from what you're trying to build. If you have questions or concerns about finances, speak to your coordinator.

Besides the frequency and length of showers and baths, hosts often complain about their students' uncanny ability to make a

♥

Chris gets her students doing their chores around the house within a few days of arrival, but she makes it fun.

───────

huge mess in the bathroom. While a good deal of this behaviour comes down to the individual and what they've been taught at home, it could be their custom to bathe in "wet rooms."

"Wet rooms" are bathrooms that are designed—as the name suggests—to get wet. All of the fixtures are waterproof and the walls are covered in tile. The surfaces slope toward a central drain in the middle of the room. Not only do wet rooms make the most efficient use of space in small dwellings, they are also easy to clean; everything gets sprayed and the water goes down the drain. Some are equipped with built-in heated dryers and automatic self-cleaning functions to avoid harmful mould or dampness.

Wet rooms originated in Japan, though now they can be found all over the world in countries like South Korea, Sweden, many parts of Europe, Nepal, and Costa Rica. Apparently, they are making headway in the US as well, as evidenced by headlines in popular home design magazines.

Hosts may need to explain, demonstrate, and remind students that their bathrooms are not designed to get soaked from floor to ceiling. Shower curtains must be placed inside the tub, and surfaces must be wiped down with a towel before leaving the bathroom. One host leaves a stack of washcloths on the bathroom counter for this purpose, asking her students to drop them in the laundry bin after use.

Tamara, a host from Victoria, says her biggest challenge is explaining how to use the bathroom. She tries to do this on arrival day, though she knows students are exhausted from travelling and overwhelmed by the language barrier. Even after they've been with her for a few days, it takes a lot of patience to work with students to break old habits. "We found that they were washing their undergarments in our bathroom sink. Some of them were impressed with how the washing machine can wash undergarments as well. I'm not sure if I was putting our way of life too much on them, but I think most of them were okay with it in the end." If it's a shorter-term placement (two weeks or less) Tamara doesn't even address it. But when she does, she is mindful and empathetic: "I never want to make them feel that they're doing wrong, because this is probably something right in their own country. I never want to make them feel uncomfortable. So I always talk to them in a very nice manner. I never get mad at them, never raise my voice or get angry because they've done something that I asked them not to! I don't want to make them unhappy in their homestay."

For these tips and more, many hosts have had success posting illustrated (and laminated!) signs with text translated into multiple languages. Again: these students may be unaware of the impact of their actions, but that does not make them negligent. Patience, empathy, and repetition will go a long way.

Sex Education

In addition to teaching about bathrooms, housework, and hygiene, hosts have a precious opportunity to teach their students how to be safe. This can include topics that might seem like common sense, but aren't: water safety (especially around the ocean), keeping valuables secure, media literacy, and so on. As Mama Lee discovered, some students will need help keeping themselves physically safe, too. Chris is still amazed, even after hosting female students for over twenty years, how few of them know about their bodies, or know how to talk about physical intimacy in the context of romantic relationships.

Chris doesn't broach this topic too soon. She knows that she needs to get to know them, to have trust and openness. She waits a few months, and then starts a conversation by saying something like, "Did your mother ever talk about sex? Do you talk about things like that in your house?" A teenage student from Vietnam once told her in reply, "My mother said my husband will tell me everything I need to know." Chris wants to make sure they don't have to rely on their future husband, or Google, for information that will keep them safe.

"Sometimes these girls get boyfriends while they're here, and don't know anything. You should know everything about your body. You have to figure out the girl, and how she feels about things. So they're not embarrassed about it, because I've built up a relationship. We have movie night, and they'll say something sexual [in the movie], and the girls..." Chris smiles and rests her forehead on her hand for a moment before continuing. "They might say, 'What's a blow job?' And I'm thinking, 'How do I explain that?' But she feels comfortable asking me. I don't make it a big deal. So I say, 'I'll tell you after the movie.' About a week or so ago, my [student] wanted to know what 'jerking off' means." Chris laughs and waves her hands around her face, as if to cool herself off. "And of course, you see, I tell them."

No Shame

It's understandable that students may experience embarrassment or guilt when talking about sex or dealing with a bodily mess. Students who menstruate or experience wet dreams (nighttime ejaculation) may feel ashamed for soiling their sheets or undergarments, and not know the best way to remove the stains. Bedwetting can also be a challenge, especially when hosting younger students. Keep in mind that some of these patterns of thought and openness to conversations are informed by both culture and families of origin. "Whatever relationships they have with their family carries into our family," Jen says.

But it's not okay if they feel ashamed or humiliated. The difference between these emotions comes down to self-talk. In a Western context, when you say to yourself, "I did something bad," you are experiencing guilt. If, on the other hand, you say "I am bad," you are feeling shame. Guilt can motivate a person to change their behaviour in a positive way. Shame, on the other hand, is destructive in cultures where it is a "wrong" emotion, and is highly correlated with negative behaviours such as addiction, violence, aggression, depression, eating disorders, and bullying.

When a mess is caused by a normal part of life and/or puberty, make sure your student knows there's nothing to be ashamed of, then simply show them how to clean up. To avoid having to replace mattresses, CHN recommends that all hosts invest in a waterproof mattress protector just in case. Patience, empathy, and repetition are essential for gently correcting problems, as the situation could be embarrassing or trigger feelings of shame for the student.

Then again, sometimes all you need is a blunt statement of fact.

When Jen and Stew were hosting the two sixteen-year-old boys, one of them, Toby, formed a unique bond with Stew. Toby's father was a high-powered, successful scientist who led an important intergovernmental organization in Europe. Stew and Jen's impression was that Toby's father wasn't around a lot for him, as he had to travel so much for his job.

"Toby couldn't get enough of Stew, because it was a father connection that he hadn't experienced before," Jen says. "We were still young parents, and we were fun. We would crank the music and dance and be silly, and he loved it. He didn't leave our side. It was a deep, pure, open love bond. It ticked a box for him that he wanted at that stage."

This deep connection was essential when Jen and Stew found themselves needing to teach Toby some important life lessons.

One night, as they were sitting in the living room with Toby (because Toby was always there), a foul smell permeated the air. It didn't take them long to realize it was Toby's socks. Jen nudged Stew, giving him the "You have to say something" look.

"Toby, your socks stink," he said.

"What?"

"Yeah, they smell. You're going to have to wash them. You can't keep wearing the same socks."

And that was it. No shame. Just the facts.

Of all their students, Toby is the one who felt most like a third son to them—despite only staying for five months. It's been seven years since then, and Toby's family still send Stew and Jen advent calendars every December.

CHAPTER SUMMARY

- Asking students to help with simple chores can alleviate your stress. But don't assume they've been taught tasks that come easily to you.

- Toilet habits vary from country to country. Teaching your students to flush the toilet paper and sit on the seat may take some explaining and a lot of reminding.

- Shower length and habits also differ around the world. It can help to explain the environmental impact of showering and the importance of water conservation.

- It's okay to talk about physical intimacy and teach your students about their bodies, but it helps to build up trust and rapport first.

- When a mess is caused by a normal part of life and/or puberty, make sure your student knows there's nothing to be ashamed of, then simply show them how to clean up.

- If personal hygiene is an issue, approach it directly and without shame like Stew did with Toby's smelly socks.

8

That's Not What I Meant
Communication and Language

We have found that students with the cultures most similar to ours have been the easiest. The more different the culture, the more challenging the communications, the unwritten expectations, and developing a respectful, two-way relationship.

DEBORA AND KEITH, hosts from Ottawa, Ontario

BACK IN THE DAYS when my parents were the only ones who answered the CHN phone outside of office hours, my dad, Fraser, took a call from a Japanese student in Toronto whom he had met at the language school orientation the week before. With no preamble, she said she wanted to move to a new family. Immediately.

"Okay, I'm listening," Fraser said. "What's up?"

"I don't feel comfortable here. I can't—I don't—I'm worried." Himari's voice was quiet, trembling.

Fraser was surprised, given what he knew of the host family. "When I saw you last week, everything was perfect! I was just telling my wife, Robin, how happy you've been. What happened? When did things change?"

"Last night, I lost my pencil."

Her pencil? Whether or not Fraser was surprised by this detail, he didn't show it. In homestay, when someone complains, the underlying issue is often something deeper.

"Have you asked your host about the pencil?"

"Oh no, no, I couldn't do that."

Saving Face

In many Eastern cultures such as Chinese, Japanese, Thai, and Korean, as well as Arabic, Indian, Russian, and other Slavic traditions, there is a sociological concept known as "face." It's a group of customs dealing with dignity, honour, morality, and prestige that guide behaviour in social relationships. Face can be lost or gained, given or taken. The importance of face cannot be underestimated. People from these cultures will go to great lengths to protect face (their own as well as others) to avoid shame. In fact, making someone lose face can sometimes insult them so much as to create an enemy for life.

Face can be lost in a number of common situations in a homestay setting, when openly criticizing, challenging, disagreeing with, or denying students; calling them out on a lie; interrupting them; or being angry at them. Both the host and the student can lose face in these situations.

Understanding the concept of face can help hosts better grasp why a student might not say what they really think, or outright lie. Many students will avoid confrontation by turning down an invitation with a vague "Maybe," "Yes, maybe," "I'll do my best," "Let's think/talk about it later," or "I need to discuss it with so-and-so first." Or they may say nothing to avoid revealing their lack of ability or knowledge (such as being able to speak English).

Himari suspected someone had taken her special pencil. In her culture, however, she couldn't confront anyone; to do so would either cause the host to lose face (by catching them in a theft) or she would lose face by falsely accusing them. Her silence avoided humiliation on both sides.

Fraser understood that Himari was trying to save face—both hers and her host's—by asking for a relocation. He also understood that his response had the power to transform this experience for Himari and her host.

"Leave this with me," Fraser said. "Give me fifteen minutes, and if at the end of that time you're not happy, then I'm going to come and get you."

Himari was skeptical. "You're not going to speak to my host, are you?"

"Leave this with me. The deal is, if you're not happy, I'll come and get you."

Fraser called the host.

"Ashley," he said, "you have to promise me you're not going to laugh when I tell you this. Under any circumstances, please don't laugh." She started to chuckle with anticipation before he began, but regained her composure when she understood his tone to be serious. "Here's the situation. Your student is nervous. She's lost her pencil. In her mind, it means something else could go missing. And she can't talk to you, because you might lose face. So, she's having trouble coping with this. It's nothing to do with you. It's to do with the difference in culture, and the relationships between people in Japan. I'm going to ask you to help her navigate this challenge. But that means you've got to be smart about how you go about this. You can't judge her. You certainly can't consider this trivial, because for her it's a big deal. It's so big that she wants to move to a new host."

"Okay, I'm listening," Ashley said.

"I want you to be prepared to help your student find her pencil. And you can't laugh. You have to take this seriously. She's being very brave."

"Got it."

"I'm going to hang up now and call Himari, and ask her to ask you for help."

When Fraser called Himari, she said she couldn't ask her host for help. Fraser encouraged her and reminded her that if it didn't work out, he would be there in twenty-five minutes to pick her up.

"Now, you need to believe in yourself and believe in your host. Try it! Then call me back and tell me how you get along."

Himari summoned her courage and walked down the hall to ask Ashley for help. The host was ready. She didn't laugh, she didn't minimize it, and she didn't make assumptions or accusations. They soon found the missing pencil in a kitchen drawer—you know, the spot where people put the bits and bobs that float around the house and need a place to land.

It was a watershed moment: for the first time, Himari began to understand that with Ashley, she had permission to express her feelings, even if it might make Ashley uncomfortable.

Himari's story is a reminder that relationships can suffer not only because of language barriers or pronunciation blunders, but because of cultural differences. In CHN's host survey, communication issues and language barriers were identified as the biggest challenge by 17 percent of hosts. In this chapter, I will focus on three key challenges that underpin many misunderstandings in homestay: language barriers, respectful communication, and feedback (given by hosts to correct some aspect of a student's behaviour). Finally, I'll talk about how to become a better listener in service of all your relationships.

Language Barriers

Misunderstandings due to language barriers are bound to happen in homestay. Diana, a host from Victoria, BC, told me about a time when her arthritis was "acting up" and she couldn't walk very well, so she asked her student at the time if he wouldn't mind going downstairs to the laundry room to get the clothes from the dryer. She pauses when she says this, stifling a chuckle. "He came back with a bag of ice from the freezer," she says, smiling.

Many hosts can recall similar incidents with their own students. Another time, a Japanese student was called Risa by her hosts for four months before the student mustered the courage to inform them her name was Lisa.

When Philippine stayed with us, we delighted in her French accent and tried to help her improve her pronunciation of particular sounds, like "th." One night as we were doing dishes, we decided it would be fun to watch a French movie as a family. I asked Philippine to pick a few options, then find a trailer for us to watch first.

About ten minutes later, she returned to the kitchen.

"The triller," she said.

"Oh no. I don't like thrillers."

She looked mildly confused. "Why not?"

"Oh, you know," I said, knowing my threshold for tension was lower than a lot of other people's. "They're too scary!" Her expression was still blank, so I tried again. "I hate them. You know, I'm the person watching who wants to yell at the screen, 'don't go in there!'" I laughed. "They're too suspenseful!"

Philippine's face contorted further, her brows furrowing. "Triller," she said again. "You come? To watch?"

That was the moment when it dawned on me.

It takes tremendous
effort and energy
to translate every
word in a new
language all day long.

———————

"Oh, you mean *trailer*!"

In the next second, we all burst into laughter at what was *my* mistake.

Liz, a host from Ottawa, had a few students whose English was so elementary they could hardly speak. "There was fear and terror in their faces whenever I talked to them," Liz says. To support them, she used a lot of "show and tell." She would point to a spoon, and say "This is a spoon." Same with the chair, table, and so on. "You go right down to the basics," she says. "So, when I asked, 'Can you put the plates on the table?' they understood 'plate' and 'table.'"

"How long would it take?" I ask, wondering if I could do this. I've hosted students with low English, but never this low.

"Oh, we would be carrying on a conversation within two or three weeks."

Indeed, as one host said on CHN's survey about the challenges of hosting, "One of the difficulties is you need to learn how they pronounce words to understand what they are saying, but this will come as you listen to them every day. Remember, the student is also here to learn English, so encourage that. Keep talking and you will soon understand each other."

As much as this is a lot of work for the host, language immersion is even more exhausting for the student. It takes tremendous effort and energy to translate every word in a new language all day long, and to constantly worry about the impression you're making. This fatigue explains why many students, much to their host's chagrin, avoid talking at dinner and retreat to their bedrooms as soon as the table has been cleared. My daughter, Morgan, can relate. "It was a lot of work all the time," she says of her own experience abroad. "You're listening and thinking and trying to get the general gist of what they're saying without knowing all the words, but you also have to respond. It would be awkward if I had to ask them to repeat it. I didn't like doing that. Sometimes I just faked that I knew what they were talking about. At dinnertime I didn't want to talk... I knew it was better to be part of that, but it was tiring."

Lionel Laroche, an intercultural communication expert and consultant, studied abroad as a teenager. He also remembers dinners being quite difficult: "When there are eight people around the table and you end up with three parallel conversations, and English is your second language, it's difficult to separate the conversations in your mind and block the noise of the others."

Some students behave poorly by not engaging with their family, not trying to improve their English, or insulting their hosts on purpose. Likewise, some students have genuine struggles with shyness, trouble sleeping, or other personal issues that may be cause for concern. Nevertheless, the best response for hosts when dealing with language barriers is to start with cultural awareness rather than assuming there's a personality issue. Not only do you give your student the benefit of the doubt—fostering a sense of safety and trust—it's easier to come up with solutions when you're both sitting on the same side of the problem.

Respectful Communication

As I discussed in chapter 2, people tend to interpret the words, body language, and behaviours of others through a cultural lens—and they usually don't notice they're doing it. When the man in Beijing stood next to me in line to buy a ticket, my first reaction was to consider him rude. This is also true when speaking: behaviours that appear disrespectful or display a lack of manners may be explained by cultural differences rather than personality. When hosts and students don't know each other very well, these misinterpretations can threaten already tenuous connections.

For example, in many cultures, it's not customary to say please and thank you to your family. When one of these students doesn't thank a host for their dinner, a North American, British, or Australian host may assume the student didn't like the meal. At worst, they may interpret the student as being rude or disrespectful. Meanwhile, the student likely thought they conveyed their appreciation by *not* saying anything.

Alex, the Chinese student who lived with Mama Lee, told me he had to learn to say thank you when he moved to Canada. "In China, you're not supposed to say thank you to family, but to everybody else you always have to say thank you."

Susan learned about manners in China from her student Haley, who played the guqin. Haley explained that saying please in China "takes you down socially." Susan understands that students have to learn to say please and thank you without "demeaning" themselves. "You have to have patience with that," Susan says. "If you don't talk about these things, you're never going to find out. You cannot know unless you're immersed in it."

Even cultural psychologist Batja Mesquita, who studies culture and emotions for a living, had to learn this custom when she first moved to the United States. Mesquita, who was raised in the Netherlands, described her reaction after a dinner party with her new American friends: "It seemed to me that this could be the beginning of a real friendship; that is, until my guests left and thanked me for dinner. I felt crushed, because it had now dawned on me that we had failed to make a true connection. The way I was raised, where there is gratitude (i.e., *thanking* someone for dinner), there is no room for friendship. 'Thank you for dinner' felt to me as an act of distancing, rather than an expression of appreciation. I would have liked my guests to say that they were looking forward to spending more time with me, that they really liked the evening together, or that they felt happy or connected to me." Instead, the experience felt transactional.

Another example of a communication norm that may be seen as disrespectful in some cultures is the amount of silence people leave between listening and speaking. For instance, North Americans take turns speaking, whereas people from Latin America tend to jump in more quickly and East Asians tend to allow for longer silences. Again, these cultural differences in conversation style lead to misunderstandings on all sides. Laroche explains: "Everyone interprets the behaviour of people who leave a shorter silence than they do (or jump in before they would) as 'rude/interrupting/finishing my sentences.'" The opposite issue—leaving longer silences or not jumping in as quickly—is also problematic, and can be seen as "not interested/not engaged/not participating enough/cold."

Hosts can also be on the lookout for differences in directness. Some people are naturally blunt, but this is also a hallmark of a cultural communication style in places like France, Germany, Italy, Russia, and many Middle Eastern and African countries. On the other hand, the opposite is true in East Asia. If you've ever hosted a student who couldn't seem to give you a straight answer to a simple question, or they contradicted themselves later, you may have encountered this dynamic, which is often married with the concept of face. HR consultant and multicultural expert Caroline Yang explains: "In Chinese, there are four kinds of yes—Yes, I hear you; Yes, I understand; Yes, I agree; and Yes, I will do it... You have to listen to what else they say besides yes. If they say yes and bring up a glitch like 'It will be disruptive,' 'It will be difficult,' or 'We will have to do something unusual to make it happen,' they are really telling you that it won't work. In order to understand the message they are sending you, you need to listen carefully and read between the lines."

It takes a lot of self-awareness and curiosity to pay attention to the impact others have on you, and if it seems out of alignment with your expectations, to stop and clarify. One way to reframe how you think about respect is to talk to students about the "platinum" rule rather than the "golden" rule. Instead of *doing unto others as you would have done to you*, try to *do unto others what they want you to do unto them*. If your students don't know what that means, teach them. If you don't know what that means for your students, ask.

Giving Feedback

I don't think it's an exaggeration to state that all hosts will need to give feedback to a student at some point. While many students will understand and accept your comments, knowing you're trying to guide them to a more satisfying, successful experience, some will misunderstand such feedback, and may resent or reject it outright. Giving feedback is hard, even when you're from the same culture as the other person. Understanding a few key cultural differences in communication can make you more effective when it's time to correct a student's behaviour.

Here, I'll highlight three factors to consider: how direct to be, how to frame the feedback (i.e., using feedback "sandwiches"), and what vocabulary to use. Any or all of these three communication dynamics can lead someone to misinterpret the strength of the feedback, how much effort they should put toward the problem, and how quickly they should take corrective action. As Laroche told me, "It's easy for people to either under- or overestimate how big of an issue the behaviour is. If you underestimate, you don't take enough action, or not soon enough, and that drives the other person crazy." Does this sound familiar?

Directness

Again, both personality and culture can predict how direct people are. If you imagine feedback on a continuum from negative to positive, there is a neutral area in the middle of that line. Here's the thing: the width of the neutral zone varies across cultures. Whether or not something feels direct or not depends on where the feedback lands relative to that neutral zone.

CROSS-CULTURAL FEEDBACK CONTINUUM

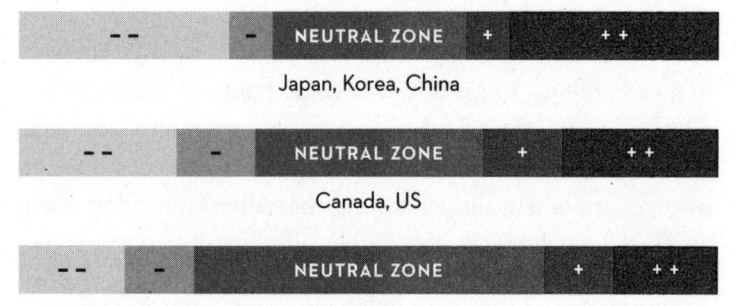

| - - | - | NEUTRAL ZONE | + | + + |

Japan, Korea, China

| - - | - | NEUTRAL ZONE | + | + + |

Canada, US

| - - | - | NEUTRAL ZONE | + | + + |

France, Germany, Italy, Russia, Romania, Israel, Egypt, South Africa

People in France, Germany, Italy, Russia, Romania, and many Middle Eastern and African countries are known for being direct *relative to North America*, because the neutral zone in North America is smaller than in these cultures. Before Morgan went to France, she knew French people have a reputation for being candid. All the same, when Sophie corrected Morgan's grammar on the subway ride from the airport—just hours after she had arrived—it felt a bit harsh to her. Sophie thought she was giving neutral feedback to Morgan, but it landed well outside Morgan's neutral zone by her North American standards.

Likewise, if a North American host were to give slightly negative feedback to a student from one of these cultures, it may come across as so mild as to be neutral and therefore inconsequential. Laroche told me about a time when he almost lost his job at Procter & Gamble because of this. "My manager gave me negative feedback but it wasn't strong enough for me to understand there was a problem," Laroche says. "So he said it again, but it was still not strong enough for me to register. My boss interpreted this as 'Lionel does not want to understand.' I understood the words, but I didn't understand the magnitude of the problem this was creating." For students from these more direct-style countries, feedback requires a firm hand.

Many years ago, CHN was matching a high volume of students from Saudi Arabia who were participants in the King Abdullah Scholarship Program (KASP), which provided funding for education abroad, including English language studies. The program was a huge success for Saudi Arabia, but many hosts found the cultural differences difficult to navigate. For instance, gender roles are highly patriarchal in Saudi culture. As a result, our team had a limited number of hosts who were willing to take Saudi students.

One afternoon, a Toronto host with two young Saudi men (around nineteen or twenty years old) called CHN's homestay coordinator Deirdre to ask for help with their rude, disrespectful attitude in the home. Deirdre consulted with her colleague, Christie. Due to our limited host capacity, they didn't want to move the boys. Instead, they would talk to the students about the host's concerns. They knew they would need to convey the message firmly. As a show of strength, they approached the students together: Deirdre would be the "good cop," and Christie would be the "bad cop."

"The boys were really worried when they saw two coordinators coming to talk to them," Deirdre says. "I remember all of us sitting around the table—I can still see them—and we launched into our little discussion. I said they were being very rude, and they weren't saying please and thank you, and they weren't helping with the house. We talked about what we expected the students to do."

Every so often, Christie would interject and say, "If you don't help with the dishes you're going to get kicked out, you know!"

"It was hilarious," Deirdre says. "It was like, back and forth. Christie was so firm."

The two young men listened. At the end, Deirdre and Christie asked them if they could live in homestay, understanding the expectations. "They said yes," Deirdre told me. "They knew they should say please and thank you, help with the family, clean up their rooms, and tell their host if they wouldn't be home for dinner. All the things."

Later, the host called Deirdre in surprise, asking what they had said to the two boys. Apparently, the intervention had worked.

Deirdre will be the first to admit that it doesn't always work. Culture is often a major factor, but when you zoom into the individual level, it's true that some students don't have the best attitude. In those cases, the student's teachers will usually notice problems in the classroom as well. In any case, "I don't think it hurts to try," Deirdre says. "Because sometimes you get through."

When comparing North America to East Asia, the opposite dynamic is at play. The majority of students from those countries may think their Canadian or American hosts are very direct, and will hear feedback much more strongly than you may intend. Like Morgan, they may be able to brush it off, but it can also lead to hurt feelings and distance in the relationship. Some students may rebel against feedback that feels disproportionate to their actions.

If you're concerned about how to give feedback in a way that helps move people forward, focus on strengths. Remember Fred, the student who ate several loaves of bread every day? Everyone has positive qualities, and those qualities are potential resources.

Framing

The second factor that influences how someone interprets feedback is related to the way you frame the feedback. In North America, the UK, and Australia, when someone does something mildly bad—no big deal, but something should be said—people tend to use a "feedback sandwich." To soften the harshness, they'll sandwich a negative comment between two positive comments. When the problem is a little worse, they might use an "open-faced sandwich," with one positive comment and one negative comment. Things are getting serious when there are no positive comments, and pretty dire when more than one negative comment is given.

It may surprise some readers to learn this feedback pattern is unique to North America, the UK, and Australia. In contrast, feedback in other cultures is either good or bad, but not both. Instead, people use completely different indicators to convey the severity of the problem. For example, in Italy, more serious feedback is communicated with a louder voice and more arm gestures; in France, it's volume and frequency of tone modulation. In Japan, you know you're in deep trouble when someone uses long silences and stern facial expressions. Again, the result is that some international students will assume they are doing fine (no corrective action required) and others will be devastated by their host's comments (though this can be mitigated depending on how those comments are delivered and how well they know each other).

Vocabulary

The third indicator used by North Americans to calibrate the intensity of their feedback is choice of words. A simple example is the difference between a "concern" and a "disaster." As Laroche explains, "Americans and Canadians have about fifteen different ways to tell you there is a problem, an error, or a conflict. The word they choose gives you a good indication of how bad things are in their mind." Just as misunderstandings can arise when discussing emotions with people from other cultures, your carefully selected words may not effectively convey the subtlety of your meaning. A limited vocabulary is largely to blame, but even words that sound similar in different languages—like the Spanish *problema* or French *problème*—don't have the same meaning as *problem* in English. A problem in North America is much more serious than the French or Spanish translation.

Thankfully, addressing the gaps between message intended and message received caused by all three of these dynamics is straightforward.

Dealing With Communication Gaps

As with many of the tools you're learning in this book, awareness is key. When you know a miscommunication *could* occur, you can dial up your sensitivity for mismatched reactions, such as a student seeming to be disrespectful or reacting out of proportion to something you said.

Laroche recalls another experience with a breakdown in communication related to directness, framing, and vocabulary which happened when he was a sixteen-year-old French student living with a family near Boston, Massachusetts. He adored his hosts Don and John and they had a respectful relationship.

Laroche learned that his running commentary comparing the US to France was not always well received. "At one point Don just lost it," Laroche recalls. "He told me, 'Look, you're constantly saying how France is better than the US.'" Laroche agrees that French people can be much more candid than Americans, but it was more than that. "I didn't have the words to express myself, to put nuances in my thoughts," Laroche says. "I remember being extremely frustrated, because I only had one word for something I could say five different ways in French."

In this example, his English was good enough to get his point across—there was no issue with pronunciation—but the subtleties of communication combined with his lack of vocabulary led to irritation on behalf of his hosts and an uncomfortable confrontation.

If you find yourself in a situation like this, Laroche recommends four steps to move forward.

1 **Be curious and pay attention to your own negative reactions (like feeling offended, annoyed, or disrespected).** If you notice something, say something—bring yourself to the same side of the problem as your student, not in opposition to them—and be open to learning about a cultural difference. Don and John took offence at Laroche's unfavourable comments about the US, and felt irritated. At this point, they may or may not have recognized Laroche's cultural tendency for bluntness, or appreciated his lack of vocabulary.

2 **Avoid acting on the negative feelings.** It's like waiting to respond to an emotionally charged email—there are better ways to vent. Don and John avoided saying anything for a while, and it seems from Laroche's story that they didn't let their feelings get in the way of their relationship.

3. **Try to identify the words, body language, or behaviours that led to your negative reaction.** It may take some time and reflection to do so; not only is it hard for people to accurately interpret the body language and facial expressions of other cultures, but it's also difficult to recognize the unspoken rules of one's own culture. Understanding your own culture is a critical step in building cultural competence. In Don and John's case, the unspoken rule is that you don't openly criticize someone else's country, and you keep your offensive opinions to yourself.

4. **Finally, ask someone what those words, body language, or behaviours meant to the student.** This can be a friend who is familiar with your student's culture, the homestay organization, a teacher, or the student themselves.

    Presumably, Don and John were able to work through this with Laroche, as they enjoyed a positive relationship long after this incident took place.

I recognize that all of this is easier said than done, and that my recommendations may seem out of proportion to the situation you're facing. Some students are harder to get along with than others, and nobody can predict the chemistry of a placement. While hosts can ask for relocations when relationships sour, some communication problems will persist no matter which student you're hosting. It makes sense to work on intercultural communication skills, not just for homestay, but to enhance your relationships within your family, workplace, and community.

Behaviours that
appear disrespectful or
display a lack of manners
may be explained by
cultural differences
rather than personality.

How to Listen

A chapter on communication would be incomplete without some discussion of listening skills. Before you skip ahead, consider this statistic from Oscar Trimboli's Deep Listening Research: "When asked how they would rate themselves as a listener compared to others in their workplace, 74.8 percent of respondents considered themselves either above or well above average. When asked to rate the listening of others, only 12.1 percent chose above or well above average." This gap exposes a bias people tend to share about their own listening skills and reveals how hard it is to define what anyone means by "good" listening.

In addition to this self-awareness gap, everyone's ability to listen is hindered by physiology. In his powerful book *How to Listen*, Trimboli explains that while people can think at an amazing 900 words per minute, most can't talk or listen that quickly. The average talking speed is 125 words per minute and listening speed is 400 words per minute. If you've ever listened to an audiobook, sat through a recorded lecture, or watched a wordy YouTube video, this is why you may have been tempted to increase the playback speed.

Even at that faster speed, if you find your mind wanders when you're listening, you're not alone. As humans, it's natural for people to anticipate the other person's words or plan what they want to say next, and that's when they're focused on the conversation!

I encourage readers who wish to take a deeper dive into Trimboli's work to read his book or listen to his podcast (he will help your effectiveness at work, too). For now, here are four recommendations for improving listening skills that are particularly relevant in a homestay setting.

Prepare for the conversation

I'll discuss this further in chapter 10, which covers difficult conversations. For now, consider Trimboli's recommendation to take a couple of minutes to "tune in," much the way musicians tune their instruments before a performance. Turn off your phone or switch it to silent mode. Anticipate distractions, both internal (your stories, emotions) and external (noises, devices). Notice your ego and its role in the conversation, and dial up your empathy. When empathy is lacking from a conversation, Trimboli's research respondents described feeling "disrespected, ignored, judged, a problem to be fixed."

This goes both ways. If you have felt disrespected, ignored, or judged by your student, it's possible they weren't empathizing with you in that moment. This is another example of a time when the host may need to set an example for the relationship; in this case, how you show up to a conversation will create space for your student to relax, trust you, and better express themselves. Tune in, notice your ego, practice your culturally sensitive empathy skills, and see what happens.

Give your complete attention

When you approach a conversation willingly—when you can be curious, generous, and open to possibility—you will notice more and will therefore learn more. Attention allows you to notice what the other person *doesn't* say and *how* they speak. Just as when you're unpacking an emotional episode, don't make assumptions. Such deep attention will make your conversations more efficient and satisfying, as it allows you to focus on what really matters and what people really mean rather than surface-level dialogue.

Remember that emotions are always present

I'll look at this in chapter 10 as well. While you may not be able to fully understand what someone else is feeling, you can pay attention to their facial expressions, words, and body language and simply notice when these things change in the middle of the conversation. Sometimes a change is overt, but other times it can be subtle, such as an audible sigh, slumped shoulders, or a downward glance. Noticing this shift will reveal something important in that moment. Be curious, not judgmental.

Listen between the lines

Recall that people can think seven times faster than they can speak; what they say at first may not be the most effective way to express themselves. When compounded with cultural influences such as directness or the concept of face, there are countless examples in homestay of students or hosts saying one thing and meaning another. Himari can't ask her host about her missing pencil. A student who complains about the food and requests a relocation is feeling ashamed of a fight she had with her host sister the night before. Lionel didn't have the right words to fully express his meaning. As the host parent, your role is to create space to allow the student to process their thoughts and find the words to express themselves more fully. This takes time, patience, empathy, and silence.

Prompting your student to explore more deeply can be as simple as saying, "Tell me more," or "What else?" Then wait. Don't be afraid of the awkward pause. Embrace it. If you are hosting a student from an Eastern culture where silence is cultivated and embraced as a foundational part of communication, your skilled use of silence will foster respect in your relationship.

The same is true for you—you also need time to collect your thoughts and ensure that your message has been received. This is all the more important if you are delivering some piece of information that is complex, challenging, or confrontational. Trimboli recommends three phrases you can use to pause and ensure shared understanding:

- "Let me pause."
- "What sense does that make to you?"
- "What does that have you thinking?"

These skills take time and practice, like anything that requires a shift in habits. And it's worth the effort. As Trimboli says, "When you are in the presence of a great listener, they not only make you feel different, they also create an experience that changes you permanently."

The next time you encounter a communication breakdown, remember Himari and her missing pencil, Morgan's struggles in France, or the Saudi boys who needed a firm hand. Be the host who doesn't laugh, the one who considers how direct they're being. Help your student see that the people who love and care for them will be there regardless of the outcome. Learning is hard for both of you, but it can be a little easier when you give each other the chance to try, fall down, try again, and do better.

CHAPTER SUMMARY

- When Himari lost her pencil, she was trying to save face. Making someone lose face can sometimes insult them so much as to create an enemy for life.

- Communication is a lot of work for the host, but language immersion is even more exhausting for the student.

- Behaviours that appear disrespectful or display a lack of manners may be explained by cultural differences rather than personality.

- Giving feedback is tricky in any culture. Consider how direct you're being, how you're framing it (with a feedback sandwich?), and what vocabulary you're using.

- Laroche and Yang's four steps for addressing communication gaps:

  1. Be curious and pay attention to your own negative reactions.
  2. Avoid acting on the negative feelings.
  3. Try to identify the words, body language, or behaviours that led to your negative reaction.
  4. Ask what those behaviours meant to the student.

- You can be a better listener by tuning in to yourself, giving your complete attention, noticing emotional shifts, and listening for deeper meaning.

PART THREE

Know Yourself

9

Being Good-ish
Fighting Bias

---

*Our family and friends are of diverse cultures
and races... We are conscious of attempting to check
the biases we all possess. Hosting a person from
another culture reminds us to consistently work on this.*
LINDA, host from Toronto, Ontario

LIONEL LAROCHE, the multicultural communication expert introduced in the last chapter, had a wonderful first impression of his hosts. Don and John, who were in their mid-forties, had a genuine interest in the world outside the US. They were a great match for him intellectually: Don was a mid-level manager in a large organization, and John was a professor of English medieval history at a top-rated university. As a sixteen-year-old boy whose "interest in women was starting to awaken," he also found it "absolutely fascinating" that his hosts were surrounded by women all the time.

Lionel grew up in Paris and had lived in homestay in England a couple of times before, but this was his first trip to North America. He was travelling with a group of fifteen teenagers for a summer language immersion program in Sharon, Massachusetts, just outside Boston. His cousin and sister were part of the group, but were placed with different families.

When Lionel arrived, Don was home with their two dogs, a German shepherd and a tiny poodle. John was on vacation with his sister, and didn't arrive until a few days later. "My initial interpretation was these two roommates were womanizers, having a great time, like playboys," Lionel says. Nothing seemed out of place to him until John arrived, and he realized the two men were sharing a bedroom. "We're talking 1981," he says. "Homosexuality was not as openly discussed then as it is today. It was not on my radar." But he was happy with his placement, so it didn't occur to him to say anything to his parents. After all, making a transatlantic phone call in those days would have cost a fortune. "At the time, I don't think I worried about it too much. I didn't see a problem."

About two weeks after his arrival, his mother found out that Don and John were a couple. Lionel still doesn't know how; he says he must have mentioned it to his cousin or sister, so he assumes one of them made a call. "My mother freaked out. She called the organizers at 2:00 a.m., because she forgot the time difference," Lionel says. "I never got the full story as to what happened during that phone call. I remember the organizers telling her what time it was. I think they were able to calm her down, made her feel like, you know, I wasn't being molested or anything like that. That I was having a great time."

I asked Lionel what he thinks would have happened to his placement if his family had been informed of Don and John's relationship status in advance of the trip. "There's definitely a good chance that prejudice would have taken over," he says, reflecting on my question. "It wouldn't have been me making that decision, as I was still a minor. On the other hand, if my parents had known Don's and John's occupations, and had a picture of their house, which was beautiful... if they had some information about the situation, I don't know what would have happened."

As Lionel points out, attitudes about homosexuality have changed significantly since the 1980s. But chalking this up to old-fashioned attitudes is an inadequate explanation for his mother's behaviour: there are more fundamental mechanisms at play.

Mindbugs

Early humans lived in a world where they had to make rapid risk assessments of their environment to stay safe. In time, humans evolved to use mental shortcuts to process the eleven million bits of information that our brains receive every moment. Most of this information—99.999996 percent—gets processed unconsciously.

These shortcuts lead to errors in "how we perceive, remember, reason, and make decisions." Such errors explain how optical illusions work, as well as dozens of other misplaced judgments about time, past events, frequency of events, inherent value, risk, danger, and more. In their book, *Blindspot: Hidden Biases of Good People*, psychologists Mahzarin Banaji and Anthony Greenwald refer to these errors in perception as *mindbugs*. Far from being a mistake of evolution, these automatic processes are exceptional adaptations that allow humans to function in a complex world. In homestay, two such mindbugs are easy to spot.

The first is known as the *availability heuristic*. This mindbug—also knowns as a cognitive bias—convinces us that when one type of event comes more easily to mind than another, the more familiar event must be more common. When combined with the tendency to remember emotionally charged events with more clarity than others, people jump to conclusions. For example, after dealing with a male student who breaks curfew and smokes in his room, a host may become convinced that boys are more troublesome than girls.

The second mindbug is called *confirmation bias*, and refers to our tendency to notice information that supports an existing hypothesis. The next time that host takes a male student and something goes wrong, she will accept the experience as proof of her assessment that all boys are trouble—despite having hosted several other male students with no issues. Humans approach the world with a certain point of view, which leads us to discount or not even notice information that contradicts our point of view.

It's plausible that Lionel's mother was passing judgment due to her cognitive biases. But where would these originate in the first place? Biased behaviour is also a result of how our society works.

The Smog of Bias

Modern society exposes people to stereotypes through the daily news, social media, books, computer games, television, movies, music, and so on. Psychologist Beverly Daniel Tatum likens these stereotypes, omissions, and distortions to a kind of smog. "We don't breathe it because we like it," she says. "We breathe it because it's the only air that's available." Our digital world spreads this smog of stereotypes even further, amplifying the human tendency to sort people into *us* and *them*. It's a slippery slope from *weird* and *normal* to *safe* and *dangerous*, *human* and *not-human*.

Stereotypes about LGBTQ+ people were far more prevalent in the 1980s than today, but they still exist—and they are still dangerous. Some hosts who identify with the LGBTQ+ community are not comfortable accepting students from certain cultural groups, due to their society's views. This isn't the only example of stereotypes in homestay.

Stew and Jen, hosts from Victoria, looked after a Brazilian student who had full-time maids and cooks back home, and expected Jen to perform these duties. Many hosts have dealt with students whose views on the role of women in the home is challenging and at times offensive.

Kenda, a host from Ontario, has felt discriminated against by students who don't want to live on a farm. Here, there was an urban-versus-rural bias. "They can't get it in their head that it's a multi-million-dollar operation. They judge the class of the family. Farmers are poor. Scum."

Another survey respondent said, "When the foreign agent realized we were not white, the student was taken away even though she already told the agent that she liked living with us." (Much like you might hire a travel agent to advise you on vacation plans, many students and parents hire international education agents to represent them with the educator and homestay company.)

It's not just the students and agents. Nora, a Swiss student, started dating a Black student while she was in homestay. Not long after, Nora's friend Julia said her hosts wouldn't let Nora come over anymore. When Nora's host found out, she was "astounded." She said Nora's boyfriend was a kind young man. "It's hard to believe that these prejudices still exist, but obviously they do," she said.

The smog of messages spread by our society also explains why people associate things like *old* with *fragile*, or *women* with *family and home*. And when the brain takes these shortcuts, simplifying data by discarding variables to make quick, superficial judgments, people end up making errors. This is known as implicit or unconscious bias. The research suggests that unconscious bias can shift depending on what's happening in the moment, but it tends to fluctuate within a fairly stable range.

Bias is also reinforced by our social groups. A Public Religion Research Institute (PRRI) survey looked at the diversity within social networks in the US. They asked participants to look back over the previous six months and consider those people with whom they discussed important matters. The researchers found that 75 percent of white people, 65 percent of Black people, and 46 percent of Hispanic people had homogenous networks composed exclusively of people sharing their own race. This tends to create echo chambers where there are few surprises and no contrary information to shake one's beliefs. Furthermore, psychologist Drew Jacoby-Senghor found that in addition to spending time with people of our own race, we are also drawn to people who share our implicit bias.

While one's explicit and implicit attitudes are related, there are differences—and people are often surprised to discover their implicit biases. The suggestion that bias exists in the first place can elicit strong reactions in people who see themselves as open minded, lacking in prejudice, and embracing diversity and inclusion in their homes and workplaces.

In response to CHN's survey question about bias, 38 percent of hosts denied any prejudice or said they couldn't think of anything. For example:

- "I don't know of any. All of my friends and family members are empathetic and most dedicated to eradicating any prejudice and discrimination, so none has had to overcome bias."

- "I have not experienced bias or prejudice in my home, my circle of friends, or in my community. All are very accepting of new people."

- "We never experienced this issue in the past and we can't see it happening in the future. We are both immigrants from different backgrounds and we don't allow prejudice or bias in our home. We treat everyone equal, the way we are treated."

Yet, everyone has biases. The discomfort people feel with questions like this is because we have what psychologist Karl Aquino and Americus Reed call a "moral identity." Moral identity, as they define it, is organized around a set of moral traits which help us conceptualize who we are. It does not, however, automatically translate into how we behave.

Moral Identity and Self-Threat

I think it's fair to say that hosts share a moral identity of being good people. CHN's 2022 survey revealed that 24 percent of families started hosting in order to support the students. As one host put it, "I am a loving and caring person and I treat all who enter my home like family. I am a teacher and I love encouraging students." The opportunity to be a good role model for young people is not just about sharing values and life lessons, it's also about love and care.

Even though many people believe in the promise of equality and equity, diversity and inclusion, our moral identity can get in the way of seeing ourselves clearly and identifying how we could be better. Part of the problem is that people evaluate their identity in a very binary way; they are either good or bad, racist or not, ethical or not. But nobody can be perfectly ethical and unbiased all the time.

Consider the last time you saw a name that looked difficult to pronounce. What was your reaction? If you were reading it in a book, did you skim over it or sound it out? If it was on a new student profile, did you secretly hope your student would choose an English name when she arrives? Did you default to using her first name and avoid the problem of botching the pronunciation of her last name entirely? Or were you like one of Seamus's hosts, who announced on his second day that she would just call him Sam? (His name is pronounced Shay-muss and rhymes with famous.)

Mary, a host from Victoria, BC, found it hard to pronounce the name of a student from Argentina. It bothered her so much that she still winces at the thought. "I would avoid saying his name, or whenever I did, I had to think about it," she says. Mary knew she wasn't being the host she wanted to be. She also used to work in radio, and prides herself on her verbal skills, so her struggles conflicted with her perception of herself. "I'm big on enunciating and pronunciation, and I kept messing up his name. It broke my heart each time."

When one's moral identity is challenged in moments like this, psychologists call it "self-threat." When students ask for a relocation because they aren't getting along with their hosts, the hosts will feel self-threat about their identity as good host parents. If a student values being seen as open minded, they will feel self-threat when their host mother judges them for not trying a new food they've been served. Self-threat does not bring out the best in people. Researchers have found that people morally disengage, their performance deteriorates, they make poor behavioural choices, their health suffers, they become defensive, and they don't treat others well.

Knowing and using someone's name is critical to building meaningful relationships, but when that name is difficult to pronounce, some may think it's easier to avoid it. The good intention—of dodging offence or embarrassment by mispronouncing the name—can have a bad impact. If you only use names that are familiar to you, you end up sending a message that the foreign-sounding name does not belong. This just alienates the person you are trying to make comfortable.

As psychologist Dolly Chugh, author of *The Person You Mean to Be: How Good People Fight Bias*, explains, "Our bodies are built to fight off bacteria and our minds are built to fight off self-threat. This does not make us bad people, but it does make us unlikely to recognize when we do bad things... It is easy for us to see this in other people and much harder for us to see it in ourselves."

One of the ways people try to shore up their moral identity is to look for affirmation—in fact, they need it so much that it in one study, researchers found that participants were willing to pay for it. When hosts *do* try to pronounce their student's name correctly, they want kudos and praise. People often look for these acknowledgements of their good intentions—like little gold stars on their homework—even when it's not good for the person giving the gold star. Unfortunately, when you want others to validate that you are a good person, you make the situation about you, and not about them.

Looking for affirmation can show up in many ways. Hosts want students to notice when they make rice for packed lunches or buy kimchi at the Korean market. When hosting a Chinese student and celebrating Chinese New Year, a host wants to tell their Chinese friends. After hate crimes—like the mass shooting at a mosque in Quebec City on January 29, 2017, or the mob that attacked LGBTQ+ activists at a peaceful protest in Sydney in March 2023, non-Muslim or straight people want to tell their Muslim or gay students and friends how sad it makes them, or how angry they are. In every case, when looking for gold stars, you end up forcing others to make room for you and your emotions at the expense of the genuine support you were trying to provide.

By embracing being "good-ish," you give yourself the grace to see your true complexity and the opportunity to learn.

The way to show up as your best self is to get rid of the impossible binaries about your identity. As Chugh says, "Being a good person means trying to be better, rather than believing in the illusion that you are always a good person." By embracing being "good-ish," you give yourself the grace to see your true complexity and the opportunity to learn. It can be hard to know the right thing to say or do about race, or any other form of bias, in order to be "good," or "anti-racist," or "an ally." Don't let a quest for perfection impair your quest for growth. Embrace your capacity for change, learn from setbacks, and then try again.

Trying to Be Better: Willful Awareness

The first step in trying to be better is to pay attention. Instead of slipping into old habits, letting your confirmation bias sway your opinions and judgments, you can choose "willful awareness." Chugh describes this process of self-reflection as staying with hard topics, listening when you'd rather leave, looking toward rather than away, and acknowledging your role in the system that keeps people marginalized: this is where the learning happens.

Curiosity is at the heart of willful awareness. One host, who works as an ESL (English as a Second Language) instructor for the Toronto District School Board, wrote on CHN's survey, "I have seen and been dealing with racial/cultural misunderstandings for decades. I find that in almost every case, misunderstanding is solved by curiosity. Questions break down bias or preconceived ideas."

When you engage with people in a curious way, the conversation can help you see new things. Ask your students what the hot-button topics on campus are. Ask your children or your grandchildren what "old-fashioned" perspectives you're holding. Ask yourself how you can learn on your own, without putting the onus on a marginalized person to educate you.

Willful awareness means noticing your own bias and how it shows up in your relationships. Ann, a retiree from Toronto, started taking students because she enjoys being connected to a younger generation. All her friends are her age and she doesn't have children of her own. She used to work as an occupational therapist at the Centre for Addiction and Mental Health (CAMH), Canada's largest mental health teaching hospital, to do something meaningful. She recalls an impactful relationship with a Chinese student who was "very good company" and loved to practice her English. Ann helped with homework and encouraged her student to invite her friends over to her home. She taught her student how to make banana bread and, in turn, learned how to cook some Chinese dishes. When I ask Ann what she values about herself, she says, "I see myself as a person of great integrity, open, and receptive." Yet in the next breath, she catches herself: "Although, this program has shown me I have some hidden, minor prejudices," she says. "I don't think of myself as a person of prejudice, but I realized that everyone is, really. It's unfair to judge a person by the policies of their government. She taught me about that. I actually cried when she left, and she did, too." Ann was practicing willful awareness.

Sometimes we just need to hear ourselves talk to notice our biases. One host shared this story of self-awareness in her home: "We are a multigenerational household. My eighty-two-year-old father is kind and open to everyone (he spent twenty-five years in the Canadian Armed Forces, many as a UN peacekeeper), but some of the phrases he used in the past were definitely from his generation and not politically correct. In the early days of hosting, sometimes a student wouldn't understand what he said and as he explained it, I could see he began to realize how it sounded. After having international students for many years, he has adjusted his vocabulary."

Another survey respondent also learned about her biases from a student. "My first homestay was an eighteen-year-old Persian/Iranian female," she wrote. "My original impressions, mainly formed from the media, are now substantially revised. As a product of a patriarchal society, I assumed she would be simpler, reticent, introspective. Actually, she was self-assured, sophisticated, and much more like the average teenager here in North America." Noticing when you've absorbed a stereotype like this is part of paying attention.

While stereotypes are often negative, they can also be positive. But even a positive stereotype ignores individual differences, is judgmental, and is based on assumptions. For example, Japanese girls are often perceived by their Canadian hosts to be quiet, polite, and studious. When a new Japanese student arrives and she is none of these things, her hosts risk excluding her, treating her more like an object or category than an individual. When someone assumes their Chinese student will be good at math, they miss the possibility that he might love basketball.

To be fair, students will also have expectations and assumptions about what host families will be like. Another host from Ontario told us, "I am Jewish and have hosted students of the Muslim faith. Some of them arrive with pre-existing prejudices about Jews. When they leave for home, it's always with a different perspective, a better one on both sides. We're both happy to have met and learned from each other."

Overcoming these stereotypes, like any form of bias, requires curiosity and openness, and a willingness to see each other as individuals.

Take a few minutes to imagine where your biases might show up in your work as a host.

- Look at which students you prefer to host—ages, genders, nationalities.

- Consider the assumptions you make about your students when they don't behave according to your expectations, and how you explain your expectations and the consequences of not adhering to them.

- Think about how you respond to complaints from students and if your response differs across ages, genders, and nationalities.

- Look at the household chores you expect of your students—of all genders.

- Consider the conversations you have with other hosts and the explanations you give for the challenges you're facing.

Trying to Be Better: Celebrate Difference

In addition to practicing willful awareness, hosts who are trying to be better are good at noticing difference. Some people would rather emphasize how we are all the same, deep down, like the hosts who made these comments from CHN's 2022 survey:

"At my household my family doesn't believe in prejudice. We treat everyone equally."

"People are just people, regardless of place of origin or ethnicity."

"I was brought up to see everyone as equal."

While it's true that looking for common ground can unite people from opposite sides of an issue, people who care about equality cannot be blind to the realities of inequality. There are vast differences in how people experience life based on their race, ethnicity, gender, and so on. To ignore these differences in an attempt to connect will actually have the opposite effect. In one study, participants who played a game modelled after Guess Who? were *more* likely to be viewed as racist when they *didn't* talk about race.

Charlene and her husband, Chase, live in Fredericton with their son, Mason. They started hosting because they wanted to provide housing and share their home life, but also to expose their adopted son to diversity in their own home. Charlene explains: "Our son is seven, and he's starting to notice that his skin colour is completely different than ours... Before Mason started saying, 'Mummy, why is my skin so different?' I never looked at that... He's just my son... I started saying things like, 'Well, I didn't even notice.' Until a girlfriend said to me, 'You need to. Because this is who he is.' And so that made me step back and go, oh yeah. He's Indigenous... he's a different person, and we have to embrace and acknowledge what that is."

She elaborates, "That's the number one reason we started hosting. So that he can see that there are other kids out there who are flourishing, who are of a different background, who have mums and dads who look a little different and talk a little different, and that's okay. At the end of the day, we're family."

Perhaps it's more than okay. It could be exactly what we need: a reminder that being different is worth celebrating, and we are all worthy of love, no matter where we're from, or the language we speak, or the colour of our skin.

Trying to Be Better: Say Something

Willful awareness and celebrating difference are important and necessary strategies that start with you and your own growth toward the person you mean to be. However, being better also means speaking up when you notice biased behaviour, as hard as it can seem. As Reverend Dr. Martin Luther King Jr. wrote, "We will have to repent in this generation not merely for the hateful words and actions of bad people but for the appalling silence of the good people."

I have felt the discomfort myself. I'm guilty of looking the other way when my aging cousin made a racist comment. *He's always been like that*, I've said to myself. *He's just an old man. He won't change. What's the point?*

Yet the research shows, again and again, that saying something *does* matter. Confronting people may not appear to matter—in fact, you may feel like me, that it would make things worse—but your words can impact future behaviour and attitudes. This is true even when people react defensively in the moment. In my case, I could have tried something like, "I'm saying this because I love you. I want you to know that what you just said is not okay. I know you didn't mean anything by it, but it can be hurtful."

Saying something helps for two reasons: it builds awareness, reminding people of their values and who they want to be, and it disrupts social norms, a process that leverages external pressure on people who want to be seen in a favourable light.

Building awareness is about bringing to light the narratives that people have absorbed from the smog of society, lingering beneath the surface of their consciousness. Your comments don't have to be complicated or heavy-handed to be effective. Sarah, a host from Quebec, told us about a student who didn't want to go outside much because her culture had taught her to be scared of "getting dark"—becoming too tanned. Little did the student realize the impact this had on Sarah, until Sarah said something: "I had to make her realize that this perspective could be seen as prejudicial, especially since we are people of colour with dark skin."

Another host shared an anecdote in CHN's host survey about an acquaintance who made a racist comment that she confronted over time, with a longer intervention. "He said that my student from India would make my house smell and not in a good way," she wrote. She took the opportunity to discuss religion and culture with him and invited him over for a curry dinner to get to know her student. This is risky if the person is lacking any motivation to change, and it puts the student in a vulnerable position. However, her student embraced the opportunity, sharing photos of her home in India, talking about her studies, and teaching him about some aspects of her culture. It worked: "He got to know her and changed his opinion to a positive one."

When you have a close relationship with the person you're confronting like this, the potential for your impact is even greater. Don't underestimate the power of your influence when talking to close friends.

Emma, a Canadian high school student, understood this when talking to her friend Alex about LGBTQ+ rights. Alex was born in Beijing and was living in homestay with Lee and Danny at the time. "The way I was raised," Alex said, "boys are supposed to pair up with girls." Emma disagreed. She encouraged him to respect an individual's right to choose whomever they want to love and told him that boys could pair up with boys, or girls with girls, or any gender with any other gender.

It was hard for Alex to accept this at first, but he cared about Emma's opinion, and her friendship was important enough for him to listen carefully. "It got me thinking. What you think is right may not be what other people think is right. If [being gay] doesn't hurt anybody, and they're doing it out of love, they should have the right to do it." Alex draws a parallel between what he was learning about LGBTQ+ rights and his personal experience with racism. "Especially during COVID," Alex says. "People were saying, 'You're from China—you should go back to China right now.' That hurt my feelings about Canadians. But now I know, it's not all Canadians—it's one of them. The one person with the mean voice cannot represent all Canadians."

Alex credits Emma with opening his mind about LGBTQ+ rights. He recently graduated from university, and he's still finding ways to pay it forward. He told me about a time when he was driving down the street with a friend who had just arrived from China, and they spotted a gay couple holding hands. Alex's friend said, "Ew! That's not right!" Instead of laughing along, Alex chose to say something. "I try to help my friends understand that [their comment] might hurt other people. They don't have to be okay with it. All they have to do is respect it. It's like standing up against bullies. If one person stands up, they might change what they do."

Alex is pointing out the second reason saying something works: it disrupts social norms. When other people are listening or watching, social pressure will sway behaviour. This explains the success of curbside recycling programs. Nobody wants to be the only family on the street who doesn't recycle.

In the same way that saying something clears the smog that people absorb from the world around them, it also disrupts assumptions about what's okay and what's not okay in a given home, workplace, or group. When I nodded and smiled and didn't speak up in response to my cousin's bigoted comments or racist jokes, I reinforced a message about the kind of behaviour

The suggestion that
we all have bias can
elicit strong reactions
in people who
see themselves as
open minded.

———————

that's allowed in his home. Research shows that people act in prejudiced ways when they think it's okay to do so. Humans are social creatures, habituated to follow the norms of the group. If I had said something, I would have been sending a signal that it's not okay to speak like that, and this shift in norms may have been enough to change his behaviour.

Just be wary about public shaming, which doesn't work to inspire change—at least, not in Western cultures such as those in North America, the UK, or Australia. Keep the comment brief, respectful, and polite. It's not about winning an argument; it's about disrupting the norm.

Host Laurie from Cornwall, Ontario, had to create a new norm for a Korean student who kept expressing a bias against Chinese people. After a Chinese student joined their family, "at first the Korean student was polite but curt and did not want to help out the Chinese student," Laurie says. "We asked that he look past the student's nationality and give him a chance to show his true self to us, without any prejudice, the same as we did when he arrived. They became friends." We've heard many similar stories of students from two historically adversarial nations coming together in homestay, and in the context of this new environment—with its different norms—learning to overcome their differences. Another survey respondent said, "I hosted two students at the same time, one from Taiwan and one from China. Despite the longstanding cultural and political tensions between their home countries, these two young ladies forged a deep and continuing friendship that has lasted over four years." When you shift the norms, you shift behaviour.

If I wasn't the only one who spoke up about my cousin's comments—if someone else in my family had also reacted—the shift would have been even more powerful. The same is true for people who hold particular status in the group—for example, the popular kids at school. When they speak up, the impact is also more effective. In one study at a high school, researchers found that bullying was reduced by 30 percent when the cool kids spoke out against it. This remarkable change was far more effective than the usual, broad-based efforts. The study also found that it wasn't necessary for anyone to change their attitude about particular kids. As long as the norm was changed, the bullying decreased.

The only catch when speaking up for others is the potential to slip into "saviour mode." In this mode, people let their desire to help others morph into a rescue mission where they are the hero and the other person, people, or causes are victims. They forget that there are real people behind the problems, prioritizing their need to feel good—what social scientists call the "warm-glow effect"—over the needs of others.

There's nothing wrong with helping others. But if you find yourself feeling an ego boost after helping a student, and that student hasn't had a chance to take the lead or learn a new skill by solving their own problems, you may be centring your needs over theirs. It's okay to want to advocate for your student—especially if they are the victim of discrimination in your own home—but there's a difference between advocacy and saviour mode. INvolve, a global firm that consults with organizations on building more inclusive cultures, explains the difference on their website: "Advocacy is recognizing the power of one's own voice to fight for others... Saviorism is [where] one believes they have all the answers and solutions... and an assumption that they inherently know best."

In other words, do not speak for people, but don't be afraid to say something even if the target of the bias is present. Chugh explains how: "One approach is to turn to the target and simply ask... 'Would it be okay if I jumped in here?' Or 'I'm happy to take this one,' or 'Say the word if I can help.'" And remember: don't look for the gold star of affirmation that you've done something good. It's not about you.

Malvina and Kelly, hosts from Saskatchewan, are comfortable saying something, but their story also highlights the importance of allowing individuals to speak for themselves. In addition to hosting for many years, Malvina has worked as a homestay coordinator and is an intercultural communications professional with expertise in bias and prejudice. One of Malvina and Kelly's most profound experiences happened while hosting two students—Kenzo from Japan and Manuel from Mexico. Manuel had several friends who would hang out at Malvina and Kelly's house. One of these friends, another Mexican student named Santiago, "held many prejudices against Asian students and would make a lot of racist comments," Malvina wrote. "We did not allow this type of behaviour in our home and would challenge Santiago when he said anything." Malvina told me this wasn't done with a lot of pressure; the atmosphere in their home was fun loving and light. Nevertheless, "These challenges were always met with defence and resistance to change. He would not admit wrong-doing."

Malvina and Kelly persisted in their conversations with Santiago. Eventually, Kenzo got involved in one of these conversations. He wanted to understand how Santiago could make such racist remarks against other Asians while appearing to be friendly with him. "Santiago's initial response was, 'You're not like those other Asians,'" Malvina says. "Kenzo wouldn't let that fly. He said, 'If you're my friend it's because *you see all of me*.' This led to a more constructive, impactful conversation about how to recognize and address the racist comments. Once a more personal connection was made, Santiago began to take some responsibility for his words and actions. Ultimately, he was friendlier."

This story reinforces several effective approaches when confronting bias: the hosts raised awareness, they leveraged their personal relationship, they spoke up as a group, they shifted the norms and led by example, and they encouraged the student being discriminated against to speak for himself. For them, it was about accountability, not shame.

To put others at ease and ensure your message is persuasive, keep the following strategies in mind:

- Acknowledge your own growth. Admit that you aren't perfect, you still make mistakes, or, like Ann, you are learning about this stuff, too. This is hard work, and mistakes will happen. That's okay! It's part of the process. The fact that you're still here, sticking at it, is what counts.
- Use humour. If you are close, you could try a gentle tease. If not, self-deprecation can hit the right tone, but it has to be authentic.
- Use stories, not facts. The human brain is hardwired to think in story. It's how we make meaning from the world around us and all those millions of pieces of data that we filter every moment. Your ability to share a personal anecdote, or a story you've read in this book or heard from a friend, will have a bigger impact than a lot of facts ever will.
- People who lack motivation to become less biased are not ready for growth. To find out if someone is ready to grow, Chugh suggests asking a simple question, calmly and respectfully: "I see it differently. Are you open to listening to my perspective?"
- Remember, when you challenge both hidden and explicit biases of a person who sees themselves as essentially "good,"

you will probably challenge their moral identity, which will trigger self-threat. If the person who has made the prejudiced claim or cracked a racist "joke" resists your invitation to explore your perspective, you will be wasting your time trying to change them. But if others are listening, it's still helpful to state your dissent, then leave it there.

It's Worth It

As you may have imagined, Lionel's story about living with Don and John didn't end with his mother's frantic phone call in the middle of the night. Looking back on it now, as an expert who has had decades of experience helping organizations manage a multicultural workforce, he says it was one of the most positive experiences he's ever had. "I think they wanted to experience having a child," Lionel says of his hosts. "They were lucky, because they got to choose a kid who suited their personality. And I was lucky, because if I had been with another family I would have been bored to tears. I wanted in-depth conversations with people. It turned out to be a fantastic arrangement."

When Lionel tells this story, the detail regarding his hosts' sexual orientation was not the point. For him, it was about the way they connected over their shared interests and forged a strong bond. Lionel stayed with them again two years later, outside of any organized program. No money was exchanged; his parents paid for his plane ticket and he lived with Don and John for a few weeks again. Don and John also came to Paris for a vacation and stayed with Lionel's family.

It wasn't until I asked Lionel if that summer changed him that he said, "There is no question that my perspective on homosexuality was greatly influenced by this experience. That's the best way I can put it. After that experience, I saw homosexuality as... you're just born with it. It doesn't make you a bad person. So, I would say it had a profound impact on me from that perspective."

I didn't ask if it changed Lionel's parents' views at all, but the fact that Don and John were welcomed to their home years later says a lot to me. "The only awkward moment for my mum was when they were going to bed," Lionel says. "Other than that, we had a great time." Lionel shrugs, smiles, and adds, "Honestly, from a diversity, inclusion, and equity perspective, it was a fabulous experience."

The stories from students like Lionel and Alex are about "growing and grappling," as Chugh says. People like you and me all over the world are scoring small wins for humanity—one student, one host, one conversation at a time.

CHAPTER SUMMARY

- We all have bias; it's part of being human.

- Modern society exposes people to stereotypes through every form of media. These messages act as a kind of smog that we breathe every day.

- When one's moral identity is challenged, psychologists call it "self-threat." When you notice this, embrace being good-ish and be open to learning.

- People will often look for acknowledgement for their good intentions. This just makes it about them, not the person they're trying to support.

- Curiosity is at the heart of willful awareness. Try to notice your own bias and how it shows up in your relationships and your work as a host.

- Saying something works by building awareness and disrupting social norms. When speaking up, it helps to acknowledge your own growth; use humour; use stories, not facts; and avoid speaking for people (and don't be afraid to offer your support).

10

When It's Harder Than You Expected
Difficult Conversations

---

*Sometimes students stay out too late,
forget to tell me they are not coming home for dinner,
keep the lights on, talk loudly on the phone
after 9:00 p.m... But it's all worth it in the end!*
GINETTE, host from Ottawa, Ontario

VALENTINA AND CAMILA were part of a group of thirty-four Spanish teenagers who visited Ottawa from September to mid-December, 2019. On Thanksgiving weekend, their regular host was away, so they were placed in a temporary "respite" with Nicole and her husband, Charles.

Despite their short stay, Nicole remembers them well. Their personalities were a stark contrast to the couple's long-term student, Alexia, who was also from Spain. Valentina was chatty and friendly, but Camila was "surly." Nicole says she always looked mad, and had a "shruggy" attitude. Camila would laugh, but she didn't participate in their family activities and she avoided eye contact.

Nicole and Charles hosted a Thanksgiving dinner with their whole family, as many Americans and Canadians do. This celebratory weekend often includes extended family who travel from afar, rich traditions that stretch back generations, and a mountain of food. During dinner, Camila continued this behaviour pattern, speaking Spanish and rolling her eyes now and then.

In this situation, how would you feel? What would you be thinking?

Nicole's mother, who was there for dinner, was unimpressed. *Why won't Camila engage with the family? What's with her attitude? Are these girls talking about us behind our backs?*

"She was so *rude*," Nicole's mother said later. Not that it mattered much. Camila would be leaving the next day.

Homestay Can Be Hard

Nicole's story is an example of the ordinary, everyday, commonplace conflicts that happen in host families all the time. These challenges tend to revolve around a few predictable themes. In CHN's 2022 host survey, we asked, "What is the most difficult or challenging part of hosting?" Responses were coded and grouped into nine themes.

I've already addressed five of these in earlier chapters: helping students get settled and adjusted to their new life and routines, the emotional burden of looking after minors and being "on" all the time, various concerns related to food, dealing with chores and managing activities, and communication and language.

Three of the remaining four themes were reported by relatively few hosts. Some hosts (5 percent) complained about surprises: students filling in their applications incorrectly—on food preferences, hobbies, family composition, medical conditions, etc.—and unrealistic expectations. Other hosts (another 5 percent) find the most difficult part of hosting is unrelated to themselves or the student, naming issues such as administrative red tape, the homestay organization's support, other hosts providing substandard care, and various stressors caused by the pandemic. Six percent of hosts identified an overall mismatch as their biggest stressor. Examples include personality clashes, a misalignment of hobbies, or typical teenage behaviour. In this "mismatch" category, there weren't special problems to address. It reminds me of a relocation in rural Ontario because the student didn't like the flies and ladybugs, and another student who requested a move because he kept hitting his head on the sloped ceiling in his bedroom.

However, as Nicole's story illustrates, sometimes the most difficult part of hosting is managing the student's behaviour. A third of respondents (34 percent) identified this as their biggest challenge.

All of these challenges underscore the importance of remembering that homestay can be difficult for both hosts and students. I'd argue that accepting this reality—despite not knowing what might happen—is a prerequisite of becoming a host. The good news is many of these difficult parts get easier with time, through a combination of shifting mindsets and practicing the skills and awareness you're learning in this book.

Student Behavioural Issues

At the most benign end of the spectrum of behavioural issues, hosts describe having to deal with "quirky habits," but even those require some patience and perspective. As I've discussed, sometimes it's enough to give the student some culturally sensitive feedback—for instance, if the host feels disrespected because the student doesn't say thank you. Feedback and consequences can work with students who spend too much time on their phones, playing video games, or talking to their friends late at night; hygiene issues; and chores.

Behavioural issues are often interpreted as a "poor attitude" or "sense of entitlement," but it can be hard to know if a behaviour is driven by personality or culture. There are a few techniques to make this assessment—a critical skill when dealing with people from other parts of the world, especially when you don't like their behaviour. The simplest approach is to ask questions. When you begin with genuine curiosity rather than judgment, it can feel less awkward. You can also ask your homestay coordinator or someone else who's familiar with that culture. Doing your own research online is helpful, but can be incomplete. Over time, the more students you host from a particular culture, the more awareness you'll develop about their behaviours—and the more you'll learn about your cultural norms, too.

Some behaviours are clearly not cultural. One host wrote on the survey that the hardest part is when "some kids don't have the right information. They think they're in a hotel and hosts are paid to serve them anything, anytime." Disrespect can show up in many ways. Susan from Ottawa, whose student Haley played the guqin, recalls a different student who "put on a smiley face" but "adamantly refused" to take any of her advice or recommendations. "She tried to change the rules, and when that didn't work, she got her mother involved," Susan says. "The respect was gone. There has to be an authority in the house. It can't come from outside and it can't come from the student." When the respect is gone, hosts question their motivation.

Lying, deception, theft, and frequent arguments with host siblings or other students are examples of issues that may have a complex explanation and deserve some compassion, but still need to be addressed. Being empathetic and culturally sensitive doesn't mean tolerating problems.

Dealing with poor attitude and other behavioural issues can be even harder if the host feels they have little influence or ability to discipline their students. For example, one host said the most challenging part of hosting is "dealing with teenage apathy toward school, as well as their boundary testing and motivating them to get out and try new things instead of immersing themselves in Netflix... because they are not my own children."

When I interviewed Laurie, one of her students had just gotten some failing grades on her midterm report card. Laurie suspected her student was capable of doing better, so she tried some tough love using feedback and consequences. She told her student that while she's here, education comes first. Laurie says she didn't care what the marks were as long as her student did her homework and tried her best. Then she introduced a real consequence: Laurie told her student she wouldn't be permitted on the school field trip to see Niagara Falls unless her grades improved. This may sound harsh to some hosts, but setting consequences like this—that play into the rewards that teenagers crave—is an effective strategy.

After that conversation, the student started getting near-perfect scores on her English quizzes. "They thought she wasn't understanding, but it was because she was using her phone. Now she has to put it on the teacher's desk during class," Laurie says. "She needed a little hard-ass on my part." Laurie has also warned her student that if her grades slip again, she'll take away the internet and phone.

Allow me to clarify: you are allowed to set boundaries and enforce them, just as you would with your own children. Remember, treating your students as part of the family is one of the keys to success in hosting. If you don't feel comfortable, ask your coordinator for help.

With the right interventions and support, conflict can deepen connections, foster compassion, build empathy, and strengthen families.

Myths about Teenagers

Teenagers have a bad rap. In a homestay, lots of behavioural issues will arise regardless of age. And yet, in CHN's 2022 survey of hosts, several people wrote "teenagers" in response to the question about the most difficult or challenging part of hosting. Sometimes it's not the teenagers; it's a matter of learning how to parent, as this host explains: "At the time we hosted, it was before any kids. Now, we have a four-year-old. Quite a difference." But there are also times when hosts fall into the trap of stereotyping an age group, which can be just as harmful as stereotypes based on race, nationality, ethnicity, or gender.

I can think of several stereotypes about teenagers that show up in homestay. For instance, adolescents are self-centred, vulnerable to peer pressure, and risk takers who don't think through the consequences of their actions.

I bought into these stereotypes myself, dreading the teenage years as a young parent. I thought I understood the brain science of excessive risk-taking—like drunk driving, unsafe sex, or hitching a ride with strangers after a day of skiing. This is often attributed to the teenage brain's underdeveloped prefrontal cortex, the part of the brain that is responsible for skills like planning, prioritizing, and making good decisions.

The truth is more complicated. While adolescents do take more risks than children or adults, these behaviours are not always reckless. They include positive risk-taking such as raising a hand in class, or standing up to a bully at school. Or flying halfway across the world to live with strangers and study in a foreign country.

Eva Telzer studies the role of society, culture, relationships, and social media on teenage brain development. She argues that risk-taking in teenagers is less about lack of foresight and more about rewards. In fact, teens are very good at regulating their behaviour. They just make different choices based on their evaluation of the benefits.

Rewards for a teenager might be physiological, like the high they get from trying nicotine or marijuana or alcohol, but they can also be behavioural. For example, when my son sneaks out after curfew to meet a friend, the reward of seeing that friend outweighs the risk of getting caught. If you are trying to understand the choices of your teenager and want to encourage healthy behaviours, consider how their choices are rewarding them and identify other positive rewards. It also helps to ask. As it turns out, my son wanted to help a friend who was in distress. So in this case, I can suggest he invite his friends over more often, or allow him to sleep over at their house.

This example also highlights the myth of self-centredness, a negative trait often assigned to teenagers. In addition to other areas of the brain that are growing during adolescence, the regions involved in social perspective-taking are increasing. This means teenagers tend to choose activities that bring meaning and joy to their lives, since the consideration of broader societal needs is a reward in itself. This may be at a grand scale—like Greta Thunberg, who started protesting about climate change at age fifteen—but can also be as simple as helping one's family or volunteering. In fact, one study found that 98 percent of adolescents from across cultural and economic backgrounds help out their family on a weekly basis. Why? Because they want to; because their family appreciates it. There's a reward of some kind that reinforces the behaviour. This is even stronger in cultures where a high value is placed on family and social support. Another study found that teenagers from Mexico spend twice as much time helping their family every day than teens from European backgrounds. Likewise, international students who get involved in school clubs or teams are engaging in pro-social activities, gaining perspective on themselves and their culture.

I've been guilty of believing the myth that teens are more influenced by their peers than their parents. In fact, Telzer has found that parents and peers make a similar impression on adolescent decision-making, or in some cases, parents outweigh the peers. This extends to risk-taking, too. Teenagers are just as likely to follow their parents' attitudes toward risk and pro-social behaviour as their peers. Robby's hosts, Denise and Mike, ended up having a big impact on Robby, despite his friends accusing them of having unreasonable rules. Hosts should take heart in knowing they can have a positive influence on the choices of their students.

Telzer's work has also revealed the role of culture on teenage behaviour. For example, in Western cultures, stereotypes about teenagers lead youth to see this period in their lives as a time of decreased family responsibility, disengagement from school, and risk-taking. In contrast, researchers have found that in China, the high school years are viewed as a time of family obligation and educational motivation. These stereotypes and views of adolescents are often self-fulfilling prophecies. When Chinese students want to please their parents, particularly when it comes to academics, they are fulfilling their culture's expectations for their role in society. In some ways, I wonder if this explains the phenomenon noticed by many hosts, wherein students arrive and begin taking risks and testing boundaries. Is this a cultural adaptation to a Western norm, after all?

Conflict Transformation

Anything that interferes with student and host engagement deserves to be addressed. Problematic behaviours create distance, when the reason families chose to host was to cultivate a relationship. As one host said, "We want to know you, we want that connection. When we bond with you, and when you leave at the end, we don't want to forget you. Let's not forget each other."

And let's not remember each other for the wrong reasons, either.

But how? Many hosts would agree with the respondent who said it's difficult to know how to approach students "without making things awkward." As a result, some hosts end up ignoring problems, or leaving them so long that the only option is to move the student.

Michelle Buck, clinical professor of leadership at the Kellogg School of Management at Northwestern University, has spent the last twenty years teaching conflict transformation, which she differentiates from conflict resolution. She understands that many people want to avoid the discomfort that conflict brings, but reminds us that the only way to restore harmony is to address the issue. Conflict is a challenge to be embraced. In our organization, we believe that with the right interventions and support, conflict can deepen connections, foster compassion, build empathy, and strengthen families. It allows the chance to learn more about each other than before and requires perspective-taking. It's our team's first step in dealing with most homestay complaints.

If you've never seen a relationship improve after working through a conflict, or this approach is the opposite of what you've been taught, or you think you'll never convince your spouse or kids—or yourself—to go along with this, I get it. Feelings about conflict are deeply ingrained, culturally informed, and reinforced with experience. Learning new things requires faith in one's ability to grow and change, belief that the upside is worth the effort, and a willingness to make mistakes.

You can do this. It could be transformational. It's okay to stumble.

The important thing is to try.

Addressing Conflict: A Cultural Perspective

When you try to address conflict, keep in mind that your efforts are influenced by culture. When I spoke to intercultural communication expert Lionel Laroche, I asked him to explain how conflict differs around the world. To a large extent, the differences are a matter of process, which leads to a secondary problem: besides the issue itself, people also run into conflict about how to confront it.

Laroche explained that conflict resolution is something we learn as teenagers, when we become social beings and interact more in teams. He believes that when a teenager travels abroad at age sixteen or seventeen, they have already started to learn how to resolve conflict in their own culture. "So when suddenly the rules change, that is really confusing," Laroche says. "For a host to help guide them, though, they need to understand these differences."

For example, some people want to have frank and open discussions, hashing out their issues directly. This would sound like a full-blown argument to others. Cultures differ in their norms about whether or not the conflict should remain between two people or involve others in the family. Some people think an authority figure—the patriarch or matriarch, for instance—should weigh in to resolve the issue. Other families and cultures avoid confrontational topics entirely, sweeping them under the rug unless it's absolutely necessary to discuss them. Some families see compromise as positive; it means they found something they can all live with. In other families, compromise is negative; it means someone didn't get everything they wanted. Clearly, everyone's approach for communicating ideas, resolving disagreements, and dealing with emotional upset can differ.

Author, business leader, and professor Mitchell R. Hammer has developed an assessment tool, the Intercultural Conflict

Style Inventory (ICS)®, to measure an individual's core approach for solving problems and resolving disputes. When I teach groups about intercultural conflict, this is one of my favourite resources. You can take the assessment in about twenty minutes, for a small fee. The ICS is a four-quadrant model. One axis covers how *Direct* or *Indirect* you are when communicating. The other axis considers how *Restrained* or *Expressive* you are when dealing with emotional upset.

INTERCULTURAL CONFLICT STYLE MODEL

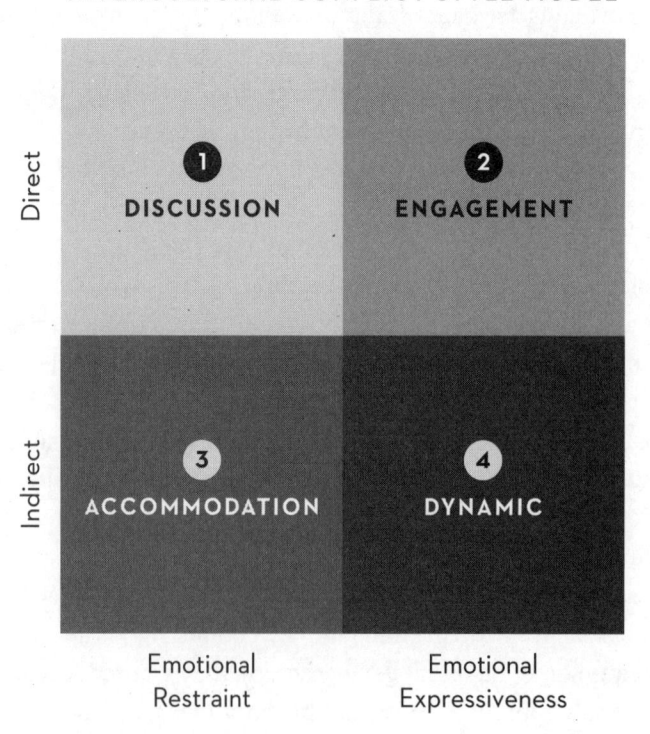

	Emotional Restraint	Emotional Expressiveness
Direct	① DISCUSSION	② ENGAGEMENT
Indirect	③ ACCOMMODATION	④ DYNAMIC

Cultures that prefer *Direct* communication use precise and explicit language to convey their ideas, prefer one-to-one meetings, speak their minds, verbally assert their opinions, and attempt to persuade the other person through reasoned arguments. Their focus is on the disagreement. Many readers will recognize themselves in this style; indeed, Europeans, North Americans, and Australians tend to land on the Direct side of the Direct-Indirect axis.

In contrast, people who use an *Indirect* communication style tend to prefer more ambiguous language, expecting the other person to read between the lines. They rely on third parties to resolve their disagreements, use discretion when voicing goals, and talk around the disagreement instead of facing it head-on. Their focus is on repairing the relationship; attempts to persuade depend on saving face. You may recognize Himari and her reluctance to confront her host about her missing pencil in this axis; Japanese culture tends to favour the Indirect style.

In the emotional upset axis, *Expressive* cultures display their feelings overtly. They control their emotions by externalizing them, both verbally and non-verbally. People want to express their feelings, sometimes at the expense of hurting others; trust and credibility are built through expressiveness. Italian and Greek cultures prefer this style.

Cultures who value emotional *Restraint* disguise and control their emotions by internalizing them. They are sensitive about hurting other people's feelings. Trust and credibility are built through emotional maturity and suppression—though Batja Mesquita would argue that emotional suppression is itself a Western notion. Nevertheless, the contrast stands. Chinese, Japanese, and Thai cultures favour this approach.

When combined, there end up being four intercultural conflict styles: Discussion (Direct + Restrained), Engagement (Direct + Expressive), Accommodation (Indirect + Restrained), and Dynamic (Indirect + Expressive). All such patterns exist in all cultures, but some are preferred more than others. Likewise, each family and individual will have their own conflict style, and it may change depending on the context (my approach to conflict is different if I'm talking to my husband than if I'm at work).

Speaking generally, then: many Europeans (specifically, people from the UK, Sweden, Norway, Denmark, and Germany), North Americans, and Australians tend to fall into the Discussion style (direct communication and emotional restraint).

Countries that tend toward an Engagement style (direct communication and emotional expressiveness) include France, Greece, Italy, Spain, Russia, and Israel.

Indigenous people of North America tend to prefer the Accommodation style (indirect communication and emotional restraint), along with Mexico, Peru, China, Japan, and Thailand.

The Dynamic style (indirect communication and emotional expressiveness) is preferred in the Arab Middle East (Saudi Arabia, Egypt) and parts of Asia, like Pakistan.

The lesson you can take from this, other than insight into your own family's and culture's conflict resolution styles, is that understanding both personal preferences and cultural differences around conflict is critical. If your student is trying to resolve conflict in a completely different way from you, the conflict could be exacerbated. Instead, it can help to recognize that you are both trying to do something within your power, knowledge, and skills to make the situation better.

Learning Conversations

Douglas Stone, Bruce Patton, and Sheila Heen from the Harvard Negotiation Project, authors of *Difficult Conversations: How to Discuss What Matters Most*, offer an approach to conflict that gives you a chance to better understand the other person by creating a "learning conversation."

Learning conversations require a genuine interest in your student. This approach also assumes you are both committed to working together to find a solution. It reminds me of two ground rules for dialogue proposed by Simon Greer, the American labour and community organizer. One of Greer's projects was a cultural exchange program between a group of progressive Jewish New Yorkers and several conservative Christian corrections officers from Michigan. On their first evening together, Greer said, "We're going to take seriously the things everyone holds dear," and "We're not going to try and convince each other we're wrong." I think these principles are relevant to all aspects of homestay, though they have particular importance when planning for a learning conversation.

Learning conversations are so powerful that I teach this process to our team of homestay coordinators every year. How does it look in practice? The following six steps are adapted from the work of Stone, Patton, and Heen. In order to move through the steps, I'll use a hypothetical situation.

Step one: Check your purpose and timing

Why are you having this conversation? Why now? Sometimes, it turns out that all you need is to vent with someone, to give yourself the chance to feel heard and seen after a tough situation. If you aren't ready to learn from the other person, or to brainstorm together to find a solution, there may be a better way to approach the problem.

If you just want to correct your student's behaviour by telling them what they *must* or *should* or *ought* to do, you aren't alone. Psychologist Thomas Gordon, who is widely recognized as a pioneer in teaching communication skills and conflict resolution methods, calls this "sending a solution message," which includes ordering, directing, commanding, warning, admonishing, threatening, exhorting, preaching, moralizing, advising, and giving suggestions.

My imaginary host, Seema, is upset with her student, Rafael, about his routines around dinner and dishes. She might say, "You must be home for dinner." Or, "Can't you clean up the kitchen when you're done making lunch?" These would be solution messages.

Some hosts incorporate language that sends a "put-down message," by communicating blame, judgment, criticism, or shame. As you might guess, not only do these commands miss the mark due to cultural differences, they just don't work. Students resist their hosts' efforts, or feel misunderstood and unfairly treated, or get defensive, or lash out. Their self-esteem is threatened, and they could feel rejected. The problem with this language is that it conflates the behaviour and the person, blurring the line between *you did something bad* and *you are bad*. Where is the potential for change, growth, learning, or trying new things if the people who are meant to support you through these experiences have shamed and labelled you? As I've already explored, shame is not an effective tool for change.

In addition, behavioural issues can mask an underlying problem that can't be corrected with "solution messages." For example, as Robby's story illustrated in chapter 1, a bad attitude or rule-breaking may arise because the student has been forced to travel abroad. Poor grades or repeated absences could be due to genuine academic struggles, or the opposite: a lack of challenge. Mental health concerns, homesickness, and conflicts with friends can also manifest in a range of behavioural problems. The only way to find out if there's a deeper issue behind a problematic behaviour is to have a learning conversation.

When you are clear on your purpose, ask yourself if this is the right time. If your student is from a culture that prefers indirect communication and you prefer direct communication, are they prepared to confront this issue with you or would they rather work through (or with) a third party, such as your homestay coordinator? If you are normally emotionally expressive, and you're on fire with your frustration and anger, do you need to cool off first?

Step two: Get curious and identify your story
If you're ready to proceed, getting into a curious mindset is essential for learning conversations. Curiosity cannot live with judgment; it builds trust where judgment breaks it down. Amanda Ripley, author of *High Conflict: Why We Get Trapped and How We Get Out*, recommends asking yourself several questions as you prepare. Here are some of her favourites:

- What do you want to understand about the other side?
- What do you want the other side to understand about you?
- What's the question nobody's asking?
- Where do you feel torn?

I would add:

- What role is culture playing in this conflict—yours and theirs?
- What are you feeling, and what do you think they're feeling? As I reviewed in chapter 8, it's safe to assume that feelings are at the heart of the matter. Acknowledge them without judgments or attributions.
- What are your student's intentions? You can't know this without asking, and intentions are often more complex than we think, as Stone, Patton, and Heen point out. Getting curious also means recognizing your student probably doesn't know the impact they're having on you.

- Finally, what is the story you're telling about this situation? When facing conflict, it's natural to make up stories about the other person to help make sense of the situation. Getting curious about your story can expose the fact that you don't have all the information yet. In a learning conversation, it's important to acknowledge that each person owns *part* of the truth about what's going on, but not *all* of it. Considering these different viewpoints helps create possibilities that did not exist before.

In my hypothetical example, Seema's story is that Rafael leaves a mess on the counter after he makes lunch, expects her to clear the table after dinner, and never offers to help with the dishes. He often stays out late with his friends and doesn't call home until after she's gone to the trouble of preparing his dinner. She works full time and wants a little respect. She thinks Rafael is selfish, ungrateful, untrustworthy, and doesn't care about her family's rules. She wants to say, "If you keep making such a mess and forgetting to call me about your plans, you'll have to move out."

Rafael's story is that Seema works late and never has time for him. She's a neat freak; if he doesn't clear the table immediately she does it herself. Given his family's availability, he would rather talk to them right after dinner instead of doing the dishes. The few times he has done the dishes, she rewashes them because they aren't clean enough. As for his plans with friends, he often doesn't know what he's going to do until after school. Besides, it's lonely when he goes straight home and there's nobody there. He's embarrassed, frustrated, and scared to talk to her because he thinks she gets mad easily.

These are Seema's and Rafael's stories about each other and the situation.

Recognizing when you're making up a story about someone requires you to slow down and acknowledge the dynamics at play, your emotional responses, and your reactions. Was it the other person's words or actions? Or the way they spoke? Are you reacting to a recurring pattern of behaviour or habit? Once you have some perspective, it's easier to see where you have jumped to conclusions about the other person's thoughts, intentions, and feelings.

Your story also reveals what's at stake for you. Conflict can threaten our identity, triggering self-threat: What does this issue say about me, and does it contradict my self-image? Some hosts may ask themselves: If I don't connect deeply with every student, does that mean I'm not a good host? If I can't manage their behaviour, does that make me incompetent? If they complain about me to the homestay company, does that mean I won't get any more students?

Be gentle with yourself. Remind yourself you are a good-ish person, trying to do better. Offer compassion to your student, recognizing that what's on the line for their identity may be culturally informed and/or hidden below the surface.

I understand that a lot of conversations happen spontaneously, and the idea of slowing down to ponder your purpose, consider if the timing is right, ask yourself questions, and identify your story may seem stilted, artificial, or too time-consuming. I also understand that it may feel like a luxury when you're faced with a crisis. Please don't skip these two steps. They don't have to take long—just a few minutes, in many cases—and will get easier with practice. If you have time to talk, you have time to prepare.

Step three: Begin like a friendly observer

There is usually a gap between the host's story and the student's story. As Stone, Patton, and Heen say in *Difficult Conversations*:

"Think like a mediator." If someone else was describing the situation in neutral terms, how would it sound?

In our example, if Seema approaches this conversation like an observer, it would start with the acknowledgement that both she and Rafael have a valid perspective, and that they have different implicit rules about how people should act. A potential *third* story would sidestep judgment. It might sound like this: "Rafael, I wanted to talk about the dishes and planning ahead for dinner. You and I seem to have different preferences and different ideas about what is appropriate. I want to understand how you see things and share my point of view."

Seema has extended an invitation to Rafael to engage in a conversation to find a solution. It's up to Rafael if he wants to accept, modify, or reject that invitation.

Notice that this approach uses what many experts refer to as "I" statements, rather than "you" statements. This keeps the focus on Seema and what she needs—which is why this conversation is happening at all. By being honest and open about her needs, she fosters honest and open communication about all sorts of issues. It also reminds the student of the attitudes and perspectives of other people, which is necessary for developing a sense of social responsibility.

Step four: Listen with genuine curiosity

The next step is to listen. You'll have a chance to share your side of the issue in step five. Stephen Covey, renowned businessman, educator, speaker, and author of *The 7 Habits of Highly Effective People*, asserts that the single most important principle in the field of interpersonal relations is to "seek first to understand, then to be understood." If you want to influence people, they need to trust you—and in order to trust you, they need to feel safe, understood, and seen. Listening to someone with the intent to understand is a form of empathy, as it helps you see the world through their eyes and connect with their heart.

Covey notes that people are naturally inclined to evaluate, probe, advise, and interpret when they think they're listening. Instead, to demonstrate curiosity, he recommends you *rephrase* the content of what you've heard and *reflect* the feeling behind the message.

Seema might begin by inquiring about Rafael's perspective. By moving past the debate about who's right, she'll create space for Rafael to feel comfortable opening up to her. She might ask, "Can you say more about how you see things?" Or, "How do you see it differently?" Or, "What impact have my actions had on you?"

Note the difference between inquiring and probing. An inquiry is an invitation to say more: to help you understand how they see things differently, and explain how your actions have impacted them. Probing is asking questions from your frame of reference, like playing twenty questions.

Ripley agrees. In her book, she shares the story of Gary Friedman, a conflict mediator, author, and former trial lawyer, who pioneered a new approach to mediation. Much of his process involves deep listening, which he calls "completing the loop of understanding," or "looping." In addition to playing back what he's heard (paraphrasing), he also *asks if he got it right*.

When Rafael responds, Seema can paraphrase the content. "So, part of the problem is that I expect the dishes to be done immediately." "You feel like my standards of cleanliness are too high." "So, you're afraid that I'll get mad if you talk to me." To loop effectively, she needs to add, "*Did I get that right?*" When Rafael responds, her job is to listen, rephrase, and ask again—looping until she gets it right.

When you create space to hear the other person's perspective, don't be surprised when they point out ways you *contributed* to the situation. This is not about blame. When you consider your contribution, you ask yourself, "What did I do that helped cause this situation?" If it's not obvious, consider whether or not you have avoided the issue until now; been unapproachable (which is about how others perceive you, not how you mean to be); have unspoken expectations about communication and relationships; or have made assumptions about roles and responsibilities (like assuming the student would come to you first).

Gabrielle Hartley, lawyer and conflict resolution expert, explains that there are several other ways people contribute to conflict. Some people cut off the other person before they have a chance to explain themselves, leading to confusion and erroneous conclusions. Some stir the pot, complaining to people outside the conflict. Others step away from the relationship, creating more distance and making it harder to come to any understanding (in homestay, this can be emotional distance or a relocation). People can become defensive, lashing out at the other person from a place of hurt. Or they roll their eyes, look at their phones, raise their voice, stomp around the house. It's tempting to bring up issues from the past or introduce new and unrelated issues. People also contribute to conflict through habitual thought patterns and behaviours. Much like habits dictate your actions, your ways of perceiving and interpreting the world around you are also habitual.

Acknowledging the way you've contributed to a problem can be challenging. Nevertheless, it's a necessary step in hearing the other person. As Ripley explains, "When people do feel heard, magical things happen. They make more coherent and intriguing points. They acknowledge their own inconsistencies. Willingly. They become more flexible... When people feel understood, they trust the other person to go a little deeper and keep trying to get it right." This is not about needing to agree; people can feel heard even when they know you disagree.

Curiosity cannot
live with judgment;
it builds trust
where judgment
breaks it down.

———

Effective listeners also acknowledge feelings. As I discussed in chapter 4, when dealing with people from other cultures, you can't assume you understand their emotions from their words, facial expressions, or body language. Instead, you need to ask what the situation means to them—why it matters and what's at stake. If they can articulate their feelings in English, don't assume you understand what those words mean. You can ask questions such as, "Is this the 'right' emotion to have in a situation like this? Does it help you be the kind of person you want to be? What does the emotion try to accomplish? How will others in your family respond to it?" In other words, slow down. Ask questions. Listen.

For instance, Seema could say, "It sounds like you're relieved to finally talk about this." Or, "It sounds like talking to your family after dinner is important to you." Or, "I can see why you might be annoyed."

Step five: Speak to the heart of the matter

Only after you have inquired for more understanding and perspective, paraphrased the content, and acknowledged the feelings behind the words will the other person feel heard. You may discover that your assessment of the problem was incorrect. Sometimes, when given the chance, students come up with their own solutions.

In any case, this is the stage when you can share what matters most to you—it's your turn to be understood. If emotional restraint is your preference, you might begin by acknowledging that this is new for you, or you feel awkward. If you prefer emotional expressiveness, it's helpful to name that, too. Use "I" statements to explain your emotions and the impact of the student's behaviour on you. It's much more powerful to say, "When you didn't come home on time and didn't call to say you'd be late, *I* got worried," than "It was inconsiderate of *you* not to call."

The first centres you, your feelings, and your needs. The second judges, evaluates, and assumes. In Seema's case, she could say, "*I* feel hurt, annoyed, and disappointed when you don't do the dishes or don't call me before I make dinner. *I'd* like to spend more time with you."

If you've felt disrespected by your student, this process can be even more difficult. Disrespect is a broad term that encompasses several underlying emotions that will vary depending on the person, culture, hierarchical status, and the situation. Feeling disrespected can include fear, anger, shame, confusion, uncertainty, isolation, self-doubt, depression, etc. In Seema's case, she was annoyed at having to prepare a meal for someone who didn't eat it and disappointed that she had to eat alone (again).

Marc Brackett, founding director of the Yale Center for Emotional Intelligence, explains that when people use general, broad terms like "angry," "fine," or "happy," they are missing a lot of information. Labelling your emotions with more granularity legitimizes and organizes your experience; it helps others meet your needs; it helps you meet the needs of others; and it connects you with other people. Just be mindful of how the words translate into other languages, and don't assume that what you mean by "angry" is the same as what your student would think of as "angry." You can get better at articulating your emotions with practice. If you'd like to try an app, Brackett has contributed to the How We Feel app and the Mood Meter app.

Putting your feelings and needs at the heart of this conversation is a powerful way to be genuine and present. As family therapist Jesper Juul explains, "expressing feelings maintains a warmth of contact. We often forget that the warmth that exists in any relationship arises from two sources: what joins us together and what causes friction. Both are always present, and both can be equally warm."

Step six: Work together to find options

In a learning conversation, finding a solution to the problem is a collaborative process. Make sure the problem under discussion is still the problem; so many issues are hiding deeper truths that may not have surfaced yet. Be open to possibility, and encourage your student to do the same by listening, looping, and gathering information.

If you are still entrenched in two different places, say what would persuade you to change your mind and ask what (if anything) would persuade the other person. Sharing where you agree and what you've learned in this conversation can also help. You can't force someone else to change. Paradoxically, they are more likely to change if they feel free *not* to, and if they can see that you're willing to change. Keep coming up with more options and repeat this cycle until you can reach an agreement.

Seema and Rafael have several options to consider, none of which would have been possible if Seema had confronted Rafael with rules and ultimatums. They came up with a new routine with dinner so that Rafael could talk to his family at a reasonable hour. He agreed to text Seema right after school about his plans. Rafael also offered to cook dinner some nights to give Seema a break. They were both relieved to discover that they truly enjoyed each other's company.

Stone, Patton, and Heen recommend agreeing to a set of principles or standards. This is one of the reasons CHN includes curfew recommendations in our host guide; it removes the need to debate what's fair. Likewise, Seema found out that Rafael was using cold water when washing the dishes—he had never been taught how to do them properly—and when he switched to hot water, she was happy with the result.

If you still can't agree on a solution, consider your alternatives. One viable option is to reach out to your homestay coordinator. They are there to help; it's not an inconvenience or hassle. At CHN, some of the most difficult cases arise from situations that escalate without our involvement, leading to a situation where a relocation is the only viable option. I'll look more closely at relocations in chapter 12.

Some clues that it's time to call for help include feeling threatened (which prevents you from being able to get curious); feeling humiliated (which jeopardizes your sense of self-worth); feeling enraged (step away!); or feeling stumped about how to move forward. Psychologists Julie and John Gottman have studied conflict in married couples, and have found that when everyday positive interactions exceed negative ones by a ratio of five to one, the couple finds it easier to maintain healthy conflict. It's why people say good morning, even before they've had their coffee. It's why families share meals, talk about their days, play games, watch sports. If you find this "magic ratio" missing in your interactions with your students, it's time to call for help. Hosts do not have to suffer through challenges alone. And as I've already shared in other stories, the intervention of a skilled coordinator can make all the difference.

Nicole and Camila

In the case of the rude Thanksgiving, Nicole helped her mother through parts of this process, without realizing she was doing it.

First, she decided not to confront Camila at all. She felt it wasn't necessary to have a difficult conversation for a weekend placement. Neither did she command Camila to change with a "solutions message."

In terms of the facts and assumptions, Nicole's mother made up a story about Camila: that she was a rude, unhappy teenager.

Camila rolls her eyes, so she must have a bad attitude. Camila speaks Spanish in front of us, so she must be hiding something. Nicole, on the other hand, didn't make up a story. She knew she didn't understand the whole truth about the situation. She reminded her mother that Camila's and Valentina's English wasn't as good as her long-term students'. She didn't let Camila's actions bother her, or allow herself to jump to conclusions about what Camila was saying in Spanish.

Nicole's curiosity allowed her to withhold judgment. "I think it's just her teenage vibe right now," Nicole says. "You don't know what their home life is like, what their experiences are. You don't know what they're going through. All you can do is be kind and patient and hope it makes a difference."

Nicole found out later that Camila had said her favourite homestay was with Nicole and her husband. "So even though you think she's having a terrible time... she did have fun."

Many hosts are motivated by the possibility of making an impact like this, which is one of the reasons why it's worthwhile to learn about yourself and how you can create the conditions for an optimal relationship with your students. Yet coaxing a student like Camila toward a more mature, positive attitude is one thing; dealing with betrayal feels altogether different. In the next chapter, I'll take a closer look at second chances. I'll discuss why it can be difficult to get past mistakes and what a good apology looks like.

CHAPTER SUMMARY

- It's reasonable to set boundaries and enforce them, just as you would with your own children.

- Be open to the role of culture in conflict; people have different styles and preferences for directness and emotional expressiveness.

- Conflict can be an opportunity to strengthen a relationship. Ask for help if you're feeling stuck!

- Curiosity cannot live with judgment; it builds trust where judgment breaks it down.

- Here are the six steps for a learning conversation:

    1. Check your purpose and timing.
    2. Get curious and identify your story.
    3. Begin like a friendly observer.
    4. Listen with genuine curiosity.
    5. Speak to the heart of the matter.
    6. Work together to find options.

11

We're Not Perfect
Second Chances

*My host treated me like I was their daughter.
Even when I got like mistakes, they never really
say something to me. If I'm so sad and mad,
they never got mad at me. They understood me.*

KIHO, student from Japan

IN DECEMBER 2014, after a big winter storm hit Fredericton, New Brunswick, holiday shoppers were braving the colder temperatures. Lee wasn't out shopping—she had to pay a utility bill. She was in line before she realized her wallet was empty. Twenty or forty bucks could have been overlooked, but she had withdrawn over three hundred dollars to pay this bill. She had to assume one of her four students had taken it.

As a mother of three adult girls and an experienced host, by this time Mama Lee was no stranger to teenagers pushing boundaries. In these moments, as she demonstrated in her handling of May's breach of curfew and Fred's appetite for bread, Lee wants to help her students grow up. And growing up means making mistakes.

The missing money was a teaching moment.

Lee and Danny were hosting four boys at the time: Fred from Bangladesh, Johnny and Ming from Vietnam, and Alex from China (who was introduced in earlier chapters). Right away, they assembled the four boys and told them what had happened. The hosts said, "Talk to us, or write us a letter. We want to know why you needed the money. And if you need any more, you can always come and ask. But you have to pay it back." They said if the boy who took the money came forward and explained why, there would be no repercussions from Lee or Danny. They also told the boys they were welcome to stay, but if they wanted to change homes, that was okay, too. "I made no bones about it," Lee says. "I gave them my word."

The next morning, Alex came clean in a handwritten note. He promised to repay them, and they forgave him. Nevertheless, he was fourteen; Lee had to tell his mother, who "was beside herself," as she grasped the ways this mistake could jeopardize Alex's standing. In fact, our homestay coordinator recommended to Lee that we remove Alex from the program—but Lee wasn't ready to give up on him.

Lee's story would put many people off hosting. *That's not what I signed up for*, they'd say. Of course not! Theft, or breaking the law in any manner, is unacceptable. As I'll explore further in the next chapter, CHN students are required to read and sign a Participation Agreement, a code of conduct with consequences. Our organization has a well-documented, progressive discipline process involving probationary measures for the student, communication with their parents and agent, and time-bound follow-up to ensure compliance.

Again, these extreme cases are the exception, not the rule. All the same, a lot of hosts in Lee's shoes would feel so betrayed, so upset that their trust had been broken, they would not be able to repair the relationship. I asked Lee how she was able to look past this incident and keep Alex.

"We all do stupid things," Lee says. "Sometimes we believe we're doing the right thing at the time, and it's the wrong choice. I was raised to believe that people make mistakes, and they can be corrected. That's just the way it was in my world."

I told Lee that my dad taught my brothers and me the same thing. "He always says mistakes are opportunities in disguise, and he wouldn't be where he is today if it weren't for the adults in his life giving him a second chance."

"Exactly. We're not all perfect. We think we are, but we're not."

As Lee points out, students aren't the only ones who make mistakes. Hosts do it all the time. And that's okay, too, because failure is not always bad. In fact, innovation and progress—both personal and professional—depend on it.

If you assume, like Lee, that someone will mess up at some point, you can move past the shock and disappointment that inevitably surfaces when someone lets you down. And when you choose to see the potential for growth in these situations, failures become lessons rather than losses.

Amy Edmondson is a professor of leadership at Harvard Business School and studies psychological safety and teaming. Her book *Right Kind of Wrong: The Science of Failing Well* explores how to think about, discuss, and practice failure wisely. While Edmondson argues that avoiding mistakes is both unrealistic and undesirable, she clarifies that not all failures are the same. The "good" kind—the ones that lead to advancements in science, for instance—are the result of careful experimentation in pursuit of an opportunity or goal. I introduced the idea of "intelligent failures" in chapter 1, and I will revisit this concept again in the next chapter.

The other kind of failure—what Edmondson calls "basic failures"—happen in homestay, too. These are preventable and unproductive, yet inevitable. They are often caused by inattention, faulty assumptions, overconfidence, or neglect.

Inattention is carelessness; it's students spilling hair dye on the rug or leaving the door unlocked.

When May (from chapter 1) didn't call Lee to tell her she would be late, it was an example of a faulty assumption—that Lee wouldn't care where she was or when she got home.

Overconfidence leads people to make decisions without reflecting on the implications, such as hugging a student without asking, or attempting to cut your own hair, like Robby.

When someone puts something off too long, it's an example of neglect: not studying enough for a test, not leaving enough time to get to the airport, not checking the bathroom to see if your student is actually cleaning it.

As unproductive and potentially dangerous as these mistakes are, they are still valuable. According to Edmondson, basic failures offer people a chance to "practice feeling okay about the fact that mistakes will happen." When you feel okay about your mistakes, it's easier to confront and learn from them, thereby preventing them in the future.

Since Alex's actions were intentional, Edmondson places them in a different category, referring to them as "mischief" or "sabotage," or a "violation" of a law or rule. Intent matters.

I couldn't help but wonder about Alex's motivations, and if that had any bearing on Lee's assessment of the situation. Was it mischief? Sabotage? A violation?

"Did he tell you why he took the money?" I asked Lee.

"Alex wasn't given much money from his parents when he stayed with us," she said. "He hung around with a lot of Chinese boys who were all rich. He used it to buy Christmas presents."

Intent matters.

If mistakes are good for us, why is it so hard to get past them? Understanding that failure can help us grow and build resilience is helpful, but most of us still try to avoid failure and feel embarrassment, shame, guilt, and/or humiliation when things go wrong. This is normal. The survival of our species depended on early humans evolving a disproportionate response to potential threats. Not only did this produce the visual, memory, and social mindbugs that protected our groups, humans also learned to favour negative information over positive. Recall the "magic ratio" for healthy marriages from the last chapter: it takes five positive interactions to balance every negative one. This illustrates *negativity bias*, a tendency to notice mistakes and failures more readily than successes.

Aversion to failure is painful and very human. When combined with confusion about different types of failure and fear of the social stigma of failure, it's clear why failing well is so hard. It's also hard when others fail us. For hosts, I think there are four factors that contribute to the possibility of granting second chances: *your role* in creating psychological safety in your home, the *other person's reaction* to the conflict, the *breach of trust* that can seem impossible to recover from, and securing a *meaningful apology*. By exploring these in turn, I hope to provide a new way of thinking about second chances and a deeper understanding of why and how Lee was able to forgive Alex.

Your Role

I discussed the concept of contribution in the last chapter, as a way to move away from blame and create a learning conversation. To the extent that mistakes generate conflict in the relationship, both parties must examine how—not if—they have contributed to the situation. The exception may be the rare student who is deliberately deviant by sabotaging a situation or intentionally hurting someone or something. These cases are more clearly blameworthy, but even then I would argue that it's unusual for there to be no other precipitating factors (which may have nothing to do with the host).

When it comes to mistakes, the contribution you need to examine is the extent to which you create—or jeopardize—a sense of psychological safety in your home.

Edmondson coined the term *psychological safety* to describe the atmosphere in workplaces where people feel comfortable talking about mistakes, asking questions, or generating half-baked ideas without fear of repercussion or damage to their reputation. If you want to create an environment where students are willing to admit when they're wrong and learn from their mistakes, it begins with you. Not only do you need to normalize discomfort, as I discussed in chapter 1 on setting boundaries, you also need to normalize failure.

Creating a sense of psychological safety requires everyone to talk about failing—frequently and clearly—before it happens. In innovative companies, leaders create mantras, like design and consulting firm IDEO's "fail often, in order to succeed sooner," which are repeated over and over again. You can do the same in your family.

Psychological safety is enhanced with a policy of "blameless reporting," which says *we want to hear from you when things go wrong* and *you won't be penalized for coming forward*. Normalizing failure requires curiosity about the outcome and a willingness to reflect on lessons learned from the experience. Punishing people for failure, on the other hand, sends it underground—where it's shameful and hidden. In turn, this actually increases the likelihood of failure. Instead, families can work together to solve their problems, looking for ways out of the setback and creating systems to prevent future errors.

When it comes to mistakes, the contribution you need to examine is the extent to which you create—or jeopardize— a sense of psychological safety in your home.

Some host parents may wonder how they can make failure safe without relaxing accountability for mistakes. Edmondson points out the false dichotomy in this concern. Families can be psychologically safe *and* still expect their students to do their homework, clean their bathroom, and engage with the family. As Edmondson says, "Learning happens best when we're challenged *and* psychologically safe enough to experiment and to talk openly about it when things don't work out as we'd hoped."

Lee was skilled in minimizing her role in the conflict with Alex. She didn't escalate the problem by making false accusations of blame (even though she suspected Fred, not Alex). Neither did she assume intention, or make up a story about why any of her students would steal from her (*he must not care about us/be entitled/not know right from wrong*). She knew she didn't own the whole truth about the situation.

Most of all, she created psychological safety. She calmly and respectfully created a policy of blameless reporting while setting a boundary (*there will be no repercussions if you come clean, tell us why, and pay us back*) and waited for her students to do the right thing. She engaged them with care and gave them the benefit of the doubt. She created the conditions for an optimal relationship, even in the face of betrayal.

Their Reaction

It's hard to imagine forgiving someone and moving past a conflict when they push your buttons. We all have our pet peeves—for me, it's when someone walks away from a conversation. For my husband, it's being forced to think out loud, on the spot. For others, it's people who talk back, talk over, or don't talk at all.

It's been more than ten years since Bella lived with Chris and her husband, but Chris still remembers this story as if it happened yesterday. Bella was a beautiful teenager from Brazil who stayed with them at the same time as two other girls, one from Japan and one from Taiwan. Her story started one afternoon when Chris caught sight of a sticky note on the mirror in the students' shared bathroom. It read, "If you want toothpaste, ask me." She found this puzzling, but let it go.

Not long after, her Japanese student came to Chris with her shampoo and conditioner in hand; she had bought them the day before and suspected someone else had used some. When the student from Taiwan overheard them, she told Chris that she was the one who left the note about the toothpaste.

After concluding that Bella must be the culprit, Chris asked Bella if she had been using the other girls' shampoo, conditioner, or toothpaste. Bella denied it. Using them was the first mistake. This was Bella's second mistake, in Chris's eyes.

Where Lee offered a way out, Chris dug in. She came up with an idea for a "sting operation." With the other girls' help, she drew a line on the shampoo bottle at the level of its contents. They timed their showers so Bella would be the last one in the bathroom. Sure enough, she used both the shampoo and the conditioner—and now they had evidence.

Chris was livid. She confronted Bella again. "Are you using Yuka's shampoo?"

"Oh no, I wouldn't do that."

"Oh, yeah?" Chris held up the bottle with the black line clearly marked on it. A lecture ensued, in which Chris asked Bella how she'd feel if someone came and took something of hers.

"Well, it wasn't like it was money. What's the big deal?"

"Yes, it was! You need to apologize to the girls, and you need to buy them replacement products," Chris said. When Bella tried to make it up to them by giving them some little soaps she had brought with her from Brazil, Chris wouldn't let it go. She insisted on Bella buying the replacements.

Chris called Brenda, her homestay coordinator, for help. Brenda understood that Chris was furious and felt she could never trust Bella again. Brenda offered to relocate Bella, but since Bella was scheduled to leave not long after this happened, Chris just let her stay.

Chris says the damage to their relationship was due to the way Bella reacted. "You know, the crying and blah, blah. She said 'Sorry' and 'Please don't send me home' and all that," Chris says. "But she still didn't think it was a big deal that she 'borrowed' the shampoo."

When you're having tough conversations—when you have to confront someone who has broken your trust—you want them to cooperate. It's natural to want them to sit still, listen patiently, agree, apologize.

But when people are on the receiving end of that feedback or criticism, the last thing they want to do is sit still, listen patiently, agree, or apologize. When someone fails, their brain tends to catastrophize about rejection, self-worth, and status—all of which humans are hardwired to protect. These physiological and emotional fears are tied to one's safety in the group. In a 2011 study funded by the National Institute of Mental Health and the National Institute on Drug Abuse, researchers found that physical pain and intense experiences of social rejection are expressed in the brain in the same way. In other words, the pain of disconnection is real pain.

Not only do people experience fear and pain, they also experience self-threat—a challenge to their identity. As I've explored, it's natural to react poorly when your self-image is called into question. In the face of failure, it's easier to deny what happened or justify what you did rather than admit you're at fault. Listening to feedback about your failure can trigger feelings of guilt, embarrassment, humiliation, or—in many cases—shame.

In cultures where shame is a "wrong" emotion, it triggers a survival instinct to fight, flee, or freeze. People may feel a response in the body (pounding heart, upset stomach, tunnel vision, etc.) or the mind (racing thoughts, misplaced anger, replaying conversations). Everyone responds slightly differently, though there are common threads. Linda Hartling of the Stone Center at Wellesley says people tend to adopt one of three general strategies to deal with feelings of shame, though many people use all of them depending on the context: moving *away* (withdrawing), moving *toward* (seeking to please), and moving *against* (being aggressive or deflecting).

Your student keeps eating food in his room despite your repeated requests not to, and when you confront him he *moves away*, looking at the floor and avoiding a response, then retreating to his room.

Your student is being bullied at school, so she *moves toward*, doing everything the bullies demand in an attempt to please them—at her own expense.

Or perhaps your student is stealing shampoo, conditioner, and toothpaste from her fellow homestay students and *moves against*, first denying it, then deflecting by brushing it off and saying it's no big deal.

On the other hand, it may not even be shame that you're witnessing; in a cross-cultural context, people often misinterpret the body language of others. The downcast eyes, slumped shoulders, and silence could be a sign of respect, not guilt. Holding one's gaze and speaking firmly or yelling could be an attempt to preserve one's honour, not defiance or disrespect.

These reactions can get under your skin even when they're minor. As I've discussed, people bring their whole selves to difficult conversations, baggage included. Your student's behaviour can trigger feelings of shame in you, too—masquerading as anger—when your identity (as a good person/caring host/attentive parent) is called into question. If you think you have failed somehow, even at an unconscious level, it's normal to rise to protect yourself—especially if there are witnesses. I recall an incident when a host phoned our team in a panic and threatened to sue us over the police cruiser that was parked outside their house. The reason for the police presence wasn't their primary concern—it was the fact that the neighbours would see it and assume the worst of them.

Even Chris, the same wonderful host who created an environment where Rika could belong, and who loves to teach sex ed and life skills to her students, has complicated human reactions. In this case, she cornered Bella. It's my opinion that giving someone a "chance to come clean" when you know they've betrayed you is not a gift, it's a trap. While others might interpret it differently, I would say this was a win-lose situation, and Bella was the loser—regardless of what she said. There was no blameless reporting offered here. If Bella admitted to her mischief, she expected rejection, criticism, and punishment. If she denied it, she risked rejection, criticism, and punishment.

Giving someone a second chance requires us to have compassion for them as they move through their experience, as well as cultural sensitivity. Recall the way Himari's host handled the case of the missing pencil, and the importance of face in East Asian cultures. Through the way she handled the theft, Lee created the optimal conditions for Alex to save face while taking accountability. Disclosing his financial limitations would have triggered self-threat in Alex, but he was able to come clean due to the safety Lee created. Besides the concept of face, there is another cultural dimension to Alex's story. In Chinese culture, gifts are exchanged for special occasions, same as in North America, the UK, and Australia. But gifts are also used to build and maintain relationships with others, and in a collectivist culture like China's, this is critical.

You also need to offer compassion to yourself. When you notice the denial, blaming, half-hearted apologies, deflected accountability, or disconnection, take a breath. If you need to remove yourself from the situation, do so. It's okay to pause a heated conversation. People tend to think more clearly and can get more of what they want from conversations when they approach them after some reflection and when they're emotionally grounded.

When you're ready to talk, embrace the opportunity for a learning conversation. You may be surprised at what you discover about the other person and what you share about yourself, both of which may bring you closer to being able to rebuild trust.

A Breach of Trust

As you've heard from me and many hosts throughout this book, enjoying the experience of hosting requires us to extend trust from day one, with healthy boundaries and reasonable expectations providing guardrails. Homestay requires a certain amount of faith in humanity, a belief that the student will come with an open heart, a willingness to learn, and an interest in a genuine intercultural connection. This is why recovering from a breach of trust is so hard. Saying, "You broke my trust" is just the beginning.

If you want to feel comfortable offering someone a second chance, it helps to be able to talk about trust more specifically. For that, I'll use Brené Brown's seven elements of trust. Brown uses the acronym BRAVING to remember the seven components: boundaries, reliability, accountability, vault, integrity, nonjudgment, and generosity.

If you assume that someone will mess up at some point, you can move past the shock and disappointment that inevitably surfaces when someone lets you down.

For example, when Alex chose the easy path—stealing the money—instead of asking for help, he broke trust by breaching his own *integrity*. When Lee believed that whoever stole the money must have had a good reason for it, she was being *generous*. And when Alex told Lee and Danny that he had taken the money, apologized, and paid them back, he demonstrated trustworthiness by being *accountable*.

When you can identify what aspect of trust has been breached, you can better decide if it was a mistake that will become a learning moment or a violation that has permanently damaged the relationship. Not every breach of trust in homestay can be overcome, but many can. As Brown says, "trust and mistakes can coexist." Next, I'll discuss how to improve the likelihood that others will make amends, and how to respond when you get an apology.

A Meaningful Apology

I have seen the power of apologies to mend relationships like Lee and Alex's, melting away hurts and healing disconnection. I've also seen the opportunity for a good apology squandered, leaving both parties feeling flat. When it comes to second chances, a meaningful apology is often the final test that will determine the fate of the relationship.

While apologizing is universal, there are differences across cultures in how, why, with whom, and how often people apologize. For example, in a study comparing American, Chinese, and Korean cultures, researchers found that people varied in their desire, obligation, intention, and norm to apologize, with Americans feeling more strongly about apologizing than either Chinese or Korean participants. Another analysis found that in honour cultures (such as parts of the Middle East, South

America, Eastern Europe, and the American South), people are less willing to apologize partly because they are concerned about lowering their social standing and partly because they don't think it will help repair the relationship.

Apologizing can also vary *within* cultures, and even within families. Some people view apologies as tools for manipulation, to shut down dialogue, to avoid criticism, or to continue poor behaviour. Others may want to apologize, but their self-esteem is so vulnerable that they don't have the emotional bandwidth for it. As I've explored, shame can jeopardize the ability to apologize because of the way it threatens one's sense of self-worth. It takes a solid sense of self-regard to feel empathy and compassion for someone else. Without this grounding, people can get stuck in defensiveness.

So what are you to do when you are feeling wronged and want someone to stop being defensive, get vulnerable, and make amends? You can't *make* someone apologize (and insisting they do will make it less sincere, leaving you feeling dissatisfied and them feeling humiliated), but you can navigate the conversation with skill to improve your chances of repair. Psychologist Harriet Lerner suggests the following five strategies.

Be accurate

When people are already feeling defensive, exaggeration makes it worse. Avoid escalating the criticism to a broad condemnation that's out of proportion. For example, when your student eats in their room *this week*, it won't help to say they *always* eat in their room.

Be concise

Not only do students have a language barrier to overcome, they will also lose focus and interest if you belabour the point. If it feels like you're not getting through, as tempting as it is, it doesn't help to talk more. Try keeping your request for an apology to three sentences or less.

Be calm—most of the time
While it's always a good idea to be tactful and kind, Lerner suggests that a raw show of emotion can be effective when it's a "very rare and surprising departure from your usual style—and does not harm the other person." Consider Lee's heated approach with her student May from chapter 1. How did May cope with Lee yelling and swearing, when many students would demand a relocation after such an outburst? It wasn't harmful. Lee's daughters told May, "When Mum gets mad like that, it means she really cares. She wants to make things right." Anger by itself is destructive, just as brutal honesty without kindness is destructive. Lee shows how much she cares every day: with her food, her open-minded approach to learning about cultures, her love.

Be responsible
Taking responsibility for your role in the problem is critical. If you feel like you could have anticipated the behaviour that has broken your trust, you're usually close to discovering your part. Acknowledging your contribution may be as simple as saying, "I've contributed to this problem by not explaining what I meant when I asked you to keep your room clean. For that, I am sorry." Or, "I've contributed to this problem by not telling you months ago that I don't want you to eat in your bedroom. Instead, I got more and more irritated and took it out on you in other ways. For that, I'm sorry." Being responsible also means taking ownership for your feelings and reactions to the other person's behaviour.

Say thank you
When you do receive an apology, the way you react has significant consequences for the relationship. To indicate your

acceptance of it as an effort to repair the relationship, the most graceful response is to say, "Thank you for the apology. I appreciate it." This is one of the hardest parts of Lerner's advice, in my experience—and I've been practicing it for a couple of years. It's uncomfortable, and I keep saying things like, "It's okay, no big deal." But I keep trying, because pushing through my discomfort is the best way to honour their efforts.

What if you think the apology isn't genuine? Again, resist the temptation to say anything but thank you. Don't launch into reminders of past transgressions, or instruct them on how dangerous or unthoughtful their actions were. Don't try to assess how sincere the apology was; there are many reasons why someone's tone or facial expressions or choice of words may ring hollow to you—including cultural differences. The best way to know if someone is truly sorry is their future actions.

Keep in mind that accepting an apology doesn't mean everything will instantly go back to the way it was. It doesn't mean you have forgiven the person, or that you will never discuss this again. But it should be the end of the discussion in that moment—and the beginning of moving forward in the relationship with goodwill, paving the way for future conversations.

I know this is hard work. I know it takes practice, and time, and a willingness to be uncomfortable and make mistakes. It is possible to strengthen relationships, in spite of hurt feelings. The result could change someone's life.

The Impact of Making Amends

Alex knew he was lucky. He had lived in homestay in Vancouver the year before, so he had a unique appreciation for how special Lee and Danny's home was. "A lot of families are doing this to earn money," Alex told me. "Lee and Danny know how to welcome new students and help with their needs. They rocked my mind about what homestay should be." Indeed, he stayed with Lee and Danny for the remainder of grade eleven and twelve, the last two years of high school in Canada.

When Lee forgave Alex for stealing three hundred dollars from her purse, she understood her decision had ramifications for his academic status. But she didn't fully grasp how impactful her choice was at the time.

"There's not a time, not a special occasion that goes by that I don't hear from that boy," Lee says, her voice swelling with pride. "I love him dearly. He was a great kid, and he's turned out to be a wonderful man." Alex continued his education at St. Thomas University in Fredericton, completing a four-year undergraduate degree. He received his Canadian citizenship, works at the Bank of Montreal, and is getting married soon.

"I'm so glad I gave him a second chance," Lee says. "They're teenagers. We don't know their life. We don't know what goes on. Just because they're sent here, it doesn't mean they have everything going right. I believe in giving anybody a second chance. Always." Lee pauses. "Sometimes three," she says, laughing. "That's just who we are as people, you know."

CHAPTER SUMMARY

- Mistakes are opportunities in disguise.

- When Mama Lee noticed money missing, she used it as a teaching moment. With blameless reporting, she gave her students the opportunity to come forward and be accountable.

- Basic failures are usually caused by inattention, faulty assumptions, overconfidence, or neglect.

- When people are on the receiving end of feedback or criticism, it's natural to get defensive. Poor reactions can be a symptom of shame.

- Giving someone a second chance requires us to have compassion for them as they move through their experience—as well as cultural sensitivity.

- When asking for an apology: be accurate, be concise, be calm, and be responsible. When you receive one, just say thank you.

12

When It Doesn't Work Out
Relocations

---

*The most difficult part of homestay is students
who leave because our family isn't right for them.
That is very hard emotionally.*
ERIC, host from Winnipeg, Manitoba

Content Warning: This section includes a discussion of self-harm.

As one host said on CHN's 2022 survey, the most difficult part of homestay is "conflict with students and having to ask them to move. It is never a good feeling when things go south." Thankfully, the incidences of such transfers have hovered around 11 to 15 percent for our organization—for thirty years and over ninety thousand students. In other words, the odds are good. In the vast majority of cases, homestay works.

But how many times does a host have to try and correct a behaviour before everyone agrees that the relationship is beyond repair? And what about those rare situations that are so unacceptable that immediate action is warranted? A host should not be expected to live with a student who steals their car and crashes it into their chimney, or continually treats the home like a hotel and the hosts like servants, or is suffering from a serious medical issue. Nobody wants to deal with such issues, but no amount of screening will prevent every potential source of conflict. This is where the support from a homestay organization will make all the difference for a host.

The Sudden Move

The knock at the door came near four o'clock in the afternoon, as Jason was making dinner for his eleven- and eight-year-old daughters and his eighteen-year-old student, Dean.

"Is there a problem, officers?" Jason asked, his younger daughter hovering close behind. The police officers—one male, one female—were dressed in navy cargo pants and heavy black boots, navy shirts, and Eisenhower jackets with utility vests. Their guns were safely holstered at their hips. Jason was a bit confused about what was going on.

"We're looking for Dean," one of the officers said.

"Is something wrong?"

"No. Is he here?"

"Yeah, I'll go and get him." Jason left them on the front porch while he fetched Dean from his bedroom. "Hey, Dean," he said, knocking on the door. "The police are here looking for you. Is everything okay?"

"I don't know," Dean said, his deep baritone voice short and flat.

It was a mild evening in Vancouver, typical for March. The late afternoon sun dropped lower in the sky, backlighting the officers on the porch. Dean stared at the doormat to avoid the glare. Jason's daughter hung around the living room window, trying to eavesdrop.

Jason returned to his supper preparations, his mind wandering. Dean had only been with them for about a month. Had he done something? Was he in trouble? Jason called the homestay coordinator, Pheona. He told her the police were there, and asked her if she knew anything. She offered to call Dean's mother.

Moments later, Dean appeared in the kitchen to give Jason an update. "I'm not in trouble or anything," he said. "I just need to go to the hospital real quick."

Dean started down the hall to his bedroom and one of the officers made to follow him. Jason asked the officer if he could take off his boots in the house; he doesn't like people tracking dirt all over the carpet. The officer said no—he had to accompany Dean.

"I didn't want to make a big deal out of it," Jason told me. "I think he was pushing his authority onto me. Dean didn't do anything wrong. We didn't do anything wrong. He had no right to be in our house. But with my daughter there, I didn't want to scare her."

Dean reappeared a few minutes later with his black paramedic jacket (from a thrift store) and Doc Martens. They waited outside a while longer and Jason continued to keep his distance, torn between wanting to give them some privacy and wanting to know what was happening. When he did peek outside, he saw an ambulance parked in front of the police cruiser, and a paramedic speaking to one of the officers. Dean was in the back of the police car.

"It was quite a scene," Jason says. "I can't imagine how Dean must have felt... it seemed like everything was blown out of proportion."

Dean would have agreed with Jason. Yes, he had told his counsellor earlier that day that he was having thoughts of self-harm, and yes, he understood she was worried about his well-being. But the police? And an ambulance?

"I didn't have a choice," Dean says. "I felt powerless and annoyed that the whole thing was happening in the first place. It felt like it was unnecessary. I didn't want to go to the hospital, but I couldn't do anything about it."

All Canadian provinces and territories have legislation to treat and protect people with severe mental disorders and to protect the public. While most people needing psychiatric support are admitted to hospital voluntarily, these laws exist to help those individuals who refuse to seek treatment. In Vancouver, Car 87, also known as the Mental Health Car, is staffed by a police officer and a psychiatric nurse who work together to respond to mental health concerns. They de-escalate situations, provide crisis intervention, and connect people to community services, like the hospital. Once there, a physician can determine whether or not the person should be admitted to the hospital for treatment and/or observation.

The US also has programs like these, often called Mobile Crisis Intervention Teams. Such teams have been in place for decades in Oregon, Arizona, and Georgia. Other states have started programs more recently, such as the one in Minneapolis that was created in the aftermath of George Floyd's killing. The Biden administration has invested close to a billion dollars into such community-based services as part of its mental health "Unity Agenda." Australia's service goes by different names—Crisis Assessment and Treatment Team, acute care team, Mental Health Triage Service, or Mental Health Intervention Team—but all can be reached by calling the local hospital or the state's mental health crisis line. The UK has similar services which can be accessed in the same way.

Dean sat on the hard plastic bench in the back of the police cruiser. The seat was moulded like an amusement park ride, but this was not a fun experience. It was cramped, intimidating, dark; there were no door handles on the inside. The windows were reinforced with wire mesh. A rifle was fastened in a plastic case on the driver's side of the barrier separating the front from the back, in plain view of the passenger. Dean was silent, wondering if Jason thought he was a criminal. "Creepin'" by Metro Boomin—an R&B pop song about betrayal—played on the radio as they drove to the hospital.

After Dean was taken away, Jason had a lot of thinking to do. He didn't know anything about Dean's mental health, or that he had a counsellor. He had enjoyed having Dean in his home. "The girls loved talking to him," Jason says. "I think my oldest really connected with him. They had common interests, like YouTube and Minecraft. I liked that they played games together. During dinnertime, they would chat. After dinner... he would show her some stuff on YouTube, or they did some art stuff. It was good."

Jason had noticed that Dean slept a lot during the day and stayed up all night, but he had assumed it was normal behaviour. "Not that it bothers me," he says. "I chalked it up to college kids. I did the same thing. We stayed up all night playing video games or whatnot, slept, and then went to school. So it wasn't a big deal."

At least, not until the police came. He realized he couldn't be 100 percent certain that Dean would be fine. "As much as I'm sure that it wouldn't be an issue, I felt like I wouldn't be a good dad to have him stay," he explains. "Just that possibility, as small as it is... I didn't want to put my kids in that situation again."

He called Pheona and told her Dean could not return to his house that night.

When Pheona reached out to Dean, he was still at the hospital, waiting to be seen by the emergency room physician. He says it felt rude. "He didn't even talk to me," Dean says, his voice quiet. "Like he was punishing me for something that I didn't plan, that I didn't want to have happen in the first place. We were on the same side, but I was still being kicked out for it."

Jason sent a text message to Dean at 10:30 p.m. that night: *Hey, I hope everything is okay. Sorry about the moving out thing. It's just a bit too much for the kids with the police around.*

"I don't like him thinking I'm a liability like that," Dean says. He didn't respond to the text.

Dismissals

When it's time to remove a student from a home, the options include moving the student to another host, expelling them from the homestay program (but allowing them to stay in the country, if they have a local support system), or sending them home. Choosing between these options can be complicated, but it may reassure the reader to know that there are a handful of situations that preclude a student from remaining in the program.

All homestay programs should require students to sign an agreement or code of conduct which sets out behavioural expectations and explains the consequences of a breach. While every homestay organization is different, I believe there is general consensus among us that homestay is a privilege, not a right.

Students who abuse that privilege through their actions are not entitled to endless chances—and educators who keep such students in school can jeopardize the reputation of their entire program. Word travels fast among host families, especially in small communities. These breaches don't have to be serious on their own, but when they happen repeatedly, a dismissal is warranted. Pam, a retired guidance counsellor and one of our coordinators, told me about one such student. "She drank, she smoked, she snuck out, she hibernated," Pam says. "I kept sending messages to her mother, and they kept making excuses."

Breaches don't have to happen repeatedly for a dismissal to make sense. For instance, our team will remove students from our program if they did not disclose or if they develop serious physical or mental health conditions that require the care and supervision of a physician and, arguably, their own parents.

The following breaches are rare—in CHN's experience, they've happened only a handful of times—but I include them to clarify our stance and manage host expectations.

Acts of violence, harassment, or abuse are not tolerated and will result in dismissal. Racism and discrimination, when used as a form of aggression (and not out of ignorance), are also grounds for immediate relocation and, possibly, termination. Sexual conduct between students and any members of the host family, even with consent, is unacceptable, as is sexual harassment or abuse of any individual, whether or not they are part of the family. Finally, drug or alcohol abuse are grounds for dismissal. It's important to distinguish cases requiring professional help from "normal" teenage behaviour (experimenting with intoxication).

This discussion would be incomplete if I overlooked the fallibility of host families; students are not the only participants who are subject to behavioural expectations. Families will be removed from CHN's network of active hosts if they break any of the rules above. CHN will also relocate students if there is a sudden divorce or similar domestic upheaval in the home, student neglect (leaving students without care or meals), unsuitable accommodation, disclosure of criminal behaviour, lack of adequate communication with our organization, providing false statements, inability to provide an English (or French, in some locations) immersion experience, or repeated issues with their hospitality or commitment.

Knowing that there are such boundaries makes all the difference for many hosts and students. Most families on both sides of the placement want to know what will happen if things don't work out and feel reassured by our organization's promise to support them with a change, if it comes to that.

Yet deciding to make that change can be complicated, especially when a student's mental health is at stake.

Mental Health

Jason is not alone in having to grapple with questions around his duty of care versus his comfort with keeping a student like Dean who may have been at risk of harming himself. Our team's anecdotal impression that mental health issues in teens have grown over the last several years is supported by research from the US Centers for Disease Control and Prevention (CDC), the Canadian Institute for Health Information, the World Health Organization, and others. Studies comparing data from the last twenty years have shown increases in reports of sadness or hopelessness, diagnoses of depression and other mental health disorders, rates of suicide, the number of interactions with Kids Help Phone, and how many mood and anxiety medications have been dispensed.

A lot of the students who experience mental health challenges in homestay are confronting those issues for the first time, but some cases originate in their home countries. Of these, there are plenty of students who are successfully managing their illness under the care of a physician and can thrive in homestay. Others will suffer relapses under the stress of studying abroad. In any case, experiencing the safety and comfort of living with a caring family can make a significant impact on outcomes for these young people.

Susan, Haley's host from Ottawa, had a difficult experience with a different student from Mexico. Her name was Maria, her English was amazing, and she had a great sense of humour. She and Susan had a good relationship at first—Maria took a sincere interest in the family and enjoyed hanging out with them.

♥

A relocation doesn't mean there was a bad host or a bad student. It could have been just a bad match.

───────

Within a few weeks of her arrival, Susan noticed they were going through a lot of cereal and bread. Maria had told them she was in recovery for bulimia, but they recognized the excessive food consumption as a warning sign that she was not well.

Susan called our coordinator. They took Maria to the hospital together. Sure enough, Maria had relapsed and would need extensive support. When Maria was discharged, Susan and her husband took her back. They attended regular doctors' appointments, held nightly conversations about her feelings, and felt ongoing stress about the food. Everything the doctors warned them about was true. "It was a roller coaster of emotions," Susan says.

By November, almost three months after her arrival, it was clear that Maria wasn't going to succeed in the program. After weeks of regular contact throughout this process, Maria's father came to accompany her home.

Don't Wait, and Don't Rush

Susan's experience with Maria highlights an important lesson for all hosts: don't wait to call for help and don't rush the decision about your student's placement.

The support provided by your homestay coordinator could make all the difference in the outcomes for you and your student. In Susan's case, our coordinators Brenda and Hilary were there at every step—both physically and emotionally. They attended a lot of the doctors' appointments and were available for countless conversations. "You feel so responsible, but you need permission to let go if needed," Susan says. "They were a sympathetic ear. When you say something and they are as shocked as you are, you know you're not crazy... We may not choose to relocate

[Maria], but we had that perspective and were able to say, 'We can weather this because we know we have someone who understands.' Without that I'd feel lost at sea."

As Susan says, "This is emotionally hard work." For some, it's too hard. There's no shame in this. All hosts are entitled to draw a line around what they're signing up for when they agree to host. When Jason decided he couldn't keep Dean in his home, his decision was driven not by anything Dean did—they were getting along fine before Dean was taken to the hospital—but by the weight of this emotional burden.

Jason didn't wait to call; he was on the phone with our coordinator while the police were still on his porch. Again: his decision to relocate was his prerogative; it must have been frightening when the police appeared, and aggravating when they started traipsing through his house in their boots. Still, at that point, Jason didn't know what Dean was dealing with. In addition to the sense of duty he felt as a father, he rushed his decision to relocate, basing it on assumptions and fear.

Many hosts are anxious about keeping students after they've asked for a relocation. I can understand how awkward it feels to live with someone who knows you don't want them there, but for Dean, that would have been preferable. He told me that being asked to leave so suddenly didn't help his state of mind. He felt rejected at one of the lowest points in his life, with no new host available.

There's an important difference between Dean and students who need supervision in a clinical setting. The emergency physician who met Dean concluded that he was not in immediate danger. This was a chronic problem, not an acute one. She discharged Dean when he promised her and his family that he wouldn't harm himself. If he needed support, he agreed to activate his safety plan (a document that guides someone when they are experiencing thoughts of suicide, to help them avoid a crisis). He was required to visit the Access and Assessment Centre (AAC) the next day. The AAC helps connect people with non-life-threatening mental health and substance use issues to the services and resources they need.

The team at the AAC gave Dean an appointment to meet with a psychiatrist. This was good news: a psychiatrist meant a diagnosis. A diagnosis meant a treatment plan. And a treatment plan meant hope.

It took two days for CHN to find Dean a new homestay. Luckily, he was able to sleep on his cousin's couch while he waited. Our team matched him with a young couple who were happy to welcome him into their home, with full knowledge of why he was moving. Chris, the host dad, was outgoing and chatty and enjoyed video games—a natural connection point. "They've got good energy," Dean told me. "It was clearly something they wanted to be doing, and had been doing for a while. They had everything organized."

A few days later, the psychiatrist diagnosed Dean with depression and social anxiety. She admitted him to the hospital for forty-eight hours, which gave the doctors a chance to prescribe an SSRI (selective serotonin reuptake inhibitor) medication and raise the dose more quickly. He was discharged with a comprehensive treatment plan, and cleared to return to school.

Dean was welcomed back to his new homestay that evening. They told Pheona they had enjoyed having him in their home, and were happy that he was feeling better and was ready to finish his semester with them. When I ask Dean how he felt about these new hosts being open to taking him in—despite what he'd been through—he says, "I don't know why they wouldn't. Isn't that just them being decent people?"

When It's Less Complicated

One of the most important lessons we reinforce with our home-stay coordinators—after emphasizing the need for a second opinion and teamwork—is that there are more than two sides to every story. Dean and Jason had their own versions of events, as did Pheona, Dean's family, Jason's daughters, the counsellor, and so on. Understanding the layers of complexity inherent in interpersonal conflict adds nuance and texture, helping us to avoid falling into the binaries of "high conflict." Author Amanda Ripley defines "high conflict" as "what happens when conflict clarifies into a good-versus-evil kind of feud, the kind with an *us* and a *them*." I showed in chapter 9 that reducing issues to a binary contributes to bias and identity crises. In conflict, when people only see two sides to the story, they overlook details and contradictions. The resulting solutions seem to have a winner and a loser. A more nuanced view serves everyone.

However, there are times when conflict can be simple. When both host and student agree that a relocation is for the best, everyone wins. More often than not, relocations can serve as a positive reset button for students and hosts. Over and over again, we see students with problem behaviours in one home flourish in another, like Artem when he moved from Evelyn's to Mike and Lee-Anne's. Some students, like Mary's student Asuka, are looking for a different family composition. Resolving mismatches of preferences can be a swift and satisfying way to improve a student's experience. In these cases, we remind everyone that a relocation doesn't mean there was a bad host or a bad student. It could have been just a bad match.

Learning from Relocations

I touched on Amy Edmondson's notion of "basic failures" in the last chapter. Relocations are different. When a relocation happens, it meets all four of Edmondson's criteria for an "intelligent failure"—the kind that leads to advancements in science. The "right" kind of wrong.

First, much like a lab experiment, homestay happens in new territory: moving to another country, hosting a stranger, practicing cultural humility, trying a new approach to conflict. Second, it's worth the risks because of the potential upside; these are meaningful opportunities in and of themselves. Third, homestay is informed by some prior knowledge—maybe you've hosted before, or a student has travelled before, or you've read the host guide, or you've met your neighbour's students. Last, the risks are mitigated by working with an organization that will support you if it doesn't work out.

Seeing relocations as "intelligent failures" allows us to reframe them as both inevitable and helpful. To the extent that homestay is an experiment with an uncertain outcome, relocations are bound to happen. Not to everyone, but as a whole—which is why CHN's relocation rate will never be zero. Relocations can be helpful in that failure and learning go hand in hand. Edmondson explains: "In new territory, the only way to make progress is through trial and failure... [Intelligent failures] are disappointing, but never cause for embarrassment or shame." You aren't creating new vaccines in homestay, but you can gain other kinds of knowledge, if you're willing to learn. That learning is another way you create the conditions for optimal relationships... with *future* students. Just as it's important to normalize the discomfort of basic failures, it's also helpful to normalize intelligent failures. It's up to you to decide how you want to look at them.

Now's it's time to bring all these lessons together, by celebrating the heart of homestay. For 7 percent of CHN's hosts, when I asked them on our survey what the most difficult or challenging part of homestay was, they said they don't find it difficult at all. For example, one respondent said, "After hosting students for nearly twenty-five years, I have no challenges. Over the years I have learned what works and what doesn't."

Another 4 percent said the hardest part of hosting is saying goodbye.

To me, the warmth and wisdom of such hosts is an inspiration for all of us. In the end, this is about love, and all the ways we feel it, show it, and receive it with each other and our students.

CHAPTER SUMMARY

- All homestay programs should require students to sign an agreement or code of conduct which sets out behavioural expectations and explains the consequences of a breach.

- Mental health issues in teens have grown over the last several years (according to research from the CDC, the Canadian Institute for Health Information, and the World Health Organization [WHO]).

- Your homestay coordinator can provide support when you're considering asking for a relocation. Don't wait to call for help and don't rush the decision about your student's placement.

- Many hosts are anxious about keeping students after they've asked for a transfer, but sudden relocations can be very hard on the student.

- Seeing relocations as "intelligent failures" allows you to reframe them as both inevitable and helpful.

Conclusion
Remember Your Purpose Upon Departure

Absolutely the most difficult part of hosting for our family has been when we have to say our goodbyes and see them off as they head back to their homes.

NICK AND CARLA, hosts from Thedford, Ontario

"ALLEN FORGOT HIS HAT!" Wes said, as I looked up from my clipboard. "It's at the house. I can get it, but I don't think I'll make it back before the bus has to leave."

We were standing in the parking lot of the Victoria bus depot on a sunny morning in August 2012. I was managing the departure of a group of Chinese teenagers, ensuring they all boarded the shuttle on time with their chaperone. The bus would drive forty minutes to the Swartz Bay ferry terminal where they'd catch the next sailing to Vancouver and their flight back to China the following day.

"Go," I said. "I'll wait for you. I'll follow the bus to the ferry if I have to."

Wes hurried to his car and disappeared. I found Allen, a boy of fourteen from Shenzhen who was travelling abroad for the first time. I told him I would wait for Wes and the hat, though I didn't know how much he understood.

About fifteen minutes later, the bus departed on time with all our students on board... and no sign of Wes.

When Wes finally returned to the depot with hat in hand, I did some quick calculations. The bus would stop to pick up passengers at a couple of locations along the route, where I could intercept them. I thanked Wes and jumped in my car. Sure enough, I caught the bus as the driver pulled off the highway at the Royal Oak exit, and returned the hat to Allen.

Satisfied that I had done a good deed, but also feeling that it was just part of my job, I assumed that would be the end of this story.

The next day, there was an email waiting for me:

> Hi, I'm that Chinese guy who left my hat in my homestay. My name is Allen and I really wanna thank you for helping me, but I don't know how, so I get Ur email, hope U don't mind. And I even wrote a diary about U.

Allen relayed his recollection of the events of that morning, including the moment when I appeared on the bus with his hat:

> Suddenly the bus stopped on the road, and my benefactor appeared, she brought my hat and came to me, at that moment she seem like a angel! and I dumbfounded, so I sat there and said "thank you," she answered "you are welcome!" and gone. after a few minutes, I felt very guiltily, I have no idea what's going on at that time ... it's very rudely. I really want to do something for that lady... but I don't know how...

So began an email exchange with Allen that lasted more than four years. We are still in touch on Facebook, over a decade later.

Allen hadn't known what to expect when he came to Victoria. He was "very curious and a little bit scared" about getting along with the family and speaking English. In hindsight, he thinks his low expectations contributed to the great outcome. "When we are hungry, the food tastes more delicious; the same notion applies to this situation," Allen said. "The kindness and hospitality of my host family literally blew me away."

Nonetheless, when I asked him what his best experience in homestay was, he wrote, "That whole hat thing, which definitely is a once-in-a-lifetime experience. I'm putting my foot down to say this is the most special thing that happened to me." He could remember all the details of that day when I asked him about it, years later. He had bought the hat as a souvenir in Victoria, but had given up hope of seeing it again as the bus pulled away. He wrote:

> The moment you handed my cap to me, to be honest, I was shocked and absolutely had no idea how to act. Since it happened really fast, I thought about it over and over again after you were gone... No dramatic words, YOU and what you've done are the main reason why I love Canada so much. My dear homestay family and you were involved in this. There's no words for me to express how grateful I am.

I learned two lessons from my experience with Allen. First, don't underestimate the impact you can have on someone in the smallest of gestures. Second, a goodbye doesn't have to be forever. Homestay placements must come to an end, but the relationship doesn't have to.

Surprise! You Make a Difference

Indeed, I've heard again and again that many hosts don't realize the full impact of their hospitality until their student is about to leave—or long after their departure.

Host Laurie says, "I think they appreciate [us] more, and what they learned, after they're gone. Like your kids going off to university, they say, 'You know what I really miss?' Or, 'Remember when you told us how to do such and such a thing, well I do it all the time now.' That brings me a lot of pleasure."

Likewise, Kenda says the thing she values most about her "work" as a host is when she gets a "random email" from a student they've hosted, saying how much they miss her and Canada and the family—especially when it's out of the blue. She recalls one student from Brazil who spoke no English and attended the local high school. "I felt so bad for her. She was the only international student at her school. She was always smiling; she just wouldn't speak. I remember the day she left, she broke down and started to cry and gave me a big hug and kiss and said, 'I'm going to miss you.' I was so surprised. Then she sent an email and said she missed the family."

Liz and André have a story about another high school student who stayed with them—Aaron, a fifteen-year-old from Germany. "He was an arrogant little shit when he got to our house," Liz says. "He was terrible. Any time you said anything to him, he would say, 'NOOOOO.'" When Liz imitates Aaron's voice, her tone drops to a low growl. Liz and André couldn't tolerate this for long. About three weeks after Aaron's arrival, André had had enough. He was in the kitchen, listening to Aaron go off about something in his growling, contradictory way. He slammed a pot down and said, "Do you ever get tired of your voice? Because I sure as shit do."

"I think that broke his veneer," Liz says. "And then we started to seep in." He ended up staying with their family for eleven months—one month longer than a typical high school year. The extra month allowed him to wait for his parents to take him on a mini-holiday in Canada. They were gone for several days, visiting Niagara Falls, Toronto, and Montreal. When they came back, his parents had a brief visit with Liz and André. "His mother came up and hugged me," Liz says. "She said, 'You gave me back a new son. He is so polite.' And I thought, that's probably the nicest thing anyone's ever said to me. So, yeah, I'm pretty proud of that."

When a Departure Is Not a Goodbye

Sometimes, the gifts of hosting arrive in unexpected ways, long after departure. The winter of 2014 was arduous for Laurie. She had taken a break from hosting to travel with her husband, Shawn. With their five children all grown up and living their own lives, Laurie felt lonely without a student around. Then, over the Christmas holidays, her father passed away.

Ji-Hun, a Korean student, was visiting at the time. It had been four years since he had lived with Laurie and Shawn; after high school he went to university in Philadelphia to study media communications, but he still came back to see them regularly. He was scheduled to leave on the day of Laurie's father's wake. Laurie said her goodbyes to Ji-Hun before her son drove him to the train station.

Unbeknownst to Laurie, Ji-Hun had second thoughts about leaving. When he arrived at the wake, she was surprised and moved to tears. Not only was he dressed in a suit, but he had also brought a gift for Laurie's father, who had been a Korean War veteran. When the time was right, Ji-Hun stepped up to the open casket and fastened a Korean War memorial pin to Laurie's father's lapel. All evening, he introduced himself as the family's Korean brother.

"For him to want to be a part of that meant a lot," Laurie says. "It touched me to think I did something that meant he wanted to come back and please us."

The families who started hosting before the advent of social media told me how wonderful technology has been, allowing them to keep in touch in ways they never could before. Chris—the host from Ottawa who enjoys teaching her students—still talks to Jessica, from Colombia, who stayed with them over ten years ago. "Yesterday, she sent an email with pictures of her wedding," Chris says. "In the email, she said, 'You were such a special person to me.'" Kenda, from Ontario, says, "We can watch them growing up and having their babies. It's a great world that we have this technology and we never lose them."

When I asked Kenda for an example of a student they had kept in touch with for that long, she told me about Andreas. He arrived for grade ten when he was about fifteen years old. Kenda had a rule in her house that her students couldn't date, but this boy developed a crush on a Canadian girl in school. They fell in love. Andreas returned to Germany at the end of that year, but he kept in touch with his girlfriend. She visited him abroad and he returned as often as he could. After graduating from high school, Andreas immigrated to Canada. Kenda helped him get a job and her husband taught him about farming. He ended up marrying his young crush; of course, Kenda and her husband were invited to the wedding. After Andreas' wife gave birth to twins, his parents bought a house up the road and soon became friends with Kenda's in-laws. Andreas is now twenty-nine years old and is expecting his third child.

In 2019, one of Liz's students from Mexico was about to graduate from university. She invited Liz and André to attend the celebration in Chihuahua. Many hosts shared similar anecdotes with me—being invited to attend graduations, weddings, and other celebrations—but not all hosts are able to accept such generous invitations. Liz and André made the trip to Mexico for eight days. One night, they went out for dinner with the student who was graduating... and *ten* other students whom they had hosted over the years. Most of the students were from the same region, some in the city of Chihuahua and others from Camargo, about two hours' drive. Some of these students knew each other through their school and the student travel agency, so it wasn't just a reunion for Liz and André. "We had a wonderful dinner," Liz says. "They didn't know before dinner, but [at the end of the meal] we treated them all. Then they took us out and got us drunk," she says with a laugh.

These lasting bonds are enjoyed not only by the host parents. Liz shared a story about another Mexican student, Alan, who developed a deep connection with her son, Ben. Alan arrived in August 2003, right before a massive blackout that began in Ohio and spread to fifty-five million residents throughout parts of the Northeastern and Midwestern United States and most of Ontario. The Ontario premier declared a state of emergency on the night of the blackout. Residents were asked to reduce their power consumption for several days as power was gradually restored to full levels.

In response to this unprecedented event, Alan (age seventeen) and Ben (age fifteen) camped out in the family's tent trailer for a week. "We used the power from the tent trailer," Liz explains. "They took the TV out there and hung out together." Alan wasn't in Canada for long—he had already graduated from high school and came to study English before going to university. Nevertheless, something clicked between the two boys. Alan had never skated a day in his life, but Ben got him into hockey. When it was time for Alan to leave, in addition to all the usual souvenirs, he also packed a hockey bag with ice skates, hockey sticks, and an Ottawa Senators jersey.

It's been twenty years—they're both married with children now—and they still talk online. "It was wild," Liz says. "They gravitated to each other. They were similar souls. It was a very tearful goodbye. Oh, there were lots of tearful goodbyes, let me tell you."

Don't underestimate the impact you can have on someone in the smallest of gestures.

———————

"It Was Part of Making Me Who I Am Today"

It was an unlikely pairing from the start: Why would anyone expect a fifteen-year-old boy from Brazil and a sixty-two-year-old man from Saint Vincent and the Grenadines to become friends?

Because that's homestay.

When two people find a way to nurture the seed of discovery between them, it will grow into something beautiful.

Alipio was fifteen when he and his mother came up with the idea to study English abroad. He also wanted to learn French and continue to study piano. He grew up in a mid-size city in the state of Sao Paolo, Brazil, and chose Canada for its safe reputation. It was a true adventure for Alipio; nobody in his family had ever done anything like this.

Our team placed Alipio with Jason and his wife, Omega, in Whitby—a small town on the north shore of Lake Ontario, near Toronto—in August 2005. They lived with their thirty-five-year-old daughter, Deirdre, and her ten-year-old son, Chevaun.

Jason worked with CHN at the time, helping us to develop the program in his community. My dad describes Jason as "the salt of the earth, the kind of person you meet and instantly feel comfortable around... He's very generous. He has an infectious sense of humour. You can't help smiling around him. There's a lightness about him, despite how much he's seen in his life."

On his first morning in Jason and Omega's home, Alipio walked into the kitchen and asked what he could do to help. Jason says that was the beginning of everything. The conversation started there, and didn't stop.

Alipio enjoyed Jason's stories of growing up in Saint Vincent and the Grenadines, immigrating to Canada in 1968, and settling down in Winnipeg; his work with the United Way, the

Citizenship Council of Manitoba, and various refugee community councils; and his experiences as a school principal, eventually moving to Ontario. "I'm not someone who goes out very often," Alipio says. "I like to talk. I think that was part of the reason we got along so well."

Alipio's English wasn't great, but Jason and Omega were patient teachers, pointing out words in the dictionary when Alipio didn't understand. They watched TV together, which also helped his English. When Hurricane Katrina struck, Alipio recalls watching it on the news and talking about it with Jason and Omega.

Jason agrees that he established a connection with Alipio immediately, that they bonded over their shared interests and love of deep conversation. "Alipio has many skills," Jason says. "He is such an outgoing person and highly intelligent... He knows about almost anything you want to talk about. I had just retired as a teacher, so I'm aware of kids, and he struck me as one of those people with many talents." He says Alipio was always seeking, inquiring. It wasn't just about relaying information, though. It was about enjoying the connection.

Alipio's time with Jason and Omega was a "true family experience." With Deirdre and Chevaun around, he was never alone, describing their home as "pleasant and lovely."

As much as he cherished being with them, the music program at his high school did not offer the opportunities Alipio was looking for. He was focused and ambitious. He researched his options and spoke to the guidance counsellor. Less than a month after he landed in Whitby, Alipio decided to move to Ottawa, where there was a better music program for gifted students. "What impressed me was how responsible [he was]," Jason says. "He was determined to achieve what [he] set out to do. That's remarkable for a fifteen-year-old."

Alipio stayed with another homestay family in Ottawa and met many other people in Canada, but Jason and Omega are the ones he's kept in touch with. When Alipio was ready to graduate from high school, his parents invited Jason's whole family to Brazil for the celebration. Jason couldn't go, but his daughter Deidre was able to get away from work long enough to make the trip. While Alipio's family hosted her, she got to meet his cousins and grandparents. Deidre accompanied him to visit the southern part of Brazil and one of the seven wonders of the world at Iguazu Falls.

One of Alipio's biggest regrets is not seeing Jason since his time in homestay. Alipio will be moving to Texas next year and hopes they will be able to arrange an in-person reunion. But the lack of face-to-face time hasn't interfered with their relationship.

"It was constant," Jason says. "It was marvellous. He was... is like a son to us."

Alipio agrees. "What I keep most from that experience is the personal connections I established," he says. "This is what really made the difference in the end, to become who I am."

I've seen dozens of inspiring examples of tight bonds being formed in short order like this. But whenever it happens, it still surprises me—and it reminds me why we do this work.

Putting It All Together

This story is one of my dad's favourites, because it represents the power of homestay to bring people from all ages, walks of life, and nationalities together. Of course, I wanted to speak to them myself, so I welcomed Jason's suggestion to bring the three of us together on a Zoom call. It had been seventeen years since Alipio's time in Canada.

When Jason, now seventy-nine, finally gets the video to work, all we can see is the top half of his face. Behind him, I have a clear view of the side of the refrigerator covered in magnets and papers along with most of his kitchen ceiling; he seems oblivious to the angle of the computer camera. He's wearing a pair of trendy metal glasses that frame his warm eyes. When he speaks, his thoughtful expression often gives way to a bright smile, soft chuckle, crinkling eyes.

At thirty-two, Alipio is wearing round wire-frame glasses, a grey dress shirt, and a tidy beard that hugs his jawline. His professional appearance aligns with his chosen career: he ended up studying economics instead of music. His English is impeccable. There's a warmth and gentleness to his face and tone that is both captivating and familiar.

At one point during the call, Deirdre stops by to say hello, waving both hands in an energetic greeting, her face cracking into a wide grin. When she notices how her dad has set up the camera, she fixes it so we can see the rest of Jason's face.

Jason and Alipio take turns swapping compliments and reminiscing. Jason says that Alipio is the only person who has ever identified the secret ingredients in his famous pancakes; Alipio remembers trying a special drink from Saint Vincent and the Grenadines but has forgotten the name. "It's called *mabi*," Jason reminds him. Alipio can't recall if he liked it or not, and Jason admits it's an acquired taste; it's made from the bark of the mabi tree mixed with sugar and spices like aniseed and ginger.

While I listen, I wonder if I'll gather some new wisdom about what makes homestay work. How is it possible that these two men had such a long-lasting connection after spending less than a month together? What can others learn from their example? While there was certainly an element of chemistry—a deep, abiding respect and admiration that was kindled very early in their relationship—there are also broader lessons that connect to the themes I've explored in this book.

First, Jason created a family atmosphere for Alipio. As he said, Alipio was like a son to them. When Alipio says how much he loved being there, Jason responds with an affectionate quip, his eyes twinkling: "He's a spoiled brat and we spoiled him even more."

"As you might have noticed in this short conversation, Jason is a very wise man," Alipio responds, not missing a beat. Jason bursts out laughing, his shoulders shaking as Alipio continues. "He reads people well. He's tolerant and patient in the way he tries to accommodate the differences. I think he's 80 percent of the reason why it was so smooth. I *was* a spoiled child coming from Brazil, and I was in a *hurry*. That's something I would change today. When you are fifteen and you have a few months to do something, you want to do it perfectly. You want to maximize everything. Nowadays you think of five months and it goes like *this—*" He snaps his fingers in the air. "And that's part of what you learn in life, no? How to let things go, and not try to optimize everything. So I think I was in that state of mind and Jason was understanding. I was lucky."

Jason agrees. He says the host family has the responsibility to create an atmosphere in which the student feels welcome. If you do that, Jason says, "the student will make the adjustments, no matter what it is. Sometimes slowly, but they will."

The kinds of adjustments Alipio made were familiar, echoing many of the stories I've heard from other students over the years. "I had to be on my own, in a different environment," he says. "I had to learn how to navigate that environment and the ways of new people. This is something that makes you a bit more aware of yourself and your place in the world."

In these two sentences, Alipio describes two themes of this book: to be your best in homestay, I've encouraged you to learn about culture and learn about yourself.

He also captures the importance of embracing the inevitability of failure and working through it, as part of being human and growing up. "You don't really know what you're going to learn when you set out to do something," Alipio says. "You have to be open minded about experiences you're going to face and try to live honestly and openly."

"What was homestay like for you, reflecting back on it now as an adult?" I ask.

"It was certainly a transformative experience for me," Alipio says. "I was fifteen. Parts of my personality were still shaping up. There are things we remember about our childhood or adolescence that embarrass us today—things we thought, or behaviours, or obsessions we had—like music, or my complaints... today I would say 'Oh, what a stupid child.' But... we're not born knowing things. We learn. Our personality is a product of a lot of experiences, so I think it was part of making me who I am today... I still think about that experience a lot. Now I'm an adult, that was part of my education. I'm already someone else, and I'm very thankful for everything that happened to me."

Finally, Alipio captures Jason's ability to follow the principles of difficult conversations I discussed in chapter 10, one of the many ways Jason created the conditions for this beautiful relationship. "Jason is thoughtful," Alipio says. "He doesn't say things randomly. That makes you feel safe. You see that he's listening, and he's not judging. He's trying to understand and see the good angle of everything, and teach you a lesson in a loving way. I can't remember any other person that has these qualities as clearly as he does... These are personality traits I value and I would like to have myself."

Jason deflects this praise, saying, "Alipio is collecting a variety of experiences to guide him as he goes along. His experience with us is just a small snippet of those he's gathered."

Strictly speaking, Jason is right. A month in homestay is just a fragment of time, a slice of life that could easily be forgotten. But in the hands of a skilled host father like Jason and an engaged guest like Alipio, that fragment became so much more. With the right conditions, Jason and Alipio's snippet of time together grew its own roots, flourishing into something strong. Something that has lasted. Something beautiful.

Something like the sound of the guqin in your living room; the taste of a new dish; the sight of a moose by the side of the road. The comforting touch when you're hit with a wave of grief. The mistakes, messy conversations, and second chances.

The love.

My wish, my hope for you and your family, is that you might have the chance to find this, too.

Acknowledgements

BRINGING A BOOK into the world is often likened to birthing a baby—a vulnerable, fragile process that needs nurturing. Some people even celebrate publication anniversaries as "book birthdays." I understand it, but as a parent and a former midwife, I find the analogy somewhat delicate. Nevertheless, this much is true: writing a book is a laborious act of creation that requires the love and support of more people than you could imagine, at every stage of the process—and long after it's "done"—because it's never really done.

To my real babies, Morgan and Seamus: You are the most beautiful and precious things I have ever made. Thank you for being part of this book, curious about my work at just the right moments, and quiet when I was on a work call. I wrote this book for you and your future; I hope your world is a little better for it.

Andrew and James, thank you for always making me laugh while offering such wise counsel. Humour is a balm for pain, an antidote to the randomness of life, and sometimes the only thing that keeps us going. You set an example for me for what family is and always should be.

I thank all the hosts, students, and experts who agreed to participate in this project. Know that this book is your doing as much as mine. To the hosts: Your devotion to your work as hosts, your willingness to share stories that weren't always easy, and your endless curiosity and love are inspiring. You see through our fear-stricken society to other ways of being. To the students: It takes tremendous courage, humility, and openness to venture abroad. Perspective is everything. Thank you all for leading the way toward deeper cross-cultural understanding; you give me hope. To the experts: Your work matters. Keep going. We're reading and listening and sharing.

Thank you to my CHN family, many of whom are represented in these pages. Your dedication to our mission and vision taught me the power of finding purpose and meaning in work. It was a privilege to serve you, and I continue to be in awe of all that you do every single day.

I started interviewing hosts for this book in 2015, making several stops and starts over the next seven years. It wasn't until I found a community of writers that I was able to finish it. Thank you Gillie Easdon, for showing me what a writing life could be and for all our adventures; Morag Wehrle, for being a creative inspiration and for flying through the MFA beside me; Frances Backhouse, Nancy Pearson, and Noga Yarmar for getting me started on my writing learning journey; my MFA mentor David Hayes, for your generous guidance and encouragement; Benjamin Errett and James Wilson for helping me find my focus in the early days; and Morag Wehrle, Alyson Soko, Emilie Adin, and Kelley Korbin for co-creating the kind of writing group that could last a lifetime (as I hope it will).

Many thanks to my beta readers for your willingness to wrestle with my early drafts and for your thoughtful and essential feedback: John Taplin, Kelley Korbin, Gillie Easdon, Stephanie Berryman, Monika Lindsay, Sheila Brandsema, Davina Bhanabhai, and Mum and Dad. My work is better because of you.

Thank you to my loyal friends and family who cheered me on: Leslie Michaels, Marika Cooper, Jennifer Russel, Michelle Chung, Heather and Mark Henzi, Josh Hammons, Brandon Nelson, Nancy and Brian Waplington, David Waplington, Michelle Chaytors and Charles Creighton, Barry Stuart, Brie Mathers, Caroline Sadlowski, Winz Casagrande, Mélanie Turcotte, and Michel Kahwaji.

Thank you to the wonderful team at Page Two who helped me make this dream come true. Special thanks to Trena White for believing in this project; Adrineh Der-Boghossian and Carmen Ho for being patient guides and advisers; Emily Schultz for your careful and visionary editorial touches; Indu Singh and Alison Strobel for giving the book its final polishes; Tessa Eisenberg for demystifying marketing and even making it fun; and Taysia Louie for the stunning cover design.

To my darling Mum and Dear Old Dad: I hope I have honoured the legacy of what you built together. Intercultural exchange offers a powerful solution to the most pressing challenges of our time; your unwavering belief that we are better together has inspired countless people. You put the heart in homestay, and we are all better for it. Thank you for always believing in me, focusing on what's right, and teaching me what it means to live one's values. I love you.

Jon, my love, my home, my heart: you make everything possible.

Notes

Introduction

p. 1   *Written accounts of the guqin:* "Guqin and Its Music," UNESCO, accessed November 1, 2022, ich.unesco.org/en/RL/guqin-and-its-music-00061.

p. 7   *how to behave in ways that facilitate understanding:* Luciara Nardon, *Working in a Multicultural World: A Guide to Developing Intercultural Competence* (Toronto: University of Toronto Press, 2017), 9.

1: Lock Your Door, Open Your Heart

p. 14   *your perceptions are based on your past experiences:* "Fighting with Your Partner? Use These 4 Phrases," *New York Times*, August 27, 2023, nytimes.com/2023/07/28/well/mind/make-up-fight-relationships.html.

p. 15   *Intelligent failures happen when you are growing:* Amy Edmondson, *Right Kind of Wrong: The Science of Failing Well* (New York: Atria Books, 2023), 201.

p. 17   *Trust is "choosing to risk:* Charles Feltman, *The Thin Book of Trust: An Essential Primer for Building Trust at Work* (Bend, OR: Thin Book Publishing, 2008).

p. 17   *If you wait to see if your student can be trusted:* Richard Fagerlin, "The Big Lie about Trust—5 Reasons Why Trust Is Not Earned," Peak Solutions, May 30, 2015, peaksolutions.com/post/the-big-lie-about-trust---5-reasons-why-trust-is-not-earned.

p. 23   *In Brazil, noise is not an issue:* Samir N.Y. Gerges, "Noise in Large Cities in Brazil," *Journal of the Acoustical Society of America* 115, no. 5 (May 2004), doi.org/10.1121/1.4784437; "The Noisiest Place on Earth," Expat.com, August 7, 2012, expat.com/forum/viewtopic.php?id=184765.

p. 28 *it's important to* normalize discomfort: Brené Brown, *Daring Greatly: How the Courage to Be Vulnerable Transforms the Way We Live, Love, Parent, and Lead* (New York: Gotham Books, 2012), 198.

p. 28 *"When you identify the discomfort:* Seth Godin, *Tribes: We Need You to Lead Us* (New York: Portfolio, 2008).

p. 29 *a fixed mindset and a growth mindset:* Carol S. Dweck, *Mindset: The New Psychology of Success* (New York: Ballantine Books, 2008), 10.

2: Don't Be a Stranger

p. 36 *easier to deal with culture shock and homesickness:* BC Government, *Health and Wellness Guidelines for International Students: Understanding Homesickness and Acculturation Stress*, https://www2.gov.bc.ca/assets/gov/education/administration/kindergarten-to-grade-12/internationaleducation/health-wellness-guidelines-international-students-has.pdf.

p. 44 *cultivating the potent cognitive process we call hope:* Rachel Colla et al., "'A New Hope' for Positive Psychology: A Dynamic Systems Reconceptualization of Hope Theory," *Frontiers in Psychology* 13 (February 2022), doi.org/10.3389/fpsyg.2022.809053.

p. 44 *talking about these issues:* "Talking to Youth about Mental Health," Kelty Mental Health Resource Centre, BC Children's Hospital, accessed June 9, 2024, keltymentalhealth.ca/info/talking-youth-about-mental-health.

p. 45 *Culture is "the way of life of a people:* Oxford Reference online, s.v. "culture," accessed November 25, 2023, oxfordreference.com/display/10.1093/oi/authority.20110901080526139.

p. 45 *how they are supposed to behave:* Luciara Nardon, *Working in a Multicultural World: A Guide to Developing Intercultural Competence* (Toronto: University of Toronto Press, 2017), 5.

p. 45 *other authority figures:* Lionel Laroche and Caroline Yang, *Danger and Opportunity: Bridging Cultural Diversity for Competitive Advantage* (New York: Routledge, 2014), 11.

p. 46 *"not because you studied them:* Steve L. Robbins, *What If? Short Stories to Spark Inclusion & Diversity Dialogue*, 10th anniversary ed. (London: Quercus, 2018), 98.

p. 46 *invisible to you until you encounter difference:* Nardon, *Working in a Multicultural World*, 5.

p. 47 *stress of adapting to their new life is reduced:* BC Government, *Health and Wellness Guidelines for International Students.*

p. 47 *still struggled to understand them:* BC Government, *Health and Wellness Guidelines for International Students.*

3: Love Is a Verb

p. 60 *defines love as "the preoccupying and strong* desire: Barbara L. Fredrickson, "Love: Positivity Resonance as a Fresh, Evidence-Based Perspective on an Age-Old Topic," in *Handbook of Emotions*, 4th ed., edited by Lisa Feldman Barrett, Michael Lewis, and Jeannette M. Haviland-Jones (New York: Guildford Press, 2016).

p. 61 *"What everyone has in common, no matter how they grieve:* David Kessler, *Finding Meaning: The Sixth Stage of Grief* (New York: Scribner, 2020); David Kessler, "Our Experience of Grief Is Unique as a Fingerprint," Literary Hub, November 15, 2019, lithub.com/our-experience-of-grief-is-unique-as-a-fingerprint/.

p. 65 *a sense of home "offers a psychological refuge:* Adrian T. Fisher, Christopher C. Sonn, and Brian J. Bishop, eds., *Psychological Sense of Community: Research Applications, and Implications* (New York: Springer Publishing, 2002), 34, 161–79.

p. 66 *prefer their first language to talk about emotional topics:* Shankar Vedantam, "Decoding Emotions with Batja Mesquita," *Hidden Brain* (podcast), September 12, 2022, hiddenbrain.org/podcast/decoding-emotions/.

4: Creating Safe Spaces

p. 79 *there's no such thing as universal basic emotions:* Batja Mesquita, *Between Us: How Cultures Create Emotions* (New York: W.W. Norton & Company, 2022), 214.

p. 79 *A smile in Japan does not always convey happiness:* "Does a Smile Mean the Same Thing in All Cultures?" Humintell, May 23, 2019, humintell.com/2019/05/the-cultural-significance-of-smiling/.

p. 79 *Holding eye contact in many cultures:* Alicia Raeburn, "11 Places Where Eye-Contact Is Not Recommended (11 Places Where the Locals Are Friendly)," The Travel, updated September 9, 2023, thetravel.com/10-places-where-eye-contact-is-not-recommended-10-places-where-the-locals-are-friendly/.

p. 79 *Nodding means "yes" in some cultures:* "International Business; How the Meanings of Facial Expressions and Gestures Can Vary across Cultures," The Headshot Guy, accessed February 2, 2024, theheadshotguy.co.uk/facial-expressions-and-meanings/.
p. 79 *Winking in Latin America is:* "International Business," The Headshot Guy.
p. 79 *If I pucker my lips:* "International Business," The Headshot Guy.
p. 80 *emotions are "social practices":* Mesquita, *Between Us*, 54.
p. 80 *know their place in the social network:* Mesquita, *Between Us*, 62.
p. 81 *anger can be a justifiable means to an end:* Mesquita, *Between Us*, 136.
p. 81 *anger (ikari) is considered destructive to relational harmony:* Mesquita, *Between Us*, 96.
p. 81 *people can grow their empathy and become kinder:* Jamil Zaki, *The War for Kindness: Building Empathy in a Fractured World* (New York: Crown, 2019), 15.
p. 81 *unpack the meaning behind someone's emotional experience:* Mesquita, *Between Us*, 201.
p. 82 *the word may not even exist in English:* Mesquita, *Between Us*, 139.
p. 90 *the well-being of the group:* "Intercultural Management: What You Need to Know," The Culture Factor Group, accessed November 2, 2022, hofstede-insights.com/models/national-culture/.
p. 90 *allowing a young person to feel seen, heard, and valued:* Brené Brown, *Daring Greatly: How the Courage to Be Vulnerable Transforms the Way We Live, Love, Parent, and Lead* (New York: Gotham Books, 2012), 145.

5: There's No Accounting for Taste

p. 98 *"what you want to cook and eat is an accumulation:* Jennifer 8. Lee, "The Hunt for General Tso," TED talk, July 2008, ted.com/talks/jennifer_8_lee_the_hunt_for_general_tso?subtitle=en.
p. 106 *the bestselling candy bar in the world:* "10 Things You Didn't Know about Snickers," Daily Meal, November 4, 2014, thedailymeal.com/cook/10-things-you-didnt-know-about-snickers/#:~:text=Snickers%20are%20sold%20in%20more,candy%20bar%20in%20the%20world.
p. 106 *"People in the UK really turn their noses up:* Harry Kersh and Joe Avella, "We Compared the Differences between US vs UK Snickers," *Business Insider* (*Food Wars* video series), August 6, 2021,

businessinsider.com/every-difference-between-us-uk-snickers-candy-food-wars-2021-7.

p. 106 *The same is true for Pizza Hut:* Sarah Fielding, "10 Surprising Ways That Fast Food Chains Are Vastly Different around the World," *Business Insider,* January 30, 2018, businessinsider.com/how-fast-food-orders-different-worldwide-2018-1.

p. 106 *half as salty in the UK as in the US:* Fielding, "10 Surprising Ways That Fast Food Chains Are Vastly Different around the World."

p. 106 *Dunkin' Donuts, available in thirty countries:* Fielding, "10 Surprising Ways That Fast Food Chains Are Vastly Different around the World."

6: Let's Not Get Physical

p. 116 *These Western norms stand in stark contrast:* Emily Pearson, "Kiss & Tell: A Couple's Guide to PDA around the World," *Stowaway Magazine,* Brigham Young University, accessed June 9, 2024, stowawaymag.byu.edu/kiss-tell-a-couples-guide-to-pda-around-the-world#:~:text=Heterosexual%20PDA-,Acceptable,explicit%20legal%20or%20cultural%20limitations.

p. 116 *"hugging is generally deemed inappropriate:* "Are Japanese People Affectionate in Private?" The Donut Whole, accessed June 9, 2024, thedonutwhole.com/are-japanese-people-affectionate-in-private/.

p. 121 *National Sexual Violence Resource Center:* For further information, please visit the National Sexual Violence Resource Center at NSVRC.org and explore more ways to learn, get help, and boost sexual violence prevention.

p. 121 *"Consent is about always choosing to respect personal and emotional boundaries:* "Everyday Consent," NSVRC, last modified March 1, 2018, nsvrc.org/sites/default/files/2018-01/everydayconsent_onepager_508.pdf.

p. 122 *In infants, skin-to-skin contact has been shown:* Diane Spatz, "Benefits of Mother–Baby Skin-to-Skin Contact," *The American Journal of Maternal/Child Nursing* 47, no. 3 (May/June 2022): 170, doi.org/10.1097/NMC.0000000000000818.

p. 122 *"Touch is ten times stronger than:* Tiffany Field, *Touch* (Cambridge, MA: MIT Press, 2001), 57.

p. 123 *"In general, NBA basketball teams whose players touch each other:* Dacher Keltner, "Hands On Research: The Science of Touch," *Greater Good Magazine*, University of California, Berkeley, September 29, 2010, greatergood.berkeley.edu/article/item/hands_on_research.

p. 123 *"even casual touch may play a more important role:* A. Heatley Tejada, R.I.M. Dunbar, and M. Montero, "Physical Contact and Loneliness: Being Touched Reduces Perceptions of Loneliness," *Adaptive Human Behavior Physiology* 6 (May 26, 2020): 292–306, doi.org/10.1007/s40750-020-00138-0.

p. 123 *refers to as "touch hunger":* Quoted in Alberto Gallace and Charles Spence, "The Science of Interpersonal Touch: An Overview," *Neuroscience & Biobehavioral Reviews* 34, no. 2, (February 2010): 246–59, doi.org/10.1016/j.neubiorev.2008.10.004.

7: This Is Life

p. 126 *The two younger boys shared a bathroom:* A minor digression on residential terminology: In Canada and the US, most homes have one room for the toilet, sink, shower and/or bathtub, and storage cabinets (often called vanities). This room is known as the bathroom, washroom, or restroom; occasionally people refer to it as the ladies' room or the men's room. A "half bath" is a term used in real estate listings to refer to a room with just a sink and toilet; these are usually in a common area of the home and may be referred to as the "powder room" in polite company. Some homes have a separate cubicle for the toilet, but this is unusual. In Australia, it's much more common for the family facilities to separate the toilet room from the bathroom. In these homes, the toilet cubicle is called the toilet or the loo; whereas the room holding the sink, tub/shower, and vanity is known as a bathroom. Ensuite bathrooms (attached to a bedroom) tend to be more like North American bathrooms with all the fixtures. Bidets are not as common in the US, Canada, and Australia, and tend to be found in higher-end bathrooms.

p. 130 *adequate sewage systems for flushing toilet paper:* "Where You Can & Can't Flush Toilet Paper around the World," Brilliant Maps, last updated March 3, 2023, brilliantmaps.com/flush-toilet-paper/.

p. 131 *frequency and length of showers:* "Bathing Habits of the World," Soakology, accessed July 15, 2023, soakology.co.uk/blog/bathing-habits-of-the-world/.

p. 131 *greatest number of showers per week:* "Bathing Habits of the World," Soakology.

p. 134 *Wet rooms originated in Japan:* Alyssa Sellors, "Seven Japanese Bathroom Trends That Americans Should Adopt," Blogcritics, July 27, 2014, blogcritics.org/seven-japanese-bathroom-trends-that-americans-should-adopt/.

p. 137 *comes down to self-talk:* Brené Brown, *Daring Greatly: How the Courage to Be Vulnerable Transforms the Way We Live, Love, Parent, and Lead* (New York: Gotham Books, 2012), 71.

p. 137 *highly correlated with negative behaviours:* Brown, *Daring Greatly*, 72.

8: That's Not What I Meant

p. 148 *best response for hosts when dealing with language barriers:* Lionel Laroche and Caroline Yang, *Danger and Opportunity: Bridging Cultural Diversity for Competitive Advantage* (New York: Routledge, 2014), 52.

p. 148 *through a cultural lens:* Laroche and Yang, *Danger and Opportunity*, 45.

p. 149 *described her reaction after a dinner party:* Batja Mesquita, *Between Us: How Cultures Create Emotions* (New York: W.W. Norton & Company, 2022), 3.

p. 150 *"Everyone interprets the behaviour:* Laroche and Yang, *Danger and Opportunity*, 46.

p. 150 *"In Chinese, there are four kinds of yes:* Laroche and Yang, *Danger and Opportunity*, 63.

p. 151 *talk to students about the "platinum" rule:* Laroche and Yang, *Danger and Opportunity*, 52.

p. 152 *Cross-Cultural Feedback Continuum [graphic]:* Laroche and Yang, *Danger and Opportunity*, 61.

p. 153 *King Abdullah Scholarship Program (KASP):* "Updated Saudi Scholarship Programme Will Send 70,000 Students Abroad by 2030," ICEF Monitor, May 3, 2022, monitor.icef.com/2022/05/updated-saudi-scholarship-programme-will-send-70000-students-abroad-by-2030/.

p. 153 *gender roles are highly patriarchal in Saudi culture:* Nina Evason, "Saudi Arabian Culture," Cultural Atlas, January 1, 2022, culturalatlas.sbs.com.au/saudi-arabian-culture/saudi-arabian-culture-family.

p. 156 *"Americans and Canadians have about fifteen different ways:* Laroche and Yang, *Danger and Opportunity*, 67.

p. 156 *the French or Spanish translation:* Laroche and Yang, *Danger and Opportunity*, 68.

p. 157 *Laroche recommends four steps to move forward:* Laroche and Yang, *Danger and Opportunity*, 54.

p. 160 *"When asked how they would rate themselves as a listener:* Oscar Trimboli, *How to Listen: Discover the Hidden Key to Better Communication* (Vancouver: Page Two, 2022), 20.

p. 161 *When empathy is lacking from a conversation:* Trimboli, *How to Listen*, 66.

p. 161 *Such deep attention will make your conversations:* Trimboli, *How to Listen*, 87.

p. 162 *foster respect in your relationship:* Trimboli, *How to Listen*, 202.

p. 163 *"When you are in the presence of a great listener:* Trimboli, *How to Listen*, 26.

9: Being Good-ish

p. 169 *These shortcuts lead to errors in:* Mahzarin R. Banaji and Anthony G. Greenwald, *Blindspot: Hidden Biases of Good People* (New York: Delacorte Press, 2013), 4.

p. 169 *the more familiar event must be more common:* Banaji and Greenwald, *Blindspot*, 11.

p. 170 *notice information that supports an existing hypothesis:* Dolly Chugh, *The Person You Mean to Be: How Good People Fight Bias* (New York: HarperCollins, 2018), 96.

p. 170 *"We don't breathe it because we like it":* "Interview with Beverly Daniel Tatum (2002)," edited transcript for the PBS documentary series RACE—*The Power of an Illusion* by California Newsreel, racepowerofanillusion.org/interviews/interview-beverly-daniel-tatum-2002.

p. 170 *Our digital world spreads this smog of stereotypes:* Seth Godin, *We Are All Weird: The Rise of Tribes and the End of Normal* (New York: Penguin Random House, 2011), 6.

p. 172 *unconscious bias can shift:* Chugh, *The Person You Mean to Be,* 50.
p. 172 *homogenous networks composed exclusively of people sharing their own race:* Chugh, *The Person You Mean to Be,* 102; Daniel Cox, Juhem Navarro-Rivera, and Robert P. Jones, "Race, Religion, and Political Affiliation of Americans' Core Social Networks," PRRI, August 3, 2016, prri.org/research/poll-race-religion-politics-americans-social-networks/.
p. 172 *drawn to people who share our implicit bias:* Drew S. Jacoby-Senghor, Stacey Sinclair, and Colin Tucker Smith, "When Bias Binds: Effect of Implicit Outgroup Bias on Ingroup Affiliation," *Journal of Personality and Social Psychology* 109, no. 3 (2015): 415–33, doi.org/10.1037/a0039513.
p. 173 *a set of moral traits which help us conceptualize who we are:* Karl Aquino and Americus Reed II, "The Self-Importance of Moral Identity," *Journal of Personality and Social Psychology* 83, no. 6 (2002): 1423–40, doi.org/10.1037/0022-3514.83.6.1423.
p. 174 *When one's moral identity is challenged:* Mark D. Alicke and Constantine Sedikides, "Self-Enhancement and Self-Protection: What They Are and What They Do," *European Review of Social Psychology* 20, no. 1 (2009): 1–48, doi.org/10.1080/10463280802613866.
p. 174 *people morally disengage:* Dolly Chugh et al., "Withstanding Moral Disengagement: Attachment Security as an Ethical Intervention," *Journal of Experimental Social Psychology* 51 (March 2014): 88–93, doi.org/10.1016/j.jesp.2013.11.005.
p. 174 *they don't treat others well:* Sally S. Dickerson, Tara L. Gruenewald, and Margaret E. Kemeny, "When the Social Self Is Threatened: Shame, Physiology, and Health," *Journal of Personality* 72, no. 6 (October 2004): 1191–216, doi.org/10.1111/j.1467-6494.2004.00295.x; Jeffery A. Lepine, Nathan P. Podsakoff, and Marcie A. Lepine, "A Meta-Analytic Test of the Challenge Stressor-Hindrance Stressor Framework: An Explanation for Inconsistent Relationships among Stressors and Performance," *Academy of Management Journal* 48, no. 5 (October 2005): 764–75, doi.org/10.5465/amj.2005.18803921.
p. 175 *"Our bodies are built to fight off bacteria and our minds:* Chugh, *The Person You Mean to Be,* 8.

p. 175 *participants were willing to pay for it:* William B. Swann Jr., "Self-Verification: Bringing Social Reality Into Harmony with the Self," in *Psychological Perspectives on the Self: Volume 2*, edited by Jerry Suls and Anthony Greenwald (Hillsdale, NJ: Lawrence Erlbaum, 1983), 33–66.

p. 175 *acknowledgements of their good intentions:* Chugh, *The Person You Mean to Be*, 5.

p. 175 *the mass shooting at a mosque:* Euan McKirdy, Paula Newton, and Merieme Arif, "6 Dead in Quebec Mosque Shooting," CNN, updated January 30, 2017, edition.cnn.com/2017/01/29/americas/quebec-mosque-shooting/index.html.

p. 175 *mob that attacked LGBTQ+ activists:* Martin Farrer and Christopher Knaus, "Two Arrested as Mob Sets Upon Protesters outside Mark Latham Event in Sydney," *The Guardian*, March 21, 2023, theguardian.com/australia-news/2023/mar/21/two-arrested-after-mob-charges-rights-activists-outside-mark-latham-event-in-sydney.

p. 177 *"Being a good person means trying to be better:* Chugh, *The Person You Mean to Be*, 8.

p. 177 *Chugh describes this process of self-reflection:* Chugh, *The Person You Mean to Be*, 132.

p. 179 *But even a positive stereotype:* Lionel Laroche and Caroline Yang, *Danger and Opportunity: Bridging Cultural Diversity for Competitive Advantage* (New York: Routledge, 2014), 14.

p. 181 *In one study, participants who played a game:* Chugh, *The Person You Mean to Be*, 157.

p. 182 *even when people react defensively:* Chugh, *The Person You Mean to Be*, 206; Alexander M. Czopp, Margo J. Monteith, and Aimee Y. Mark, "Standing Up for a Change: Reducing Bias through Interpersonal Confrontation," *Journal of Personality and Social Psychology* 90, no. 5 (2006): 784–803, doi.org/10.1037/0022-3514.90.5.784; Alexander M. Czopp and Margo J. Monteith, "Confronting Prejudice (Literally): Reactions to Confrontations of Racial and Gender Bias," *Personality and Social Psychology Bulletin* 29, no. 4 (2003): 532–44, doi.org/10.1177/0146167202250923.

p. 186 *may have been enough to change his behaviour:* Chugh, *The Person You Mean to Be*, 207; Christian S. Crandall, Amy Eshleman, and Laurie O'Brien, "Social Norms and the Expression and Suppression of Prejudice: The Struggle for Internalization," *Journal of Personality and Social Psychology* 82, no. 3 (2002): 359-78, doi.org/10.1037//0022-3514.82.3.359.

p. 187 *bullying was reduced by 30 percent when the cool kids spoke out against it:* Fletcher A. Blanchard et al., "Condemning and Condoning Racism: A Social Context Approach to Interracial Settings," *Journal of Applied Psychology* 79, no. 6 (1994): 993-97, doi.org/10.1037/0021-9010.79.6.993.

p. 187 *"Advocacy is recognizing the power of one's own voice:* Neha Vyas, "How to Act Like an Advocate, Not Like a Savior," INvolve, May 23, 2022, involvepeople.org/advocacy-vs-saviorism/.

p. 187 *"One approach is to turn to the target:* Chugh, *The Person You Mean to Be,* 214.

p. 189 *"I see it differently:* Chugh, *The Person You Mean to Be,* 210.

p. 191 *"growing and grappling":* Chugh, *The Person You Mean to Be,* xxvii.

10: When It's Harder Than You Expected

p. 196 *There are a few techniques to make this assessment:* Lionel Laroche and Caroline Yang, *Danger and Opportunity: Bridging Cultural Diversity for Competitive Advantage* (New York: Routledge, 2014), 12.

p. 199 *less about lack of foresight and more about rewards:* Kim Mills, "Understanding the Teenage Brain, with Eva Telzer," *Speaking of Psychology* (podcast), episode 203, American Psychological Association, August 24, 2022, apa.org/news/podcasts/speaking-of-psychology/teenage-brain.

p. 200 *help out their family on a weekly basis:* Eva H. Telzer et al., "Ventral Striatum Activation to Prosocial Rewards Predicts Longitudinal Declines in Adolescent Risk Taking," *Developmental Cognitive Neuroscience* 3 (January 2013): 45-52, doi.org/10.1016/j.dcn.2012.08.004.

p. 200 *teenagers from Mexico spend twice as much time helping their family:* Eva H. Telzer and Andrew J. Fuligni, "Daily Family Assistance and the Psychological Well-Being of Adolescents from Latin American, Asian, and European Backgrounds," *Developmental Psychology* 45, no. 4 (2009), 1177-89, doi.org/10.1037/a0014728.

p. 201 *in China, the high school years:* Yang Qu et al., "Conceptions of Adolescence: Implications for Differences in Engagement in School over Early Adolescence in the United States and China," *Journal of Youth and Adolescence* 45 (2016): 1512–26, doi.org/10.1007/s10964-016-0492-4.

p. 201 *These stereotypes and views of adolescents:* Mills, "Understanding the Teenage Brain, with Eva Telzer."

p. 202 *the only way to restore harmony is to address the issue:* Michelle L. Buck, "Engaging in Conversations and Reframing Conflict," *The Hill*, November 12, 2020, thehill.com/opinion/civil-rights/525701-engaging-in-conversations-and-reframing-conflict/; learn more about Dr. Buck and her research at kellogg.northwestern.edu/faculty/directory/buck_michelle_l.aspx#biography.

p. 202 *It allows the chance to learn more about each other:* Brené Brown, *Braving the Wilderness: The Quest for True Belonging and the Courage to Stand Alone* (London, UK: Vermilion, 2017), 79.

p. 204 *Intercultural Conflict Style Inventory (ICS):* "Resolving Conflict across Cultural Boundaries Using the Intercultural Conflict Style Inventory (ICS)," ICS, accessed June 14, 2024, icsinventory.com.

p. 204 *The ICS is a four-quadrant model:* Mitchell R. Hammer, *Intercultural Conflict Style Inventory: Assessing Communication and Conflict Resolution Styles across Cultures* (facilitator's manual) (Olney, MD: ICS Inventory, 2016), 10.

p. 204 *Intercultural Conflict Style Model* [graphic]: Hammer, *Intercultural Conflict Style Inventory*, 15.

p. 205 *Cultures that prefer Direct communication:* Hammer, *Intercultural Conflict Style Inventory*, 11.

p. 206 *it may change depending on the context:* Hammer, *Intercultural Conflict Style Inventory*, 12.

p. 206 *Speaking generally, then:* Mitchell R. Hammer, "Solving Problems and Resolving Conflict Using the Intercultural Conflict Style Model and Inventory," in *Contemporary Leadership and Intercultural Competence: Exploring the Cross-Cultural Dynamics within Organizations*, edited by Michael A. Moodian (Los Angeles: SAGE Publications, 2009), 226–27.

p. 207 *creating a "learning conversation":* Douglas Stone, Bruce Patton, and Sheila Heen, *Difficult Conversations: How to Discuss What Matters Most*, 3rd ed. (New York: Penguin, 2023), 4.

p. 207 *two ground rules for dialogue:* Amanda Ripley, *High Conflict: Why We Get Trapped and How We Get Out* (New York: Simon & Schuster, 2021), 259.

p. 207 *"sending a solution message":* Thomas Gordon, *Parent Effectiveness Training: The Proven Program for Raising Responsible Children* (New York: Harmony Books, 2000), 121.

p. 208 *sends a "put-down message":* Gordon, *Parent Effectiveness Training,* 120.

p. 209 *recommends asking yourself several questions:* Ripley, *High Conflict,* 296.

p. 209 *feelings are at the heart of the matter:* Brené Brown, "Brené Brown on How to Reckon with Emotion and Change Your Narrative," *O, The Oprah Magazine* (September 2015), accessed on September 20, 2023, on Oprah.com, oprah.com/omagazine/brene-brown-rising-strong-excerpt.

p. 210 *make up stories about the other person:* Brown, "Brené Brown on How to Reckon with Emotion and Change Your Narrative."

p. 210 *Considering these different viewpoints:* Susan Scott, *Fierce Conversations: Achieving Success at Work & in Life, One Conversation at a Time* (New York: Berkley Books, 2011), 22.

p. 212 *"Think like a mediator":* Stone, Patton, and Heen, *Difficult Conversations,* 180.

p. 212 *necessary for developing a sense of social responsibility:* Jesper Juul, *Your Competent Child: Toward New Basic Values for the Family* (New York: Farrar, Straus & Giroux, 1995), 150.

p. 212 *"seek first to understand:* Stephen R. Covey, *The 7 Habits of Highly Effective People* (New York: Fireside, 1990), 237.

p. 213 *"Can you say more about how you see things?":* Stone, Patton, and Heen, *Difficult Conversations,* 212.

p. 213 *playing twenty questions:* Covey, *The 7 Habits of Highly Effective People,* 245.

p. 213 *he also asks if he got it right:* Ripley, *High Conflict,* 43.

p. 214 *When you consider your contribution:* Stone, Patton, and Heen, *Difficult Conversations,* 92.

p. 214 *several other ways people contribute to conflict:* Gabrielle Hartley, *The Secret to Getting Along (and Why It's Easier Than You Think): 3 Steps to Life-Changing Conflict Resolution* (Naperville, IL: Sourcebooks, 2023), 18–25.

p. 214 *contribute to conflict through habitual thought patterns and behaviours:* Hartley, *The Secret to Getting Along*, 33, referenced from Benjamin Gardner and Amanda L. Rebar, "Habit Formation and Behavior Change," *Oxford Research Encyclopedia of Psychology*, April 26, 2019, doi.org/10.1093/acrefore/9780190236557.013.129.

p. 214 *"When people do feel heard:* Ripley, *High Conflict*, 43.

p. 216 *you can't assume you understand their emotions:* Batja Mesquita, *Between Us: How Cultures Create Emotions* (New York: W.W. Norton & Company, 2022), 201.

p. 216 *need to ask what the situation means to them:* Mesquita, *Between Us*, 201.

p. 216 *"Is this the 'right' emotion to have:* Mesquita, *Between Us*, 202.

p. 217 *How We Feel app:* This tool is available at howwefeel.org.

p. 217 *Mood Meter app:* This tool is available at moodmeterapp.com.

p. 217 *"expressing feelings maintains a warmth of contact:* Juul, *Your Competent Child*, 208.

p. 218 *If you are still entrenched:* Stone, Patton, and Heen, *Difficult Conversations*, 256.

p. 218 *more likely to change if they feel free* not *to:* Adam Grant, *Think Again: The Power of Knowing What You Don't Know* (New York: Viking, 2021), 107.

p. 219 *If you find this "magic ratio" missing:* Ripley, *High Conflict*, 200, referenced from John Gottman with Nan Silver, *Why Marriages Succeed or Fail ... And How You Can Make Yours Last* (New York: Simon & Schuster, 1994).

11: We're Not Perfect

p. 225 *The "good" kind:* Amy Edmondson, *Right Kind of Wrong: The Science of Failing Well* (New York: Atria Books, 2023), 19.

p. 225 *what Edmondson calls "basic failures":* Edmondson, *Right Kind of Wrong*, 88.

p. 226 *basic failures offer people a chance to:* Edmondson, *Right Kind of Wrong*, 89.

p. 226 *Edmondson places them in a different category:* Edmondson, *Right Kind of Wrong*, 92.

p. 227 *notice mistakes and failures more readily than successes:* Edmondson, *Right Kind of Wrong*, 27.

p. 227 *why failing well is so hard:* Edmondson, *Right Kind of Wrong*, 25.

p. 228 *Punishing people for failure:* Edmondson, *Right Kind of Wrong*, 91.

p. 230 *"Learning happens best when:* Edmondson, *Right Kind of Wrong*, 40.
p. 232 *These physiological and emotional fears:* Jancee Dunn, "Want to Thrive? First, Learn to Fail," *New York Times*, September 15, 2023, nytimes.com/2023/09/15/well/mind/failure-mistakes-advice.html.
p. 232 *physical pain and intense experiences of social rejection:* Ethan Kross et al., "Social Rejection Shares Somatosensory Representations with Physical Pain," *Proceedings of the National Academy of Sciences* 108, no. 15 (March 2011): 6270–75, doi.org/10.1073/pnas.1102693108.
p. 232 *rather than admit you're at fault:* Edmondson, *Right Kind of Wrong*, 105.
p. 233 *one of three general strategies to deal with feelings of shame:* Jessie Sholl, "How to Overcome Shame," *Experience Life*, June 7, 2019, experiencelife.lifetime.life/article/shutting-shame-down/#:~:text=Hartling%2C%20PhD%2C%20director%20of%20Human, and%20keeping%20secrets%3B%20moving%20toward.
p. 235 *can get more of what they want from conversations:* Gabrielle Hartley, *The Secret to Getting Along (and Why It's Easier Than You Think): 3 Steps to Life-Changing Conflict Resolution* (Naperville, IL: Sourcebooks, 2023), xxv.
p. 235 *Brené Brown's seven elements of trust:* Brené Brown, *Rising Strong: How the Ability to Reset Transforms the Way We Live, Love, Parent, and Lead* (New York: Spiegel & Grau, 2015), 199.
p. 237 *"trust and mistakes can coexist":* Brown, *Rising Strong*, 201.
p. 237 *the power of apologies to mend relationships:* Readers who are interested in learning more about how to apologize well when they are in the wrong are encouraged to read Harriet Lerner's book, particularly chapters 2, 3, and 4: Harriet Lerner, *Why Won't You Apologize? Healing Big Betrayals and Everyday Hurts* (New York: Gallery Books, 2017).
p. 237 *a study comparing American, Chinese, and Korean cultures:* Xiaowen Guan, Hee Sun Park, and Hye Eun Lee, "Cross-Cultural Differences in Apology," *International Journal of Intercultural Relations* 33, no. 1 (January 2009): 32–45, doi.org/10.1016/j.ijintrel.2008.10.001.
p. 237 *Another analysis found that in honour cultures:* Ying Lin et al., "From Virility to Virtue: The Psychology of Apology in Honor Cultures," *Proceedings of the National Academy of Sciences* 119, no. 41 (October 3, 2022), doi.org/10.1073/pnas.2210324119.

p. 238 *It takes a solid sense of self-regard:* Lerner, *Why Won't You Apologize?*, 62.
p. 238 *people can get stuck in defensiveness:* Lerner, *Why Won't You Apologize?*, 66.
p. 238 *Psychologist Harriet Lerner suggests the following five strategies:* Lerner, *Why Won't You Apologize?*, 72.
p. 239 *doesn't help to talk more:* Lerner, *Why Won't You Apologize?*, 81.
p. 239 *a raw show of emotion can be effective:* Lerner, *Why Won't You Apologize?*, 84.
p. 240 *the most graceful response is to say:* Lerner, *Why Won't You Apologize?*, 96.
p. 240 *accepting an apology doesn't mean:* Lerner, *Why Won't You Apologize?*, 100.

12: When It Doesn't Work Out

p. 246 *Mobile Crisis Intervention Teams:* Eli Cahan, "Mobile Crisis Teams Still Sidelined Despite Growing Need for Mental Health Services in US, Advocates Warn," ABC News, September 14, 2023, abcnews.go.com/Health/mobile-crisis-teams-sidelined-despite-growing-mental-health/story?id=103118681#:~:text=Mobile%20crisis%20teams%20have%20been,health%20and%20substance%20abuse%20crises.

p. 246 *as part of its mental health "Unity Agenda":* The White House, "FACT SHEET: President Biden's Budget Advances a Bipartisan Unity Agenda," The White House, March 28, 2022, whitehouse.gov/omb/briefing-room/2022/03/28/fact-sheet-president-bidens-budget-advances-a-bipartisan-unity-agenda/.

p. 246 *mental health crisis line:* "CATT—The Crisis Assessment and Treatment Team," Heathdirect Australia, accessed December 6, 2023, healthdirect.gov.au/crisis-management.

p. 250 *Studies comparing data from the last twenty years have shown:* "Child and Adolescent Mental Health," *2022 National Healthcare Quality and Disparities Report*, Agency for Healthcare Research and Quality, report no. 22(23)-0030 (October 2022), ncbi.nlm.nih.gov/books/NBK587174/; Sally C. Curtin, "State Suicide Rates among Adolescents and Young Adults Aged 10–24: United States, 2000–2018," *National Vital Statistics Reports* 69, no. 11, cdc.gov/nchs/data/nvsr/nvsr69/nvsr-69-11-508.pdf; "Children and Youth Mental Health in Canada," Canadian Institute for Health Information, 2022, accessed December 6, 2023, cihi.ca/en/children-and-youth-mental-health-in-canada; Natasha May,

"More Than a Third of Young Australians Experienced Mental Health Disorder in Past 12 Months," *The Guardian*, October 5, 2023, theguardian.com/australia-news/2023/oct/05/abs-national-study-of-mental-health-and-wellbeing-report-results-released-young-people-australia-bureau-statistics#:~:text=Young%20people%20experienced%20the%20highest,the%20most%20common%20at%2031.8%25; "Mental Health of Adolescents," World Health Organization (WHO), November 17, 2021, who.int/news-room/fact-sheets/detail/adolescent-mental-health.

p. 255 *Author Amanda Ripley defines "high conflict" as:* Amanda Ripley, *High Conflict: Why We Get Trapped and How We Get Out* (New York: Simon & Schuster, 2021), 4.

p. 256 *all four of Edmondson's criteria for an "intelligent failure":* Amy Edmondson, *Right Kind of Wrong: The Science of Failing Well* (New York: Atria Books, 2023), 64.

p. 256 *"In new territory, the only way to make progress:* Edmondson, *Right Kind of Wrong*, 84.

PHOTO: LEANNA RATHKELLY

About the Author

JENNIFER ROBIN WILSON is the board chair of Canada Homestay Network, her family's business. She joined CHN in 2005 and served as CEO from 2010 to 2022. She is also a writer, consultant, certified leadership coach, and facilitator. Prior to working at CHN, Wilson practiced as a registered midwife in Manitoba and British Columbia. She holds an MBA and an MFA in creative nonfiction. She has two adult children and lives with her husband on the unceded traditional territory of the Lkwungen (Lekwungen) peoples, known today as the Songhees, Esquimalt, and W̱SÁNEĆ First Nations, in Victoria, BC.

Ready to Build More Meaningful Connections?